Ma
Pu Relations

Palgrave Master Series

Accounting
Accounting Skills
Advanced English Language
Advanced English Literature
Advanced Pure Mathematics
Arabic
Basic Management
Biology
British Politics
Business Communication
Business Environment
C Programming
C++ Programming
Chemistry
COBOL Programming
Communication
Computing
Counselling Skills
Counselling Theory
Customer Relations
Database Design
Delphi Programming
Desktop Publishing
e-Business
Economic and Social History
Economics
Electrical Engineering
Electronics
Employee Development
English Grammar
English Language
English Literature
Fashion Buying and Merchandising
  Management
Fashion Styling
Financial Management
French
Geography
German

Global Information Systems
Globalization of Business
Human Resource Management
Information Technology
International Trade
Internet
Italian
Java
Language of Literature
Management Skills
Marketing Management
Mathematics
Microsoft Office
Microsoft Windows, Novell NetWare
  and UNIX
Modern British History
Modern European History
Modern United States History
Modern World History
Networks
Novels of Jane Austen
Organisational Behaviour
Pascal and Delphi Programming
Philosophy
Physics
Practical Criticism
Psychology
Public Relations
Shakespeare
Social Welfare
Sociology
Spanish
Statistics
Strategic Management
Systems Analysis and Design
Team Leadership
Theology
Twentieth-Century Russian History
Visual Basic
World Religions

www.palgravemasterseries.com

Palgrave Master Series
Series Standing Order ISBN 0–333–69343–4
(outside North America only)

You can receive future titles in this series as they are published by placing a standing order. Please contact your bookseller or, in case of difficulty, write to us at the address below with your name and address, the title of the series and the ISBN quoted above.

Customer Services Department, Macmillan Distribution Ltd.
Houndmills, Basingstoke, Hampshire RG21 6XS, England

Mastering
Public Relations

Anthony Davis

Business Series Editor
Richard Pettinger

palgrave
macmillan

First published 2004 by
PALGRAVE MACMILLAN
Houndmills, Basingstoke, Hampshire RG21 6XS and
175 Fifth Avenue, New York, N.Y. 10010
Companies and representatives throughout the world

PALGRAVE MACMILLAN is the global academic imprint of the Palgrave Macmillan division of St. Martin's Press LLC and of Palgrave Macmillan Ltd. Macmillan® is a registered trademark in the United States, United Kingdom and other countries. Palgrave is a registered trademark in the European Union and other countries

ISBN 1–4039–0783–8

This book is printed on paper suitable for recycling and made from fully managed and sustained forest sources.

A catalogue record for this book is available from the British Library.

10   9   8   7   6   5   4   3   2   1
13   12   11   10   09   08   07   06   05   04

Typeset by Footnote Graphics Ltd, Warminster, Wilts

Printed and bound in Great Britain by
Creative Print & Design (Wales), Ebbw Vale

To Wendy Curme,

for her constructive criticism
and unfailing encouragement

Contents

■ ⋈ Preface

Why is it that everyone 'knows' about public relations? That *really* anyone can 'do it', when they have the time, that is. That public relations is just PR, and everyone knows what *that* means. As in 'a PR exercise' or 'just another PR job'. And everyone *knows* there is precious little science to it, if truth were told. Which, to mention it, is not much used, as everyone also knows, when it comes to public relations. But amidst such knowing, just how much is *really* known about public relations?

Why, in short, is the management occupation that claims guardianship of corporate reputation itself held in such universally low regard, why do its detractors expend so much effort on denigrating it and why has it become an all-pervasive and invasive enigma, referred to daily by countless millions of people around the globe? And why, most significantly, do so many young people aspire to a career in it? Why is it growing exponentially, in every walk of life?

Most books about public relations tell you, often in monotonous detail, how to do it. The rest are mainly dense academic texts, explaining public relations in terms of a multiplicity of other disciplines. *Mastering Public Relations* steers a course through the middle, with a combination of theory and practice interpretation set in a 'real world' context.

There is no hidden agenda here, whether to work out some intellectual frustration over the vapidity of much published material or a determination to distil the subject into a collection of tips and neat rules for practice made perfect. The sole aim is to provide a balanced, wide-ranging introduction to a very large subject indeed, help position it in management terms and broadly consider its potential future development.

Books on the subject also tend to divide another way: towards euphoric endorsement of public relations in all its practice guises or relentless outright condemnation for everything done in its name. Both postures are absurd and unsustainable, but subjects that provoke such intense interest can have that effect. Here every effort is made to maintain a balanced view about the nature and purpose of public relations. That entails looking outside the loop as well as within it, at the views of its detractors and rivals, abusers and dissemblers, as well as at the observations and conclusions of its users, employers, practitioners, researchers and informed commentators.

Not that public relations people are blameless in acquiring their collective reputation. Some undoubtedly have done, and continue to do, more than their bit. Perhaps the rest should have spent greater time responding, instead of being in denial or in passive acceptance of what few other occupational groups would, or could, willingly tolerate. While it is the *shallows* of practice that are exposed to the daily sunlight, because that supposedly makes 'good copy', in reality public relations also has its *depths*, wherein are found intellectual vigour and a formidable battery of communication skills. And those depths, for whoever cares to consider them, are the source of much that is most interesting and stimulating about public relations.

ANTHONY DAVIS

■ ✓ Acknowledgements

Many thanks are due to the kind people who have so generously assisted me in sourcing material for this book and in giving their advice and comments.

In connection with the case studies, I am indebted to:

Charles Todd at Carlisle Process Systems
Mark Brooks and Wendy Franklin at National Savings & Investments
Sue Hyde at Dorset County Council
Richard Anderson at Puddings & Pies
Emma Jane Taylor at Aerosystems International
Barney Holbeche at The National Farmers' Union
Clare Winterton and Emma Melville-Ross at The Prince's Trust
James Lawrence at Action for Blind People.

In addition, I also much appreciate the assistance of:

- Lindsay Mason at Lindsay Mason Public Relations, for allowing me to draw on her 2002 research into use of e-mail in public relations, undertaken for her PR masters dissertation at Stirling University
- Amanda Merron at Willott Kingston Smith, for permitting me to extract from her firm's 2002 annual survey of marketing communications, *The Financial Performance of Marketing Services Companies*
- Helen Sullivan at Shell International, for providing much information about her company's worldwide activities and UK research on sustainable development, published in 2002 ahead of the UN World Summit on Sustainable Development
- Charles Stewart-Hunt at Romeike Media Intelligence, for his overview of the current size and disposition of the European media.

Many thanks also to all those other people, too numerous to mention, who have shown such interest and support in this project to capture and distil the essence of a subject that is so huge, so relentlessly topical and of such great and widespread fascination.

▪ ⌄ Introduction

Public relations is a very broad subject for study and trying to capture it succinctly can be formidable. It has several dimensions and many implications, its intellectual content being derived from a substantial number of sources and its practitioners, collectively, employing a range of skills and experience drawn from an equally wide range of occupational backgrounds.

Communication is the new mantra, and public relations is at the heart of it, but the term is susceptible to many interpretations: for instance, it may be used to describe making a telephone call, what happens in a conversation or remembering to tell everyone about a detail of work routine. Communication is a portmanteau term so widely used, and sometimes misused, as to be, ironically, the potential source of confusion. And in public relations there is much confusion also created by duplicate descriptions, over-enthusiastic creation of new language and generous one-size-fits-all adaptations to facilitate hoped-for mutual understanding.

What each chapter covers

In **Chapter 1** the *nature* of public relations is explored. Recourse is made to some of the very many definitions and to public relations culture; some widespread misconceptions are addressed and the history is traced of modern public relations throughout the 20th century. What public relations is *not* is covered here, but there is acknowledgement of its propagandist roots and of the continuing use of *propaganda* in politics and publicity, often in the name of public relations.

In an equally long **Chapter 2** the *purpose* of public relations is investigated. Here is encountered the *corporate* direction of much PR and how it fits into the context of the organization, whether that is a company or some other body. This raises matters of image, identity, reputation and business ethics, the latter a continuing topic throughout the book, and of creating shareholder value. These first two chapters, therefore, together provide *the basis to what follows* in the rest of the book.

Chapter 3 is the first of two that start to focus on the principal responsibilities and activities. Here concepts such as vision, mission, the learning organization and enterprise culture are discussed, together with managing change and other contemporary preoccupations of communication *within the organization*. In the following **Chapter 4** thought is given to how public relations communicates between the organization and its *operating environment*. There is discussion of publics and stakeholders and of risk and crisis management, and the concept of corporate social responsibility (CSR) is introduced. These two chapters together confirm that there is more to public relations than may be widely supposed.

The theory of public relations is substantially contained within **Chapter 5**, although various *theories* and *models* are discussed or alluded to throughout the book. Here, notably, communication itself, the core four models of public relations practice and the theory of public relations excellence make their first of several appearances. Conflict resolution, diffusion and effects and attitude and behaviour are also covered.

Chapter 6 is the last in the *first section* of the book. Here *research, planning and evaluation* are discussed, in terms that are more managerial than technical. In particular, there is some mention of power play impact on public relations roles and the implications of various influences on the formation of strategy. The chapter ends with a discussion of cost–benefit analysis.

The **second section** comprises five chapters that consider by turn *differing areas of public relations practice.* Owing to the high proportion of PR work that is in support of marketing – one frequently quoted guesstimate suggests 70 per cent – there are not one but two chapters specifically covering Marketing Public Relations (MPR).

Chapter 7 concentrates on the *customers*, addressing how they make their decisions, the marketing approach to this all-important public and the public relations understanding of consumer relations. Dialogues with privacy and customer lifetime value are also covered. In **Chapter 8** attention turns to *marketing communications*, the role of MPR, the concept of integrated marketing communication (IMC) and the practice of Cause Related Marketing (CRM). It ends with a discussion of the relationship between marketers and public relations practitioners.

Probably the one area of PR activity that is most readily recognized, *public affairs*, is reached in **Chapter 9**; its position so relatively late in the book is not intended as any comment upon its importance. This long chapter does not attempt to include much that is already, perhaps inevitably, public knowledge, but seeks instead to offer some critical perspectives relating, in particular, to the concept of the 'public sphere', government public relations and propaganda. There is also discussion of lobbying and issues management.

Community relations attract a great deal less attention than public affairs, but are often assigned higher ranking in PR importance by corporate strategists. In **Chapter 10** this less obvious area of activity is examined, starting with corporate community involvement (CCI) and continuing with the physical environment and community action, the growing 'community sector' of self-help schemes. There is also consideration of UK companies' expenditure, public attitudes towards it and relations between the private and voluntary sectors.

The final chapter in this section, **Chapter 11**, 'last but not least' covers *the media*. Here again the emphasis is on offering some critical perspectives, addressing topics such as media values, on-line media news and the relationship between the media and public relations practitioners. A number of controversial issues are raised, and the chapter ends with telling private research on the use of e-mails, extracted from a dissertation for a postgraduate degree in public relations.

The **third section** of *Mastering Public Relations* comprises three chapters, starting, in **Chapter 12**, with a look at *global PR*. In addition to tracing its development across the world and discussing some of the communication factors encountered, there is consideration of non-governmental organizations (NGOs), the European Union (EU) and communication conditions in the developing countries.

Chapter 13 turns the spotlight on the *occupation of public relations*. In considering its size and structure, the chapter draws on detailed annual research of marketing communications businesses in the UK, considers the person specification for public relations practitioners and surveys sample current UK salaries. It looks at the possible future development of consultancy, discusses self-regulation and concludes with a review of education and training.

With the somewhat cryptic title of 'Futures', **Chapter 14** discusses the future for public relations in connection with the Internet, the mass media, politics and globalization. Topics include the 'information poor', legal liability for Internet content, continuing media misrepresentation and abuse of public relations, media editorial standards and the globalization of communication. It concludes with a final reference to excellence in practice and asks some departing questions designed to provoke strategic thoughts for the future of public relations as a whole.

Regular features of each chapter

Chapters are arranged in a format designed to ease interpretation and cross-referencing.

In addition to text and illustrations, this format includes:

- A **summary of topics** to be covered in each chapter, which appears in italics at the beginning
- **Numbered sections**, each with a title. Some sections are further divided into **subsections**, each introduced with its own heading

Not all topic descriptions are the same as the titles of sections in which they appear:

- **Emboldened main points**, which occur in the run of text
- **Highlighted examples**, which also arise in the run of text
- A **checklist** of main points and concepts covered in each chapter, which immediately follows the body text
- A detailed **case study**, after the checklist except in the first and last chapters, describing real life applications in a variety of contexts
- **Five questions**, which conclude each chapter and are specific to its content. These are designed to offer food-for-thought, stimulate discussion, encourage further reading and assist practice benchmarking.

▣ 1 The nature of public relations

'Spin' – widespread use – definitions – persuasion – culture – nomenclature – publicity – the media – what PR is not – early development – modern origins

1.1 'Spin'

'Every day,' writes Thomas Pynchon in an introduction to a new US edition of George Orwell's classic novel *1984*, 'public opinion is the target of rewritten history, official amnesia and outright lying, all of which is benevolently termed "spin", as if it were no more harmful than a ride on a merry-go-round. We know better than what they tell us, yet hope otherwise.'

This term **'spin'** is ubiquitous and synonymous with deceit, trickery or, at best, exaggeration, wishful thinking or fanciful interpretation. Its use litters the daily outpourings of the western news media, where it has become a handy tool for the lazy journalist and broadcaster, the ready means to insinuate in substitution for reporting fact. Everything, it sometimes seems, constitutes spin, and everyone knows exactly where that comes from, because spin, they are repeatedly told, is the product of public relations.

Orwell anticipated spin, his inventions in *1984* being remarkably prescient: the Ministry of Truth that busily told lies, the Ministry of Love, which dealt in torture, the Ministry of Peace that continually waged war and the Ministry of Plenty, which perpetuated starvation. And there were the contradictory doublethink party slogans, War is Peace, Freedom is Slavery and Ignorance is Strength. So much so that when the 'real' 1984 occurred the UK Prime Minister felt obliged to make a speech denying that *1984* had come to fruition.

Public relations, therefore, has become *closely linked in the collective imagination* with politics and government, from whence emanates so much that is described publicly as spin. This in turn has led to government employees being fairly indiscriminately called 'spin doctors', whether or not they have any involvement with the dissemination of either governmental propaganda or public information.

But spin is not confined to politics. It is liberally used to describe communications from all manner of sources. Wherever, it seems, that the presence of public relations may be detected, or supposed, spin surely follows. Why, every journalist says so, repeatedly, so it must be so.

But should journalists, themselves not well regarded by society generally, be allowed to smear so freely, to weave their own web of selective 'post modern irony' without challenge? Could public relations comprise rather more than they choose to represent, could it have some redeeming features, some better or higher purpose, perhaps even more honourable and serious intent than does much journalism?

1.2 Pervasive and invasive

Public relations, as a recognizable activity, is widely undertaken by people in all walks of life, by:

- **professional practitioners** employed in every corner of the public, private and not-for-profit sectors of the economy;
- **managers** and **members of staff** whose work includes *an element* of public relations responsibility and/or activity;
- **volunteers** who undertake public relations activities *without pay* in order to obtain and increase support for their interests and causes; and
- **individuals** who wish to **advance private interests** on behalf of *themselves* or someone who they *represent*.

Public relations, or PR, as it is commonly called, is no longer undertaken solely on behalf of commercial interests, which is how it substantially began in the USA during the 19th century, nor by government, which in the UK a few decades earlier laid the foundations for its later entanglement with the burgeoning public communication media.

- It is increasingly 'done' by anyone and everyone, reflecting a growing civic pluralism, whereby many voices are heard in public via 'display-for-attention-and-advantage' (Moloney, 2000), mainly generated through wanting to gain personal attention, advance worthy causes and/or express disdain of authority in all its forms
- It is also widely undertaken by all manner of organizations, reflecting the parallel rise in commercial pluralism, resulting from ever more competition for resources, markets and advantage, owing to globalization, finite natural resources, colossal population growth and the influence of a prevalent political ideology that promotes 'me first', the supremacy of self over society.

This **universality** raises interesting questions about the **exact nature** of public relations, for, if indeed, as is widely represented, it comprises an easily learned and applied set of low-cost techniques accessible to all, can it be a serious management function or is it merely a popular means of self-expression? Is it an occupation or a hobby, a profession with barriers to entry and serious self-regulation or a trade that may be engaged in by anyone, a form of diplomacy or a euphemism for deceit and trickery? Does it have worthy pretensions or pretentious worthiness? Is it a powerful force for greater democracy or the means to brainwash the masses, central to corporate success and a significant element of an integrated approach to marketing or simply a trendy thing to do?

1.3 Definitions

Probably the simplest and most straightforward definition of public relations is: the *'management of communication between an organization and its publics'* (Grunig and Hunt, 1984). This contains three clues: it indicates that public relations is a **corporate** activity, comprises **communication** in some form or other and entails a degree of **specificity**, involving 'publics' rather than the general public at large. So far, so good, but is this adequate?

Most public relations people might think not, judging by the proliferation of alternatives offered. Of these, most aim to describe the activity, what effects it seeks or how practitioners should behave. Prominent among them is the widely quoted **'Mexican Statement'** that resulted from a meeting in 1978 at Mexico City attended by practitioners representing PR associations in 31 countries. It reads: *'Public relations practice is the art and social science of analyzing trends, predicting their consequences, counselling organizations' leaders, and implementing planned programmes of action which will serve both the organizations' and the public interest.'*

This 'sits on the fence' about whether PR is an art or a science, since in practice it combines creativity and flair with incisive analysis and measurable precision. More significantly, the statement implies that there is present (1) a strong element of **research** and (2) **responsible behaviour** that is **in the public interest** as well as that of the organization. It also suggests an element of **prediction**.

Environmental scanning, that is to say, looking-out for what is going on outside the organization and assessing the implications of what is found there, is often referred to as **issues management**, because 'one does not merely monitor change but plans to take it into continuing consideration in planning corporate strategy' (Black and Davis, 2002). It entails spotting and unravelling an issue, deciding its likely future course, following its development and seeking to influence its outcomes, most of which is more easily said than done. The Conference Board of America has defined an issue as being 'a condition or pressure, either internal or external, that, if it continues, will have a significant effect on the functioning of the organization or its future interests.'

The Public Relations Society of America offers this definition: *'Public relations helps an organization and its publics to adapt mutually to each other. Public relations is an organization's effort to win the co-operation of groups of people. Public relations helps organizations effectively interact and communicate with their key publics.'* Here there is reference to interactions between the sender and the receiver of a communication, to co-operation of the receiver with the sender and, most significantly, to facilitating mutual adaptation to each other. In other words, this take on PR is hinting at **dialogue**, not merely communication by an organization *at* someone but communication *with* them.

The (UK) Institute of Public Relations had a definition that read: *'Public relations practice is the planned and sustained effort to establish and maintain goodwill and mutual understanding between an organization and its publics.'* This emphasized that PR is an **on-going activity**, which sought, by one means or another, to **foster goodwill and mutual understanding**. This does not entail, as is often mistakenly supposed, approbation or popularity, nor does it necessitate a substantial level of exchanged communication or involvement by the receiver.

Then the Institute decided to add a bit more, about **reputation**: *'Public relations is about reputation – the result of what you do, what you say and what others say about you.'* PR practice had become *'the discipline which looks after reputation – with the aim of earning understanding and support, and influencing opinion and behaviour.'* This places corporate reputation at the centre of public relations practice, an onerous responsibility with important implications for relationships between the PR function and other departments and units. Reputation is certainly the major factor in PR, perhaps even to the extent that 'Managing the causal linkage between reputation, perception, attitude and behaviour is what PR is all about' (Stone, 1995), although this may be an overstatement.

An 'acceptable standard of definition' among practitioners (Kitchen, 1997) is: *'Public relations is the management function that identifies, establishes and maintains mutually beneficial relationships between an organization and the various publics on whom its success or failure depends (Cutlip et al., 1985)'*. This American interpretation brings us back again to interactivity, the purpose being to establish **ongoing relationships** that are **mutually beneficial**. It bears a closer relationship to the commercial purposes of marketing communications.

Given the spread of public relations activity beyond the confines of the organization, perhaps a more contemporary definition might read simply: *Public relations is communication with people who matter to the communicator, in order to gain their attention and collaboration in ways that are advantageous to the furtherance of his or her interests or those of whoever or whatever is represented.* It takes account of civic pluralism and recognizes the persuasive nature of most public relations practice.

1.4   The role of persuasion

From their earliest origins people have sought to make themselves understood, and they are still having difficulties in doing so. They began with the simplest tools and gradually developed them, achieving notable landmarks along the way, such as the inception of cave drawings and paintings, the creation of the earliest handwritten documents, the laborious production of richly illuminated religious tracts and the invention of printing.

Through a simple need to be understood by others there developed (relatively) soon a desire to *enhance* understanding, in order to push the benefits of communication beyond satisfaction of simple needs towards the **achievement of power and influence**, and the resultant benefits that might be secured. Communication came to be **used to assert identity and assign qualities such as status**, for example, through the use of heraldic symbols and the design and decoration of public buildings. In the last millennium this process unfolded at a quickening pace, resulting in the modern supremacy of the **brand**, an identification that communicates various values designed to secure advantage.

Such values do more than simply lay claim to certain qualities, such as size and commercial or military strength. They **are persuasive**, designed to *gain willing recognition, mould perceptions, develop attitudes and influence future behaviour.*

Those actions may be:

- *commercial* in nature, for instance, purchases of a product or service;
- *intellectual*, perhaps involving agreement with a particular argument; or
- *emotional*, such as making a commitment to support a social cause.

Brands are trust marks, in which it is intended that *faith may be placed unreservedly.*

Persuasion, it is widely argued, underlies all public relations practice, and certainly much of the early activity was directed primarily if not solely at winning converts to a cause, believers in a faith or loyal followers of a recognized leader. Oratory, for instance, was widely heard, in which persuasive language was used in order to influence thought and behaviour, and this form of communication widely persists to this day in many differing cultures and for many diverse purposes.

However, by no means *all* public relations activity has persuasion as its purpose. The major exception is provided by the dissemination of that **public information** which comprises simple 'need to know' facts and figures informing the average citizen or subject about the minutiae of daily life. In so far as it plays any part in public relations, strongly denied by most practitioners, **propaganda** provides an exception, as can **mediation**, which we will consider later.

1.5 The public relations culture

Stated simply, **the public relations culture** describes an organizational environment in which every participant both **understands the value and purposes of PR**, including the creation and maintenance of **favourable reputation**, and is committed to ensuring that his or her actions reflect that. In effect, this is translated into a *predisposition* to:

- speak up for the organization,
- champion its cause,
- act towards outsiders as an ambassador,
- strive to bear in mind the PR implications of every decision and
- generally to daily re-affirm commitment through both attitudes and actions.

There are many organizations, both large and small, where the culture has so permeated, but the very term 'culture' is difficult to define. It may be seen as:

- collective acceptance of a *values system,*
- a simple set of *performance criteria,*
- informally stated *customs or conventions* by which individuals 'bond', or
- a more complex interaction of *assumptions, values,* even *philosophy.*

What *does* seem certain is that the public relations culture of an organization will *reflect* its **current overall culture**, and this is particularly observable where the **leadership values** both

- incorporate a *commitment* to public relations and
- are *substantially* accepted and adopted throughout.

It is probable, however, that the PR culture will also reflect the **external environment** in which the organization functions. So, for instance, a *retailer of consumer products* may have an entirely different PR culture from that of a *hospital*, because the world that each inhabits differs according to its purposes.

Example

The shop that sells bicycles is tuned to the needs and lifestyle aspirations of different types of potential purchasers, and to all the many influences that bear upon that. The primary aim is to secure sales. Meanwhile, the hospital is preoccupied with achieving the optimum efficiency and effectiveness in handling its workload of sick and injured people that present themselves for treatment. The primary aim is patients' recovery of their health and fitness.

For both the shop and the hospital there are many external influences to be taken into account, coincidentally some arising from the activities and attitudes of each other. The bicycle seller may be *a source of fresh patients* for the hospital (should the bikes be unroadworthy, the instructions given are inadequate or the way in which the products are sold emphasizes risk-taking usage) and the hospital may be *a source of lost trade* for the shop (possibly because it is poor at repairing cyclists' injuries, it counsels its patients to take greater care of themselves or it deters patients by representing bicycling as a risky activity owing to their physical condition).

The **PR function** is also, potentially, a major influence: should its members perceive a disparity between the current PR culture and what it should become, they may seek to **mould the PR culture to better meet their requirements**, even to the extent of creating a 'counterculture'.

Marketers have their own version of this, what they call *the marketing concept*, which emphasizes the central importance of the customer: all activities are designed with the ultimate aim of satisfying customers, because they determine present and future prosperity. This 'customer focus' unites the efforts of every unit and underscores the performance and attitudes of every participant within the organization.

There is a fundamental difference, because the marketing concept is limited to satisfying the customer. Marketing activity may take an indirect route to achieving this, so that its immediate declared purpose can be to meet an interim objective that says nothing directly about sales, but its ultimate purpose is focused very firmly on the customer. By contrast, the PR culture has broader application, although there is substantial overlap, since the majority of public relations practice is directed towards supporting marketing, in which guise it is called Marketing Public Relations, or MPR, one of five principal marketing communications tools used in promotion of products and services. We shall look at MPR in detail in Chapters 7 and 8.

1.6 Communications versus public relations

The occupation of public relations is often described as being that of communications, on the grounds that they comprise the core activity. Not everyone agrees.

According to Harold Burson, a doyen of the business, interviewed in *PR Week* (19.10.01), 'The term communications has become synonymous with PR but this does a disservice to our profession by making it tactical. . . . The best term for what we do is public relations.' Long after he sold control of his consultancy, it opted for 'perception management' as a replacement for describing its service.

There is also uncertainty about whether communication or communications is preferable. The latter is widely used to refer to electronic equipment: 'I long ago adopted this form [communication without the 's'] as being more accurate and left communications to the telecommunications specialists. It's a small point but another attempt to bring clarity out of confusion.' (Jackson, 1987, quoted by van Riel, 1995).

Communication without the 's', preferred also by van Riel, better addresses the nature and range of PR-originated communications activity and appears in that form throughout this text. It is unlikely, however, to be an adequate substitute for the description public relations, whose full **practice comprises more than communication alone**. Alternative descriptions, which abound, may be perceived as attempts to more accurately describe its nature and purpose and to enhance its reputation and status.

1.7   Publicity

Historically, MPR was described by marketers as being *publicity in the editorial content* of the print and broadcast media, *as opposed to advertising*, or 'paid space' (Kotler, 1991), by which is meant space on the page that is purchased directly by the advertiser from the media owner. The term publicity continues to be widely and mistakenly conceived as an *alternative name* for public relations, and it is also sometimes used disparagingly to discount the PR communication materials of competitors and rivals.

Publicity, however, is *a part* of public relations, when it usually comprises activity that is designed to draw attention and create awareness by a means that is both credible and relevant to the underlying message. Such activity is likely to comprise a contrived **event** or some other overt act that is intended **to disturb the continuity of life** for those at whom the publicity is directed. It may be interpreted, for instance, as:

- news,
- comment or
- simple distraction,
- an invitation,
- opportunity or
- affirmation,
- a gesture,
- appeal or
- wake up call.

This purposeful publicity is undertaken in a controlled manner, but publicity may also occur as a result of **information becoming known** that by so doing may have either a beneficial or harmful consequence. The act of making known may have been purposefully controlled or unintended and thereafter found to be uncontrollable. Nor is all publicity necessarily 'good' in the sense that it is calculated to appear by its nature favourable; some publicity is deliberately 'bad', because, ironically, it is expected to provide good results, as where commercial fame benefits from notoriety.

1.8 The media

The relentless **growth in the scale and influence of the mass media** continues around the world, creating an ever-greater demand for material to fill the pages of print and the airwaves. As technology advances continue to streamline the processes used to gather and disseminate material of all kinds, notably news and its accompanying commentaries, *the demands of the media on public relations intensify.*

Public relations uses the media in order to communicate with its publics and it benefits from whatever **added credibility** the chosen medium of communication may attach to its messages.

Example

An item on a BBC television or radio main news broadcast, in the UK or elsewhere, is likely to be seen and heard more keenly and with greater respect than the self-same message coming directly from its originating source.

Time was when many people said they believed whatever they read in the newspapers, simply because *it was there.* Still, in these *more questioning* times, marketing messages that are routed through the media, *as editorial matter or in programmes*, continue to **generate higher levels of credibility** than those that go via, for instance, advertising or direct mail.

The downside to media intervention is that most if not all messages have to acquire certain immediacy, a '**news angle**', and great may be the effort to assign one that can meet journalistic requirements. To this end PR people and journalists frequently collaborate closely in order to contrive a 'peg' that may warrant publication to their mutual satisfaction.

There are many more detailed aspects of what is known as **media relations**, the interactions by which public relations communication is filtered through the scrutiny of the media intermediaries, notably the editors, sub-editors, reporters, specialist writers, photographers, producers, directors, presenters, scriptwriters and film crews. This mediated communication illustrates the value of endorsement by **opinion formers**, people whose very involvement, say in reading the news, may provide some added interest and relevance to a communication.

For their part, the media need public relations, to provide **subsidized or free**, to them, **material and ideas** with which to supply their customers. They have much space and airtime to fill and seemingly always too little real time in which to do it. They value 'copy' that is reliably sourced and ready for use, and accept that in using these outside, or secondary, inputs they abdicate some of their control over the news agenda, by which they determine what is and what is not news. They benefit from any **growth in customers** that may result from using such material, for instance, in readers attracted by competitions funded by retailers or in viewers who enjoy programmes that discuss and test cars that are supplied for that purpose by manufacturers.

The consequences of this *mutuality of interest* do not escape criticism. Journalists 'are being colonized by it [PR]. There is a PR-isation of the media happening in the UK. This is a growing identity in the attitudes, behaviours and personnel of journalism and PR. It implies a growing dependency of journalists on PR, leading to the disablement of their critical faculties' (Moloney, 2000).

Probably much the same could be said of media elsewhere in the world, but the depiction of a cosy conspiracy by public relations and journalism to 'manufacture news' and other content greatly depends upon the perspective from which it is viewed. Public relations now has to hand, in the **Internet**, a powerful means to **communicate direct**, without mediation by journalists and broadcasters, and it is also using and developing *other direct links* with publics such as shareholders, or stockholders, employees, pressure group members, local civil administrators and neighbouring community leaders. The benefits derived from **media endorsement** of filtered messages are being weighed *routinely* against those of direct communication of more closely targeted **unmediated** messages.

1.9 What public relations is not

Just as public relations can be confused with publicity, so too it may appear to be synonymous with journalism, particularly when they are closely entwined, even though the two sets of activities are distinct. Nor do the confusions end there; public relations is often mistaken elsewhere:

Marketing

Although much public relations activity is directed at support of marketing, to the extent that it *may in some instances* amount to the principal promotional tool used, it has **a broader remit**, that perceives customers as being but one public, or several disaggregated publics, *among many*. This is not to diminish the importance of customers, but rather to recognize also and allocate time to addressing the powerful claims of others, notably shareholders, employees, suppliers and the media.

Advertising

Most advertising seeks to achieve optimum persuasiveness with a view to **achieving sales**, although much is now *less directly* persuasive, designed instead to achieve interim effects that in turn will assist in generating sales; such purposes include to remind or reinforce, bring brands to 'front-of-mind' or calm post-purchase doubts. And some advertising is not at all about sales, directly or indirectly; here the purpose may be, for example, buying supplies, recruitment of personnel, announcing trading results or communicating public information.

For PR, however, achieving sales, or helping others to achieve sales, is *by no means* its *principal* purpose. It may be tasked, for instance, to:

• inform,
• educate,
• create better understanding,
• gain credit,
• encourage loyalty, or
• foster discussion.

In theory, at least, publication of editorial content *cannot be purchased directly*, unlike advertising, but has to **earn its inclusion on its merits** as those are judged by the media (although this is far from universally so internationally). Accordingly, the advertiser's **level of control** over what appears is relatively absolute and exceeds that of the public relations practitioner's over non-advertising mediated communication.

Further, *traditionally* the advertising agencies' remuneration has been mainly by **commission paid by the media** in which their advertisements appear, although in the past decade the payment by **fees** for creative work unconnected with its later appearance in the media has developed. Public relations practice is paid for by employers through **wages and salaries** and clients via **fees**.

Sales promotion

Sales promotion is directed at gaining short-term results, usually measured over weeks or months, whereas public relations is assessed over longer periods, often a year at a time or more. The former seeks to **affect a market quickly** and thereby achieve changes, whether in competitive attack or defence. The latter sets its sights on securing **results** that by their nature are **likely to take time to achieve**. Nor is PR 'free' sales promotion. They do share, however, the ability to communicate directly with individuals and relatively small groups of people.

Propaganda

It has been argued (Grunig and Hunt, 1984) that in publicity there is propaganda. 'Practitioners spread the faith of the organization involved, often through incomplete, distorted, or half-true information.' Certainly publicity often relies upon an element of self-praise and in telling rather than listening, features shared with propaganda, but in most uses of publicity those further characteristics of propaganda, such as belligerence, dogmatism and demand of unquestioning agreement and obedience, are absent. Typically, publicity is more likely to be associated with *celebrity and celebration* than with seeking uncritical following through arousing emotions and evoking spiritual responses.

It might be contended more convincingly that propaganda persists elsewhere in some nooks and corners of modern public relations, as where, for example, communication is intended to mould public opinion about a political, economic or social matter. But these are **increasingly questioning times**. Public relations people aim to communicate with convincing argument and presentation, and take great care in nurturing and defending reputations that they value.

1.10　Early development

The modern evolution of public relations has been traced back to the 18th century. On the 200th anniversary of the American Revolution in 1976, Cutlip wrote in *Public Relations Review* (Grunig and Hunt, 1984) that 'several propagandists' had incited the war against the British, among them Samuel Adams, who had used techniques familiar to public relations people today. These comprised:

- *formal organization*, using an appealing name, the Sons of Liberty ('because the revolution was not a popular uprising')
- *use of media*, mainly newspapers, sermons in places of worship, speeches at public meetings, pamphlets and letter writing by dedicated 'committees'
- *use of a symbol*, The Liberty Tree
- *use of a slogan*, 'Taxation without representation'
- *creation of events*, or 'pseudo-events', to make news; these included the 'Boston Tea Party', when tea was thrown into Boston harbour
- *partisan presentation*, to promote favourable interpretation of events such as the 'Boston Massacre', when British soldiers attacked their civilian tormentors, and
- *sustained campaigning*, in this case through all available media *over 20 years*.

It worked, and these 'public relations-like activities' continued to be used by proponents of the creation of a federal government for the whole continent, who needed nine of the then 13 states to sign up for the constitution. The successful outcome, which included the **negotiated** addition of a Bill of Rights, served to emphasize the value of such techniques. According to Black (1989), the actual term 'public relations' was not used by a president, however, until 1807, when Thomas Jefferson amended his seventh Address to Congress, or speech to parliament, by substituting public relations for the phrase state of thought.

Then in 1829 there appeared a newspaper editor in the White House, Amos Kendall, later to become regarded as 'the first presidential public relations man'. He worked for Andrew Jackson, the first 'commoner' president, a man said to be barely literate, largely unschooled and much in need of communication assistance. Possibly his reputation as one of the 'great' US presidents owes more than a little to Amos. (Grunig and Hunt, 1984).

1.11　'For as long as the newspapers [are] important'

Meanwhile, pamphlets and newspapers were becoming familiar also in Europe. British monarchs became increasingly interested in what their subjects were saying and writing about current political, economic and social issues. In 1809 the British government joined in, when the Treasury assumed the role of **press spokesman on overseas policy**. In December it sent a message to the Department of War and Foreign Affairs and to the Admiralty, the latter at that time accounting for about 20 per cent of British public spending, saying: '. . . as long as the newspapers shall continue to be considered as important as they now are, some person in each of the three departments ought to read the principal newspapers every morning, and send to the Treasury ... either a correct statement of the facts, if facts are to be stated, or a hint of the line which it is wished should be taken' (Black and Davis, 2002).

Throughout the century the techniques used by the American revolutionaries came to be adopted with greater frequency on both sides of the Atlantic. These notably included:

- use of the term **public relations**
- **publicity stunts**, often using arresting claims
- **staged events**, often to inaugurate or commemorate
- Publication of **magazines and journals** by companies or their employees
- Publication of **annual reports**.

In Britain much of the development of PR rested with government, which in the early 20th century led to the recruitment, in 1912, of lecturers tasked to explain the new National Insurance law to employers and employees throughout the country. This marked the beginning of the **dissemination of information to the public** as an integral part of government and public administration.

It was soon followed by the formation of the War Propaganda Bureau and the Home Office Information Bureau to generate propaganda during the First World War, directed at friendly foreign countries and at the homeland. In 1917 they were combined, to form the Department of Information, which was dismantled following victory, and only gradually over the following years did the government appoint press officers in each department. This is significant; in 1918 it was considered that the need for propaganda had ceased, and what emerged later was regarded instead as public relations.

The advent of the Second World War in 1939 prompted a new Department of Information, whose role included not only **propaganda** but also dissemination of **unadulterated public information** to a civilian population that was enduring war at first hand. This included:

- **practical advice** about living through a war,
- **training** in how to cope with food rationing and other privations,
- heavy use of radio to disseminate **information** and **evoke support** for the war effort and
- production of cinema films that combined patriotism with **entertainment**.

This produced a **substantial pool of skilled communicators**, many of whom, following the war, embarked upon careers in public relations and advertising, often on the same premises, with advertising agencies alongside public relations consultancies.

The two great wars also served to hasten the development of PR in the USA. In 1916, on entering the war, the president appointed a journalist friend to form a Committee of Public Information to generate domestic support for the war effort. This provided the impetus to a surge in the development of public relations, led by a group of young men newly experienced in propaganda that included press agent Edward Bernays, a nephew of the psychologist Sigmund Freud. His clients had included the singer Caruso.

1.12 The founding fathers of modern public relations

In exchange for a box of cigars that Bernays sent his uncle in Vienna, while he was attending the Versailles peace conference near Paris in the winter of 1918–19, Freud sent his nephew a copy of his latest work, *A General Introduction to Psychoanalysis*, which expounded the proposition that there lay within people hidden irrational forces. This convinced Bernays that people might be persuaded not only to support a war effort but also to adopt new ways of thinking in other directions and to adapt their 'organized habits and opinions'.

On returning from Europe in 1919 he went into business in New York with his wife, Doris Fleischman, as **public relations counsel**, a term he devised, by his own later account, *in substitution for propaganda*. He also developed and delivered the **first course in public relations**, at New York University, and, in 1923, published the **first text** on the subject, *Crystallizing Public Opinion*. Quickly the firm acquired as clients many large companies and well-known personalities.

Bernays (1892–1995) is regarded today as one of the two founding fathers of modern public relations. In addition to his distinguished uncle, several others inspired him, notably Walter Lippmann, whose *Public Opinion* appeared in 1922. Lippmann viewed propaganda as part of government and he conceived of pseudo facts, the pseudo environment and of stereotypes, 'the mental phenomena used by people in the formation of public opinion. . . . The PR counsellor creates news to strengthen, weaken or amend stereotypes' (Moloney, 2000).

Ivy Ledbetter Lee (1877–1934), acknowledged as PR's other founding father, also influenced Bernays. Lee wrote successively for three New York newspapers, including *The New York Times*, at the turn of the 20th century, at which time a group of journalists, who came to be called 'muckrakers', were busily exposing employers for their concentration on profit with scant regard for the health and safety of their employees. Lee came to specialize in writing about banking and business, through which he encountered a wide range of managers in major corporations. In 1902 he set up as a publicity writer, his first client being a political reform group, which led him to consider whether there might be a market for **publicity on behalf of business** that was designed to counter the prevailing hostile publicity against business of the muckrakers.

With George Parker, a political publicist, Lee established a **public relations consultancy** in 1904, the third to be started, the first being in Boston (1900) and the second in Washington (1902). These first firms appear to have been solely concerned with conventional publicity as it was then understood and were relatively short-lived. Lee, who had other ideas, soon parted company with Parker and continued alone, eventually establishing Lee, Harris and Lee (1916).

In 1906 he initiated a policy of '**the public be informed**' while engaged in defending coalmine owners against their striking workforces. Lee circulated a **statement to editors**, offering to assist them by supplying *whatever information they required*, itself a significant innovation, and he began to issue press releases, or handouts, that, for the first time, *stated their source and interest*. With these he appended a copy of his **Declaration of Principles**, which began 'This is not a secret press bureau. All our work is done in the open. We aim to supply news. This is not an advertising agency; if you think any of our matter properly ought to go to your business office [advertisement department], do not use it.' This was revolutionary indeed, and arguably Lee's greatest legacy.

Lee also introduced the '**facility visit**'. On the basis that publicity meant making public, he began to organize opportunities for reporters to visit the scenes of rail crashes, hitherto closely guarded secrets, where they might **investigate and report freely on what they found**, *provided* that they gave a *balanced and fair account* that included the organization's version of events as well. This practice soon began to spread to visiting other sites, including factories, or facilities.

In 1914 Lee was engaged by the Rockefellers, at that time reputedly the wealthiest family in the USA. Following a murderous gun battle that year at a coal mine that they principally owned, John D. Rockefeller Jnr *toured the mines*, itself remarkable at the time. Later John D. Rockefeller Snr began to reveal publicly his charitable activities, in order to counter allegations about his business practices. Yet again, this was a first, in building a sustained favourable reputation by *speaking openly* about matters that had been hitherto seen as being strictly private.

In their fascinating account of Lee's career, Grunig and Hunt (1984) concluded that Lee worked purely on **an intuitive sense of public opinion**, what good sense indicated. In other words, what might be expected and appropriate to the given circumstances. Bernays, they reported, once remarked that his work was based on science, whereas Lee's was based on art. Lee had never conducted an opinion survey: 'Lee's work was typical of contemporary practitioners of the public-information model. They advise management on public opinion – and often understand public opinion quite well – but they rarely do any scientific research to measure that opinion.' That is a controversial assertion likely to be refuted by many current practitioners.

Lee's career had a sad ending. Believing that openness and frankness between nations might bring **greater international understanding**, he undertook a 'personal crusade' in the 1920s to win US recognition of the Soviet Union, made official in 1933, and in the early 1930s he was engaged by a Nazi-controlled German industry association to advise it on international relations. He had pushed his experiment too far, found himself publicly vilified in the press and came under official investigation for Un-American Activities. He died prematurely in disgrace.

1.13 'Order out of chaos'

Bernays is a rather more controversial figure. He had a fondness for propaganda, which never left him. In his second book, *Propaganda*, published in 1928, he wrote of the 'conscious and intelligent manipulation of the organized habits and opinions of the masses' as being 'an important element in democratic society'. He continued menacingly 'Those who manipulate this unseen mechanism of society constitute an invisible government which is the ruling power of our country.' Later he wrote 'Propaganda will never die out. Intelligent men must realize that propaganda is the modern instrument by which they can fight for productive ends to bring order out of chaos' (Moloney, 2000).

His later title, *The Engineering of Consent* (1955), persisted in the view of public relations as being a means to manipulate and control opinion, using the mass media and visual symbols, a one-way, rather than a two-way, process of communication. Decades later, throughout a four hour long conversation in his 99th year, Bernays 'conveyed his hallucination of democracy: A highly educated class of opinion-moulding tacticians is continuously at work, analyzing the social terrain and adjusting the mental scenery from which the public mind, with its limited intellect, derives its opinions' (Ewen, 1996).

In advance of the interview Bernays had forwarded a copy of a *Life* magazine special issue, in which he was named among the 100 most influential Americans of the 20th century. During the encounter he maintained an 'unabashedly hierarchical view of society', referring to 'an intelligent few' with responsibility for contemplating and influencing the tide of history, a comment echoed in modern preoccupations with legacy issues. 'Bernays,' wrote Ewen, 'perceived me as one of these "few", so he was willing to share his outlook with me in straightforward terms. . . . [He] sketched a picture of the public relations expert as a member of the "intelligent few" who advises clients on how to "deal with the masses . . . just by applying psychology." ' The PR person was an applied social scientist who also understood sociology, psychology, social psychology and economics in order to influence and direct public attitudes.

After his death at the age of 103, Bernays's attitudes were summarized by his daughter, Ann Bernays: 'Democracy to my father was a wonderful concept, but I don't think he thought that all those publics out there had reliable judgement and that they very easily might vote for the wrong man or want the wrong thing, so that they had to be *guided* from above. It's enlightened despotism in a sense. You appeal to their desires and their own recognized longings, that sort of thing, but you can tap into their deepest desires or their deepest fears and use that for your own purposes' (*The Century of the Self*, RDF Television/BBC, 2002).

Reflecting upon Berneys's effect upon the people around him, she added 'You make other people feel stupid, the people who worked for him are stupid, and children were stupid. If people did things in ways he wouldn't have done then they were stupid. It was a word that he used over and over and over, dope and stupid.' And the masses? 'They were stupid.' Referring to her father's use of the Soviet Union's first H bomb in 1953 to manipulate public fears in the USA as a weapon in the 'Cold War', she explained 'Groups are malleable and you can tap in to the deepest desires or fears and use it for your own purposes.'

So as founding fathers go Bernays too has left this life somewhat ingloriously, provoking comments varying from the downright unflattering to the mildly distancing, such as:

- 'There is an unspoken but palpable feeling that Bernays, particularly because of his literary legacy, is an embarrassment' (Moloney, 2000)
- 'The early functions of PR concerned public contact (publicity), then research into public opinion with a view to influencing such opinions favourably. . . . During the decades following the Second World War public relations sought to change its image from manipulative and one-way to two-way, reciprocal, and interactive' (Kitchen, 1997).
- 'In any event, Bernays was the first PR academic and his influence continued throughout his long life (he died in 1995)' (Fawkes, 2001).

There appears to be little doubt that the very substantial development of public relations practice in the last half-century has not been impeded by its propagandist origins, however much they may still discomfort current PR practitioners. But equally there is little doubt that contemporary political propaganda, the source of much alleged 'spin', with which we began, is very damaging to the reputation of public relations, however far removed it may be from mainstream practice.

To the modern mind propaganda has entirely negative connotations, associated with the many dictators and repressive regimes that have strutted the globe in the last 60 years, although there was a time when propaganda was applied for positive purposes, such as the 'New Deal' in the USA of the 1930s, and when it was accepted widely as harmless entertainment. Disassociating public relations from propaganda has been a concern of many PR people in recent decades but they are unlikely to succeed until propagandists cease to claim the mantle of public relations, which is improbable, since they find it too congenial to abandon.

In his interview with Ewen, Bernays at one point retorted, on mention of commercial imagery, '"Of course, you know, we don't deal in images . . . We deal in reality." ' Perhaps at the time he had in mind his remark in a foreword he wrote some three years before: 'The phrase "public relations" is today in the public domain and anybody can use it to mean almost anything. Words today have the stability and permanence of soap bubbles' (Black, 1989).

CHECKLIST

- Public relations activities are undertaken widely throughout society for a variety of purposes relating to the furtherance of corporate and private interests.
- Practice is variously defined, including: the management of communication, an art and science, the promotion and defence of reputation, creating mutually beneficial relationships and the furtherance of self-interest through gaining attention and collaboration.
- Most public relations practice is designed to be persuasive.
- A Public Relations Culture exists where everyone within an organization understands and fully supports the value and purposes of PR.
- Communication, not communications, better describes the nature and range of public relations communications activities.
- Publicity is a type of purposeful public relations activity, not a substitute name for PR. It may also occur when information becomes known unintentionally.
- Communication through the media adds credibility but messages are filtered and have to satisfy media priorities.
- The media benefit from public relations sourcing but thereby may relinquish some editorial control.
- Messages may be unmediated as well as mediated, going direct to publics and influential third parties direct, without journalistic intervention or interpretation.
- Much public relations activity is in support of Marketing, when it is known as Marketing Public Relations (MPR), but an estimated half as much again is about communication outside Marketing.
- Public relations differs significantly from Advertising, in that it has a greater range of purposes, media space for publication of its messages cannot (usually) be purchased and it exercises less control over mediated messages.

- Although propaganda is still used in politics and publicity, most public relations activities rely instead on convincing argument and presentation.
- The origins of modern public relations practice have been traced to the seeding of the American Revolution against Britain in the two decades or so before 1776, the interest of King George III of Britain (1760–1820) in public opinion and the formal monitoring of the daily press by the British government from 1810.
- The acknowledged 'founding fathers' of public relations are two Americans: Ivy Ledbetter Lee (1877–1934), best remembered for his credo 'The public be informed' and the 'facility visit', and Edward Bernays (1892–1995), who devised the term 'public relations counsel', established the first university course on PR and wrote the first book on the subject, *Crystallizing Public Opinion* (1923).

QUESTIONS

1 In what ways might public relations be both pervasive and invasive?
2 How could its PR culture impact upon an organization?
3 Why could publicity be seen as a 'two-edged sword'?
4 Is the 'PR-isation of the media' a benefit or a threat to press freedom, and why?
5 Why in public relations might advocacy be mistaken for propaganda?

▪ M 2 The purpose of public relations

Corporate communication – communication and leadership – creating shareholder value – systems theory – environmental scanning – image, identity and reputation – business ethics and values

2.1 Corporate communication

The Confédération Européenne des Relations Publique is in no doubt about the scale of responsibility of the public relations function: 'When someone refers to "PR", he is making reference to a profession which uses its own proper methodologies and techniques to manage Corporate Communications, the total communication needs of a Company or an Organization' (CERP website 5.11.02). But what does 'total communication needs' mean in practice?

Corporate communication may be divided into three categories (van Riel, 1995):

- *Management* communication, primarily by all managers within the organization but also externally, when chairmen and chief executive officers, or managing directors, perform their ' "symbolic" role' in representing their organizations
- *Marketing* communication, all those activities that come under promotion within marketing, including MPR, advertising, direct sales, direct marketing and sales promotion
- *Organization* communication, 'a general term' to describe 'all forms of communication used by the organization, other than marketing communication' This includes the non-marketing elements of PR and internal communication both between employees and to the outside world.

Although in this analysis public relations appears to be mainly found in the third category, in reality it permeates all three:

- Modern management communication internally is primarily about persuasion in order to optimize efficiency and effectiveness of the whole outfit, and the external ambassadorial role of senior managers is commonly recognized as being the PR element of their jobs
- The support of marketing forms the majority of PR practice in the UK and many other countries; as economies grow the emphasis gradually transfers from non-marketing PR, mainly the dissemination of public information, to MPR
- Organization communication is primarily about PR, in relation to, for example, finance, human resources, public affairs and environmental issues, although expenditure is likely to be substantially lower than with MPR.

Figure 2.1 **Corporate communication**

Clearly, therefore, there is much scope for the public relations function to be involved in addressing the total communication needs of an organisation, but where does such a broad remit fit into the organizational structure and how may it realistically expect to 'manage' all corporate communication? Might not some non-PR managers contest the claims of PR, particularly in technical correspondence and instruction?

2.2 Communication and leadership

A successful leader, in any environment, has to be **an effective communicator,** in order to arouse confidence, sustain credibility and generate excitement. He or she has many tasks to fulfil through communication, particularly:

- the creation of trust in management's competencies and decision-making skills,
- the delineation of a credible and inspiring vision for the future and
- the demonstration of a willingness and ability to anticipate, initiate and implement change.

Within the organization these challenging purposes are designed in order to motivate and empower. *Outside,* they tell onlookers about the nature of the organization in ways that do much to create its corporate image. Powerful attributes may be assigned to an organization on the basis of **perceptions created through observing and hearing the chairman or CEO.**

This external communication by the figurehead is not confined to announcing annual results or shaking hands; the style of presentation and the content of the messages form a **composite picture** that investors and others carry with them in their overall impression of the organization. Those in turn inform the attitudes and behaviours of external publics towards the organization and accordingly they establish **the parameters within which the managers may develop the organization,** for instance, in raising capital, securing credit, generating commercial opportunities, accessing grant funding and fostering joint ventures.

Few senior managers are likely to go forth to communicate beyond the confines of the workplace without first recognizing the serious public relations implications. Some still trust to their innate skills without much prior thought as to the most appropriate methods, the likely consequences and the kinds of impression that they should be seeking to impart. Most, however, take good care and many of them allocate considerable attention beforehand, working to a plan that accords with the organizational and public relations objectives.

This attention to detail is necessary because the leaders's *primary* communication motive is **to secure attention from others**. 'Organizations participate [in the attention market] when they want to attract attention from their customers, business partners, investors, or employees.' And '. . . as the amount of information increases, the demand for attention increases' (Davenport and Beck, 2001).

Among *these* attentive and attention-maximizing managers there is likely to be more recognition of the potential value of public relations in the **development of corporate strategy** and its implementation. That may mean that the most senior PR person is both a director and part of the inner cabal of senior managers who in effect run the show, who is located physically close to hand, readily available to address a broad range of communication matters as they arise at this level, perhaps even specializing in management communication throughout the organization. Prominent leaders often acquire popular fame.

Example

In the UK many people readily cite Richard Branson, the entrepreneur whose name is synonymous with the Virgin brand, which over the years has been applied to, or stretched across, many diverse products and services, including an international airline, trains, music, drinks, financial services, mobile, or cell, 'phones, the Internet, clothes, cosmetics and radio. He is famous for his carefully cultivated youthful style and daring-do activities, and is a highly effective communicator of values that appeal to a variety of publics. Public relations figures prominently in Virgin's management priorities.

Success at gaining attention in order to communicate provides growing returns for the effort, to the point that relatively *less* effort may be needed in order to secure optimum effectiveness in communication. This is very familiar to corporate public relations practitioners. 'The more we have of [attention] to begin with, the easier it is to get more. . . . If I'm a very well known politician or CEO, any pronouncements I make will be covered by the press.'

2.3   Creating shareholder value

In addition to communicating the corporate values, it is necessary to spell out and explain the values of products and services in terms that are understood and appreciated by both existing and potential customers. It is here that Marketing Public Relations (MPR), which is discussed in Chapter 8, and all other marketing communications contribute to the creation of **shareholder value**.

This is based on the principle that 'a business should be run to maximize the return on the shareholders' investment. . . . Creating shareholder value is . . . essentially about building a sustainable competitive advantage – a reason why customers should consistently prefer to buy from one company rather than others' (Doyle, 2000).

The *traditional* approach to placing a value on a company is to assess its ability to produce optimum returns for investors. This encourages emphasis on short-term profits and takes little if any account of intangible assets, such as the ability of particular brands to generate sales and the quality of relationships between the company and its customers and suppliers. *Shareholder value* analysis, by contrast, looks *also* at **the strategies that are going to generate cash in the future**, to assess their prospects for obtaining greater returns than the same money would have earned for the investors elsewhere in circumstances bearing similar risks.

This more penetrating analysis of a company's future prospects has been prompted by **the growing competition for capital, as well as customers**, with which to build businesses. For investors around the world what matters most is the *quality* of prospective return on their investments, and to that end the ability of the intangible assets to stimulate future profits is a major factor.

Implicit here is the important role of marketing communication. To judge MPR within this as no more than a minor player, in terms of relative expenditures, below five per cent in the UK when compared with advertising and the other alternatives, would be seriously mistaken, for its potential impact customarily far exceeds its cost. Furthermore, it is not only product and service brands but also *corporate* brands that may constitute valuable assets for future growth. Public relations can, and often does, contribute much to their development.

2.4 Where is home?

Given the proximity of PR to senior management implicit in its role within management communication and the extent of its involvement in marketing communication, the initial likelihood that the probable home for the PR function is in organization communication now seems doubtful. This is the category that covers the routine of daily exchange, surely just the place for a function with pretensions to manage all corporate communication? *Or is it?* Here public relations is engaged on a variety of non-marketing activities, including internal communication, since within the organization there is found arguably the most important public of all, the workforce. So *just where does* the PR function operate?

Systems theory provides the clue. There are three models that offer explanations of how humans organize themselves:

- a *mechanism*, comprising interacting elements that maintain equilibrium within a closed system that exists in isolation from its environment
- an *organism*, in which each component performs a specific part that contributes to the functioning of the whole and to the maintenance of equilibrium within an open system, where there is constant interaction with its environment
- a *social system*, in which each member freely accesses and interprets information to satisfy individual needs through socially responsible, co-operative actions that resolve conflicts and produce social harmony and unity.

The first two of these are considered to be 'traditional', having been developed in the 19th century, whereas the third was proposed in the late 1960s, and 'addressed issues such as conflict, deviance and social control, which traditional models are unable to deal with' (Pieczka, 1996).

During the 1950s a general systems theory evolved, in which a system was defined as being a group of related elements organized for a purpose. When this was applied to looking at how organizations operate, particularly larger ones, three types of system were identified:

- *mechanistic* systems, with highly controlled and engineered processes
- *probabilistic* systems, where there is rather less control and more uncertainty
- *adaptive* systems, highly flexible and readily responsive to change.

In an increasingly competitive and complex world, the managerial struggle for control of processes has intensified while many of the old certainties have been lost. During the 1970s it became clear that organizations had to:

- endeavour to master their environments by contesting more vigorously what they found there and
- develop an ability to engage more robustly within their world and evolve cultures that would seek to master changes around them and exploit them successfully

While *closed* systems may be preferred for the degree of certainty that they may provide, because they fulfil their vision and mission without support or disturbance from outside, *most* organizations have *open* systems, **interdependent on their external environments and influenced by them.** Boundaries may be created, but essentially the system depends upon *a continuing flow of contacts, in and out.* Usually, the more the organization thrives upon this *the greater its likelihood of achieving enhanced performance and results.*

Within the system there are a number of **subsystems**, which may be variously described, maybe as divisions, departments, sections and units, all parts of the whole. So every organization may be viewed as **a collection of subsystems** that together work in **dynamic equilibrium**, or 'steady state' of continual response and adjustment, to influences, forces and pressures for change arising from both within the organization and outside it, in the social system comprising a variety of publics.

The public relations department is a subsystem, formed to undertake the communication work that existing managers are having difficulty in doing, or doing adequately, owing to their lack of sufficient relevant skills and available time. These first began to appear late in the 19th century in American companies. 'Typically, organizations develop a formal communication subsystem when the organization or its publics behave in a way that has *consequences* upon the other. Those consequences upon one another create a *public relations problem*' (Grunig and Hunt, 1984).

The role of the department is to **communicate both with other subsystems within the organization and with the external publics**, but there is also reciprocal communication occurring between *subsystems and publics*, both of which can have **consequences on the other**. In other words, communication outwards is not solely the job of the PR people; individual subsystems are busy doing it too, and that may, and often does, require the assistance of the public relations department.

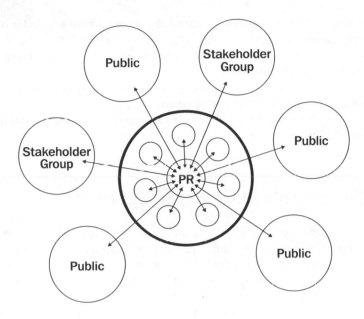

Figure 2.2 **Boundary spanning**

So the PR people find themselves working *both inside and outside the organization,* located therefore somewhere along the perimeter boundary but also *crossing the internal boundaries* between each subsystem. This **boundary spanning** is a fundamental characteristic of the function.

Most organizations have similar subsystems, and these may be described as:

- *Management* subsystems that lead, co-ordinate and control the others, sorting out conflicts between them, assigning resources and balancing their needs one with another and with the demands laid upon the organization from outside it
- *Production* subsystems, the 'powerhouse' of the operation, where what comes in is converted before it is exported out. These subsystems often comprise manufacturing and engineering but they embrace any process by which products and services are created
- *Disposal* subsystems, charged with the task of making sure that products and services are marketed and distributed
- *Adaptive* subsystems, tasked to keep on top of change, so that the organization may adapt and thereby enhance its position. These are likely to be involved in planning, research and development
- *Maintenance* subsystems that provide cohesion of effort and efficiency of operation of the whole organization. These include personnel, training and development and facilities.

So where exactly is PR among these?

1 Most often it is located within the group of *management* subsystems, where it may be close to the centre, because much of its work is concentrated on

advising senior management, or further out, reflecting a broader or more evenly spread workload.

2   Alternatively, it is likely to be found in the *disposal* subsystems, either stand-alone or as part of marketing.

3   It may be located in the *adaptive* group, emphasizing its external environmental scanning and issues management.

4   Or it may be among the *maintenance* subsystems, reflecting an emphasis on internal communication.

2.5   The organizational 'eyes and ears'

The elitism of Bernays, Lippmann and others of their generation pre-dated the advent of the Internet, the dramatic spread of education, the creation of mass tourism, 'frivolous flying' and much else; in short, the *mass circulation of knowledge* about other people and places, perceptions and attitudes, beliefs and behaviours, tastes and languages, norms and values.

Then information was still expensive and in short supply for most people most of the time, not cheap, accessible and constantly on tap. Now the world is different, and any organization, unless it is a closed system, needs to be sensitized to what is going on within the environment in which it operates, if it knows what is good for it. This is called **environmental scanning**, gaining information about the macro environment that can be turned into useful intelligence.

PR people consider issues and trends. Their aim is to gain insights about the social environment that may be interpreted correctly and used by the **dominant coalition**, 'groups [of managers] with the power to set organizational structures and strategies over a sustained period of time' (White and Dozier, 1992). These groups have 'the power to make and enforce decisions about the direction of the organization, its tasks, its objectives, and functions'.

Such groups may comprise a small proportion of senior managers, typically three or four people, or the whole of a large senior management team. Good sense suggests that public relations should be represented there, but failing that it should most certainly be permitted to contribute what it knows before decisions are taken. Public relations is prominent among the boundary spanners within the organization, and its strategic inputs contribute to the definition and re-definition of organizational purpose and direction.

At the heart of this research and analysis lies the hunt to **identify and locate the critical forces that are impacting on the organization**, whether helpfully or otherwise, and to ascertain **how each relates to the other**. The techniques are common to all planners, arguably the most popular being the PEST categorization, in which the environment is examined under four headings: Political, Economic, Social and cultural and Technological. Owing to the growing complexities encountered, some have adapted this framework to include Legal and Environmental, when it is referred to as PESTLE, others also adding Information, using the acronym EPISTLE. There are several more versions, but the point is made; this work has to be *thorough.*

In addition to environmental scanning, public relations practitioners gather **information about their publics and stakeholders**. They need to be *fully aware* of and *understand* their attitudes and behaviour towards the organization and current issues, and to *how these may alter over time*, and *with what likely consequences*. They also need to know how one public or stakeholder group might *relate to another and interact*.

To this end, in addition to using secondary research methods, PR people:

- engage with all their numerous external contacts and
- consult widely with other boundary spanners within the organization;
- also undertake **primary research** into opinions and attitudes, continually probing to assess the potential power and influence of stakeholders, their needs and wants, their expectations of the organization, *their inclination and capacity to act* and *under what circumstances they might do so*.

In this the public relations function acts as **the eyes and ears of the organization**. Because it connects widely outside it develops useful contacts, observes and hears what might well pass by or evade someone less externally active. PR provides well-attuned **corporate antennae that can pick up distant signals** as well, providing early indications of how operating conditions may change over time, facilitating future scenario planning, trying to answer the '*what if?*' questions thrown up by the scanning. This may well affect markets, but it is just as likely to have *wider* implications or possibilities.

Example

Often it has been found that ethical and social considerations are developing into a critical mass capable of affecting a market, political decisions about regulation or trade negotiations at some future time. Some issues suddenly blow up, like a storm in the desert, with precious little warning, others rumble on, yet more prove to be passing fads that fail to gather momentum.

2.6 Image, identity and reputation

So if, as Bernays asserted, images differ from reality, just *what is* **image**, a term that has entered universal usage and is widely applied with ease by people generally. An image is a **composite mental or sensual interpretation**, a perception, of someone or something; a *construct arrived at by deduction* based upon all the available evidence, *both real and imagined*, and *conditioned* by existing impressions, beliefs, ideas and emotions. Perceptions can be, often are, intuitive, relating to, for instance, aesthetic qualities, fundamental truths, absolute 'givens', basic understandings.

Images may be cultivated that are *factually accurate reflections of reality or essentially ephemeral and insubstantial*. They may be relatively honest or downright deceitful, randomly communicated or carefully contrived.

This interest in images grew rapidly, so that by the 1960s the humorous novelist J. B. Priestley conceived of 'Social Imagistics' in his satire *The Image Men*. His underlying theme was that images are bogus. 'They're part of the unreality that's swindling us,' declares one of the principal characters, reflecting the widespread view that 'The average person sees image as the opposite of reality' (Grunig and White, 1992).

For an organization, its *current* image is of keen interest, particularly if it differs from the *wish* image, how it would *like* to be perceived. **Corporate image can be as important as the image of the organization's product and service brands**, for it translates the organization into a *personality, with qualities and values* that provide **foundations to expectations of its behaviours**.

There is much controversy about image. Public relations people are criticised for using the term too freely, when referring to many differing concepts, including 'reputation, perception, attitude, message, attributes, evaluation, cognition, credibility, support, belief, communication, or relationship' (Grunig and White, 1992). Images are typically described as being vapid, imprecise, superficial, figments of reality, but 'however unpalatable . . . [image] remains a popular focus of interest. Even companies that prefer to adopt a low profile are assessing their corporate image . . .' (Oliver, 2001). And it is not only companies; **all manner of organizations** are interested.

This scepticism is acknowledged by those who nevertheless champion the development of corporate images that 'build-up goodwill and confidence in the firm, create identity and publicize the firm's strengths' (Lancaster and Massingham, 1988).

The value of a carefully constructed corporate image turns upon its **credibility** in the *varying interpretations* placed upon it, and this can have a **cumulative effect**, as these mental pictures are *shared*, often informally. Both the *rational and irrational* sets of meanings ascribed to the organization can become confused and *result in loss* *of definition*, so that the values that it is *intended to convey* have been submerged in contradiction or incomprehension.

Example

'The World's Favourite Airline' was British Airways, as it was fond of proclaiming, but it quietly dropped the claim in 2000. In August 2002 Lufthansa was formally declared to be transporting the most passengers, and Air France was in third place, closing in on BA. What happened? With such a long list of pioneering achievements, including the first jet service across the Atlantic, the first automatic landing and, with Air France, supersonic flight in Concorde, there was plenty of equity in the brand, surely more than enough to counter any damage done by spurious gimmicks such as on-board 'hot milky drinks' and revelations about dubious competitive practices.

A 'notorious attempt' in 1997, however, at adjusting the corporate image, described by its chief executive as being staid, conservative and cold, most certainly did test severely the airline's credibility and status. As part of this adjustment, out went the British national flag, the distinctive 'Union Jack', which appeared on every 'plane's tailfin, and in came a series of ethnic designs, representing different places around the world. There was a cabin crew strike that year too, but the greater damage to corporate image came in a momentary gesture by a former British Prime Minister, who, expressing what she thought about the image 'makeover', placed her handkerchief over the new-style tailfin of a model BA plane at an exhibition stand, in front of television cameras and press photographers. At a stroke she had indicated what a lot of British people *felt* about their national airline wanting to 'abandon' its roots in this way. Two years later the project was assigned to history, but not before it had become 'a national laughing stock'. The chief executive left soon after.
(*The Guardian*, 10.9.02)

Corporate identity

Corporate image differs from **corporate identity**, which 'denotes the sum total of all forms of expression that [an organization] uses to offer insight into its nature' (van Riel, 1995). Corporate *identity* is 'the strategically planned and operationally applied self-presentation of the organization (the corporate self) on the basis of a desired image.' It 'raises employee motivation, inspires confidence among the organisation's key external groups, acknowledges the vital role of customers [and of] key financial groups' (Varey, 1997a). In other words, it is **how the organization presents itself, warts and all**, which, if done artfully, may bring it benefits leading to tangible rewards.

Corporate identity is primarily thought of in the context of symbols and logos, once very popular mechanisms for distinguishing one outfit from another, although now less so, because corporate identity in the last decade has acquired a *broader inter-pretation*. These branding tools are now joined by other considerations, including:

- *Presentation*, in all its manifest details, including not only the design of all materials and the corporate colours and patterns but also such finer points as staff livery, the appearance of premises, what the vehicles look like and so on, right down to such minutiae as distinctively shaped internal door windows, choice of canteen cutlery and all the other applications of the 'corporate look' that stake out the territory, assert the corporate distinctiveness and preferences
- *Personality*, the organization's values, its mission in life, its vision and purpose, as these are manifested
- *Behaviour*, how that personality comes across in the way people within the organization behave, 'live the values' or otherwise, particularly when they are in contact with publics such as customers and shareholders
- *Communication*, in whatever form: organizations communicate with their environments all the time, by omission as well as commission
- *Connections*, the company that the organization keeps, such as various charities and political parties, the causes and interests that they sponsor and the types of celebrities and public personalities they employ or attract.

In essence, this recognizes that people consider *in the round* and they connect up the bits of information they gather about the organization: so, for instance, what they consider to be poor handling of their enquiry, whether or not that is warranted, affects what they think about the organization when next they see its logo or livery.

This broad interpretation of corporate identity can be bruising. It means that in effect **the organization is never 'off duty'**, *cannot relax if it is serious about a holistic approach to communication.* Even dirty delivery vans in bad weather, for example, can do damage if what they carry is food, no matter that the products are unaffected. And dangerous driving by the van drivers can speak reams about process standards and work attitudes.

Example

'Companies pour millions of pounds [and other currencies] into creating strong brand identities that, once released into the world, become potent but difficult forces to control.' (*The Observer*, 13.8.00). Printed corporate names in public places are often altered in attempts to subvert their carefully constructed meanings, an activity described as 'political jujitsu' by Naomi Klein in *No Logo*. 'Jujitsu is a martial art that aims to take the energy of an attacker and redirect it against his or herself.' These guerrilla tactics, or social commentaries, represent a desire to make clear to the organization that the identity presented *does not accord with perceived reality.*

'The [visual presentation] programmes that seem to be most effective are those where identity schemes are part of a total and cohesive process of change that affects everything the company does. Not only does it mean operations and communications are working together, but it tends to encourage the involvement of employees. Whatever the scope of the programme, involvement should be a core objective' (Ind, 1995). This should *anchor the result closer to reality*, and avoid the

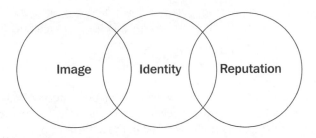

Figure 2.3   **Image, identity and reputation**

persistent tendency for some identities to be 'slapped on' the organization, as if applying a cosmetic.

Corporate reputation

Image and **reputation** are also often mistaken for being one and the same. However, *there is a key difference.* The reputation of an organization is based upon *experience* of it, which is *not* a pre requisite of deciding about its image. Experience may be:

- *direct,* as where a product is purchased and or a service is received, or
- *indirect,* when the direct experiences of others are recounted.

Those 'others' are people whose

1 judgement may be trusted, or whose credibility is plausible, and
2 whose circumstances are recognizable and sufficiently similar to be relevant.

The *quality* of the experience is assessed by reference to the behaviours of the people with whom there have been contacts, at whatever level within the hierarchy.

The most common circumstances in which reputation is established are sales and purchases transactions, hence the emphasis placed upon customer care and customer relations, but there are *many more opportunities* for the organization to alter its reputation, both with individuals and generally, through the aggregation of individual experiences, as people advise one another. The fostering of reputation is also subject to the vagaries of *rumour,* whether or not malicious, and the *quality of interpretation* of the messages received; **too much weight may be attached to gossip and innuendo and too little given to reasoned assessment of the experience.**

Image, identity and reputation are closely linked. The identity contributes to the image and both condition the reputation. It is a popular adage that **positive reputations take a long time to create but may be destroyed very quickly**, the implication being that *attention to detail* in all reputation-making situations is highly advisable.

Clearly, this has a direct bearing on the *size* of the organization, for as the numbers of contacts increase so too do the *opportunities to get it right or get it wrong.*

Example

The British National Health Service (NHS) offers an example of how difficult reputation management may become. It employs some 1.2 million people, is said to be the largest organization in Europe, and has considerable difficulties in managing its corporate reputation, with daily media reports about its under-performance, mistakes and howlers, recounted by its patients and their relatives and friends. For many years the NHS basked in the reflected glory of its pioneering founders, its *image* highly favourable, the British generally proud to have been the first to establish a comprehensive medical service accessible on demand and without charge to all residents, regardless of individual financial means. Once its *reputation* began to weaken, the NHS's troubles multiplied and it had to submit to emergency treatment, taking massive injections of state capital, experiencing successive managerial ructions, its reputation dramatically deteriorated. From being generally regarded as 'the best' it is now commonly described as being 'one of the worst' by those who have experienced similar services in other countries. The recovery of its favourable reputation may take many years.

Deficiencies of reputation, which is based on experience, may *jeopardize well-deserved and long cultivated* favourable image and identity.

Example

Boots is a UK international retailer, trading in pharmaceuticals, toiletries and related products. It is long established and has both an image and reputation as a caring employer. An internal document, 'leaked' to the press in spring 2003, revealed that a year before the formal announcement was made the company had decided to close a factory in Scotland and transfer the work to its facilities in England, France and Germany. This would cause the loss of 1000 jobs locally.

The document implied that the closure, codenamed Project Tuscan, would occur regardless of the outcome to a prior review of manufacturing options: 'We debated two possible approaches: i) announcement of Airdrie closure, ii) announcement of a manufacturing review. On balance it was agreed that approach ii) was preferable . . . This would give us a much more positive, media-friendly story to tell.' When the announcement of closure was made it was disclosed that at the end of 2002 the company had refused the offer of government funds to secure the future of the plant, because it did 'not need support.'

The document listed four audiences to be managed if the closure was not to damage the brand – employees, the media, politicians and business partners – and rated the probability of various reactions and their impact. It listed actions to control media impact and to 'limit government interference', including a suggestion that the closure announcement be timed to coincide with 'key political events'. When the company was informed of the leak it replied: 'The documents that have been leaked do not properly represent the extent of the total review process undertaken by the company. Our review was full, thorough and undertaken in keeping with our obligations.'

(*The Guardian*, 10.3.03)

Some companies *may not even much value reputation*, supposing that they may meet their objectives without bothering overly about it. Such cases are on the increase, raising ever more **questions about corporate governance**. For public relations practitioners *this trend raises serious challenges* to their assumed role as the function that is in control of the corporate reputation.

2.7 Business ethics and values

Widespread and growing distrust has implications for public relations practice. The *Concise Oxford Dictionary* defines *trust* as being:

firm belief in reliability, honesty, veracity, justice, strength, etc., of person or thing.

Interestingly, to be trust*ful* is defined as being *full of trust, unsuspicious, confiding*, that is to say, believing confidently in the veracity of another person. Trust*worthy* is to be *worthy of trust.*

When these terms are applied to organizations, rather than individuals, they strike a deeper resonance. For instance, *how many* organizations provoke *confidences* worthy of the name and how many may be accurately described as being *trust-worthy?* Are not these values cornerstones of communication, and why do they appear to be in short supply?

It is widely agreed that trust is a precious commodity that every organization needs. The arguments in favour are familiar:

- that trust in the workplace improves efficiency and creates greater enjoyment in the work
- that it creates the foundation for meaningful relationships with customers and other publics
- that it facilitates decision-taking and engenders confidence.

Trust is a product of *moral awareness of the ethical dimensions*, the rules of moral behaviour, encountered both within the organization and in its contacts with its external environment.

- But are ethical considerations to be discarded, as competition intensifies and communication becomes more complex, hurried and demanding of patience and expertise?
- Or might the widely acknowledged flight from trust be reversed, to advantage, applying some age-old truths to some very modern problems?

Utilitarianism

Probably the most commonly cited ethical principle is '*do what is likely to create the greatest happiness for the greatest number of people*,' first propounded in 1725 by Francis Hutcheson, thinking about politicians and nation states. This is the simplest form of **Utilitarianism**, the most widely used in routine 'common-sense' decision-making. It was used, for example, by the British Prime Minister in March 2003 when seeking parliamentary support for military invasion of Iraq.

Jeremy Bentham added to this, with his Principle of Utility, by which each action should be judged according to the *results* achieved by it, on how it *benefits everyone*, not just the performer. Also, he asserted that *everyone should be treated equally*, one form of happiness was not more important than any other.

Then John Stuart Mill also added that the *effects* of observing rules should also be considered where their observance would *benefit society as a whole*, and universally respected when they are framed for the benefit of everyone. He disagreed with Bentham about happiness, saying that there are higher and lower pleasures.

Public relations practitioners are unlikely to have difficulty in recognizing these precepts and in agreeing with them. But the *consequences* can be difficult to predict. 'Since you cannot be sure, ahead of time, what that good will be, or even, at times, where the greatest number will lie, you need to speculate as best you can on the consequences, or end, of your action' (Kidder and Bloom, 2001).

Among the many interpretations of utilitarianism there has arisen the theory that the *preferences of the individual* should be taken into account, unless those of others outweigh them. That is to say, the people concerned should be allowed to say what *for them* constitutes pleasure or pain. This widely applied argument has been advanced by, among others, Peter Singer (*Practical Ethics*, 1979), who advocates appropriate *equal consideration* of interests.

Utilitarianism has its *practical limitations*, owing to conflicts of interest and divergence of views. It advocates respect for individual preferences but **the final decision has to be in the interests of the majority, not the minority or the individual**. Nor does Utilitarianism:

- adequately allow for *motive*, which is important when thinking about morality
- explain why some moral rules should not be broken, *despite the consequences*, and
- does not allow fully for handling *complex* moral issues.

Categorical imperative

The second commonly cited approach is the **categorical imperative**, the view of morality that is based on knowing what *ought* to be done, having **a sense of duty**, *regardless of the consequences*. It is **absolute and unconditional**, very much suited to the person who prefers to act by the rulebook. Immanuel Kant is most closely associated with this; in 1785 he asserted that a person should only do that which he or she would be prepared for everyone else to be able to do as well. A main theme is that **actions should be consistent with treating people as the *ends* and not as the means**.

Kant was not troubled by consequences, preferring to concentrate on motive and the particular act. Expected results, he thought, could not be used to demonstrate conclusively that a proposed action was right or wrong; there would never be enough evidence and agreement about interpretation. Action should be out of *a sense of personal moral conviction*. The moral certainties of the categorical imperative may appeal, but prove difficult to follow, since *in public relations practice consequences have to be most carefully considered beforehand.*

Do unto others . . .

Given the reservations widely held about the practicalities of these two ethical avenues, a third, perhaps more simple approach, is widely favoured; simply *'do unto others as you would they do unto you'*. This advice is found in all the great religions and addresses *a universal truth* about human nature, that in behaving badly one with another people may like to give but certainly do not like to receive.

Example

Public relations is riddled with practical ethical dilemmas, so much so that the International Public Relations Association's eighth 'Gold Paper', *Ethical Dilemmas in Public Relations*, identified 20 commonplace situations that arise in practice. Typical instances that arise include:

- Promising prospective employers and clients knowingly unattainable results
- Undertaking to do what is transparently un-doable
- Leaking commercially sensitive information about a competitor or past employer
- Not offering critical advice in order to ensure a 'a quiet life'
- Telling partial facts to create plausibility and distraction
- Not replying to questions but instead reciting well-prepared alternative answers
- Implying senior attention to projects when knowing they will be implemented by juniors.

The generally acknowledged decline in business ethics pervades many aspects of corporate life, and is certainly not confined to public relations, but PR finds itself in the front line, promoting and guarding corporate reputation.

CHECKLIST

- Corporate communication may be divided into three categories: management communication, by managers both internally and externally; marketing communication; and organization communication, being all other forms of communication by an organization.
- Public relations practice occurs in all three categories, but primarily in the third.
- By their communication skills senior managers motivate and empower others internally and establish the external parameters within which they may develop their organizations.
- Those senior managers that recognize the public relations implications of their communication responsibilities acknowledge the relevance of PR to the development of their corporate strategy.
- MPR contributes to the creation of shareholder value and investment returns.
- The PR department is a formal subsystem, usually established when the activities of an organization or its publics, both internal and external, affect the other.
- The function is usually located among the management subsystems, but may be found in the disposal, adaptive or maintenance subsystems, depending upon workload weighting.

- The function spans boundaries, both internally between subsystems and between the organization and components of its external environment.
- Environmental scanning enables the PR function to ascertain, understand and record attitudes and behaviours towards the organization, evolving issues of potential consequence to the organization and the interactions of its publics and stakeholder groups.
- Image is a composite mental or sensual interpretation of someone or something that is based upon all the available evidence, both real and imagined, and conditioned by existing impressions, beliefs, ideas and emotions.
- Corporate identity describes how the organization presents itself in the round.
- Reputation is based upon experience gained, whether through direct contact or indirectly via information received from third parties who have had contact.
- Widespread and growing distrust has implications for PR practice, in which ethical dilemmas are commonplace and arise frequently.

CASE STUDY
A TALE OF TWO DOT COMS

Upmystreet.com is one of the UK's largest Internet businesses, originally a pitch promoting a consultancy, Aztec Internet, which was transformed, using £12.5 million external financing, into *the* site for all manner of local information, such as statistics on crime, the identity of elected representatives and, perhaps most importantly, given the British obsession with property, current house prices. In January 2003 alone it attracted 665,000 visitors, the same month the company went into administration, beset with severe cash flow problems. In the following April it was put up for sale, one of its founders posting the plea 'Buy my baby please'.

The company had been devising new products, including its praised 'world first in social software', a discussion board for conversation among neighbours, and had targeted services at the public sector and at business, to counter a downturn in advertising revenue, on which it is substantially dependent. But there are likely to be limits to how much local information and chat with neighbours is individually needed or wanted, and winning commercial contracts is costly and time-consuming.

This brand has been built with hardly any advertising expenditure, ironically, given the dependence upon it for income. It is rich in goodwill, intangible assets and intellectual property. And it has professional management that is positive about its future and its business model (*The Guardian*, 14.4.03).

Friends Reunited is another major UK Web-based business, founded by a married couple and their friend in a modest suburban house in 2000 to 'put people in touch with their old classmates'. Thousands of e-mails poured in daily, each one being answered individually, and soon relatives and friends, appropriately, were enlisted to help, a charge for the service being introduced in April 2001. In March 2003, still operating partly from the original tiny bedroom, the founders made known publicly that they were open to offers for the site, with its eight million registered users in the UK. Reported offers of up to £30 million came in, from companies thought to include AOL and Yahoo.

This company too has been adding to what it offers. It has GenesConnected, for people wanting to trace their family history, which also proved very successful, and is involved in online dating services that introduce strangers to one another socially. It is developing an international reach, notably into Italy, Spain, The Netherlands, Australia and New Zealand.

But Friends Reunited's owners decided not to accept an offer for the company, preferring instead to 'have other people managing it. . . . We don't really see ourselves as businessmen. . . . We describe it as an old-fashioned cottage industry.' It has reached this point with virtually no marketing or advertising. 'Basically there has been nothing spent on marketing so far, everything has been PR driven, which has been fantastic, but there is a point at which you need marketing to go further,' according to the company's new chief executive (*The Times*, 13.3.03).

QUESTIONS

1 What might be the 'total communication needs' of an organization, and why?
2 How may public relations contribute to shareholder value?
3 What might be meant by 'image is in the eye of the beholder'?
4 Why may reputations be made slowly and destroyed quickly?
5 How accountable is public relations for the quality of business ethics, and why?

▪ ⚡ 3 Within the organization

Vision and mission – the learning organization – enterprise culture – motivation – organizational structure and environment – communication channels – managing change – organizational body language

3.1   Vision and mission

The vision and mission of an organization provide the framework for all of the formal internal communication, and are therefore wholly relevant to public relations. **Vision** addresses the 'big picture', **what the organization aims to be and look like within a stated period**, typically several years ahead. It conveys a clear indication of ultimate direction for everyone engaged within the organization or connected with it in some way; *what the managers envisage being the organization's future.*

In a complex and uncertain environment, where there is **constant change**, it can be very reassuring to have a precise, clearly stated overall view of a credible, if distant, aim. As the proverb says, if you do not know where you are going any road will take you there. So the purpose of **vision statements** is to *set out clearly* the intended destination.

Mission, by contrast, is concerned with **how the organization performs at present**, specifically concerning standards of behaviour. **Mission statements** abound: some even are displayed in entrance halls and boardrooms, to tell visitors as well about the character of their organizations. When framing these statements there is an understandable temptation to *embroider reality*. Where that occurs it is the public relations task to provide employees with **valid interpretations** that they may recognize and accept as *having some bearing on their individual experience and perceptions.* This may be no easy task, but unless the mission statement has credibility it is likely to be rejected as mere irrelevant gibberish, meaningless verbiage, and this in turn can *foster doubts about other aspects of their employment.*

The *potency* of mission statements is in proportion to their credibility and the degree to which they reflect values that the organization *has in common with* its members.

- Research and corporate experience confirms that people *will* their employing organizations to demonstrate that they uphold their personal values.

Employees want to know that what they think is right or wrong in their private lives *coincides* with what goes on when they get to work. When asked for their perceptions of their employment, typical of the approving responses are comments such as

- 'They know how to treat people' and
- 'We are all a happy family'.

Where these and similar sentiments are expressed in house newspapers and other internal media, as often they are, they **must accord with employees' experience** if they are to be accepted.

This desire to see **shared values** in the workplace that foster accord and confidence goes *well beyond* the satisfaction of what seems right and proper, important though that is:

- Employees often seek reassurance that their organization *outperforms others owing to its superior behaviours*. These 'others' may be competitors, rivals or *all* organizations that are outwardly similar, including those in entirely different fields of activity.
- There is a need to know that *their* organization is superior, simply 'the best', and this has *implications* for performance and competitive advantage.

Example

The principles by which 8000 people work at Unisys, specialists in information and communications technology, translate into a very commercial core objective, to leave customers so satisfied that they recommend to friends and colleagues: *If you make a promise to a customer or a colleague, keep it and always do the right thing, however difficult it may be.* 'We all know what the right thing is and we try to encourage employees not to feel intimidated by hierarchical or political barriers.' The aim of the 'Vision On' internal communication programme is to 'get people involved in the company but to let them know that the only reason they have their jobs is that we have customers, and that everything they do has an impact on customers'. Communication is through meetings, intranet and a monthly newspaper. Information and answers from meetings, together with suggestions, 'even the less delicate ones', are posted on a website. Every comment is assigned an 'owner', a manager who is expected to respond within five days.
(*The Times*, 25.4.02)

There are four **elements of mission** (Campbell *et al.*, 1990): *organizational purpose, strategy, behaviours* and *values*, which both reflect and reinforce each other, and there are *three categories of company* where purpose is stated:

- the first is primarily concerned to maximize *shareholder value*
- the second exists primarily to satisfy all of its *stakeholders*
- the third prioritizes some *higher ideal* that all stakeholders may be proud to support and to which they contribute.

Example

A popular example in the last category is The Body Shop, a toiletries retailer dealing in 'products that do not hurt animals or the environment'.

These categories may be adapted to other types of organization. Clearly they have important implications for the structuring of internal communication, which needs to be *framed within the context of vision and mission*. The constant threat of confusion about mission and how it relates to vision compels eternal public relations vigilance, particularly since on occasion vision and mission coincide. This can occur in conditions of rapid change, where the mission may be more concerned to address desirable future rather than current behaviours.

The case for developing and maintaining meaningful mission statements is compellingly simple. 'A management team capable of defining a clear mission will have advantages over a team that has defined only its strategy. The mission team will have values as well as strategic concepts to guide it through important decisions; the strategy team will have commercial logic only. Business decisions and people decisions are often hard to take, particularly on a consistent basis. . . . In these two areas . . . senior managers need as much support as possible. A clearly defined set of values reinforcing the strategy gives this extra support.'

In developing both vision and mission statements the public relations function has a strong contribution to make and an equally strong interest in the outcome. Through their boundary spanning PR people are highly sensitive to the corporate culture *at all levels of the hierarchy. And* they are better placed than anyone else to have at their fingertips the raw data of outside attitudes and perceptions across all publics and stakeholders. *And* they have a ringside seat in seeing how other people within the organization interrelate with parts of the outside environment. All of which makes them a *key source* of input.

Furthermore, what emerges is *fundamental* to public relations strategic planning. The vision and mission statements are building blocks used for the foundations, without which any PR practice is at serious risk of being constructed on insecure premises and to being seriously hindered in its effectiveness. For public relations, therefore, the organization's current vision and mission is not simply 'nice to know' but absolutely '*need* to know'.

3.2 The learning organization

Internal communication is primarily about securing universal *motivation* and *commitment*, because **organizations are rated on their scope for leveraging assets**, obtaining more from what they have, and the human asset is potentially the richest source of enhanced performance.

- Managers in knowledge-based and in service-driven environments understand that they have to optimize the *organizational value of each person*.
- That in turn requires everyone to have his or her very own *personal development plan*, a career signposting that has less to do with jobs and more with self-fulfilment. They are the outward manifestation of a *mutually advantageous deal* between employer and employee, and where this pact works well the internal communication can assume some *very stimulating and worthwhile* dimensions.

It is this drive to enhance performance and competitive advantage through people skills that has brought about the concept of the **learning organization**. Learning may be defined as:

the process of acquiring, through experience, knowledge that leads to changed behaviour.

Expressed like that, not surprisingly many organizations want to become learning ones, in which their members routinely acquire knowledge that they can readily apply in the workplace. To qualify for the accolade involves everyone becoming and remaining *demonstrably at the cutting edge of knowledge acquisition.*

In order to attract students, some trainers advertise evening instruction providing knowledge that, they ambitiously claim, may be put to immediate use the following morning. Knowledge-based employees are expensive investments; sometimes they are sufficiently ambitious and self-disciplined to seek careers, not jobs, opportunities to learn and possibilities for applying what they know to ever more challenges. Most times they need a little encouragement, for commitment to learning can seem burdensome, particularly after another hard day's work.

The learning organization addresses this at several levels. First and foremost, it has a *vision*, one *that is shared*. Knowing where the organization is aiming for and being wholly committed to that creates a powerful combined determination to 'pull weight'. This may foster a relatively informal workplace, because, in perception if not in reality, the structure becomes flatter, as **each person exercises power through an ability to acquire knowledge and share information in a common cause**. The emphasis is on the 'learning curve', securing *up-to-date intelligence that can be used to advantage*, and on facilitation and collaboration to this end. **Creativity**, in ideas and implementation, is highly valued.

Communication has a significant role to play in enhancing this environment, for it serves information and ideas, supports and supplements coaching and mentoring and provides both advice and reassurance. 'How people listen depends on the organization's culture. . . . Culture 'refracts' communication. . . . The central skill in managing today's organization has gone from 'telling the troops' to fostering and facilitating communication. The aim . . . should be to align attitudes, share knowledge, and manage information' (Quirke, 1995).

It is observable that *an intensity of commitment* to learning often tends to be found within *smaller* organizations and units, perhaps owing to:

- the immediacy of competitive pressures,
- readier identification with core values and
- the necessity to adopt flexible work attitudes.

Small businesses in computer-related occupations or new media products offer typical examples.

3.3 Enterprise culture

Grunig and Grunig (1992) reported **four types of organizational culture** that had been identified by reference to the interaction of *two dimensions of attitude and behaviour*: authoritarian versus democratic and reactive versus proactive.

'*Systematized* cultures are authoritarian and reactive.
Entrepreneurial cultures are authoritarian and proactive.
Interactive cultures are democratic and reactive.
Integrated cultures are democratic and proactive.'

Subsequent research had indicated that nine out of ten in the sample were either *integrated* or *entrepreneurial*.

The idea of the individual taking initiative, unassisted by anyone, is deeply rooted and there is a widespread tradition of *enterprise born of initiative*, a concept that appears to thrive and is actively encouraged by some governments. The term **enterprise culture** is used to describe a **disposition towards bold, outward-going dynamic action that is based upon a set of supportive values** that has been widely described as a philosophy of 'free enterprise'. There is much talk of creating an enterprise culture, which encourages and exploits people's adventurous ambitions, as a means to achieve economic growth and wealth generation more widely.

Within the enterprise culture there abides the *entrepreneur*, who may be defined as anyone who undertakes a business activity with the chance of making a profit or loss. They are noted for their ability to:

focus, to the extent of seldom being 'off the job',
analyze what they know and believe,
demonstrate self-reliance and resourcefulness,
exercise judgement,
provide leadership and
think flexibly.

They keep *asking the tough questions* and *trying to avoid set thinking*, a kind of corporate hardening of the arteries. Often they concentrate till it hurts and they are always looking for ways around obstacles.

In *What They Don't Teach You At Harvard Business School* (1984) the entrepreneur Mark McCormack counselled that 'Running a company is a constant process of breaking out of systems and challenging conditioned reflexes, of rubbing against the grain.' This calls for lateral thinking. 'The trouble is that there is no logical reason for looking for alternatives unless we are dissatisfied with what we have. And yet in creativity it is vital to be looking for alternatives no matter how satisfied we may be. There therefore has to be a deliberate intention or exercise of will to seek alternatives. . . . Curiously we do not have a verb to describe the need to look for alternatives. That is why it was necessary to create the term "lateral thinking" ' (De Bono, 1978).

Creativity is the very life-blood of public relations, which is *closely identified with the enterprise culture*. Public relations people are required to demonstrate their ability to be creative and think laterally. *Organizations in search of a more entrepreneurial bias in their cultures look to their public relations departments to communicate some of that outlook and 'can do' approach* which characterizes their work. Public relations is expected to provide an inexhaustible flow of creative solutions that are distinctive and practitioners are generally noted for their seemingly relentless energy and enthusiasm.

3.4 Motivation

The house magazine may have a long history, but it has not been a particularly glorious one. Too often these popular components of the 'created media' have included a varied collection of management opinion and assertion, propaganda, cloying supposed entertainment and inconsequentialities. Front pages and covers invariably featured the chairman with a drink in his hand or the managing director gripping a public speaker's lectern. Inside there would be a few more photographs, mostly involving the chairman and the managing director again, the finance director too if he or she got lucky.

Sometimes merely to *glimpse* such organs seems an unwarranted intrusion upon the private lives of the senior management. Seldom did the employees *learn anything much* of substance *about management's thinking, conclusions, decisions and purposes*. Instead they probably had to be content with a concoction of instructions and heavily contrived news, *mostly filleted of facts worth having*, interwoven with a few well-placed entertainment items of the utmost banality.

All this *should* be past, for the motivational role of communication within the organization has never been clearer. Whatever the primary purpose, such as greater efficiency or customer focus, managers *need the positive collaboration* of employees in coming forward with their feedback, ideas and suggestions, so that **those whose experience tells them where changes might be usefully made inform those who have the authority to make them.**

Now the emphasis is on *involving everyone*, bringing them into the thinking, getting them wanting to come forward, creating believable futures and so on. Content standards have improved. The purpose is to stimulate a *united sense of motivation and loyalty* through a more collegiate approach that takes greater account of readers' knowledge and perceptions.

Entertainment and information remain components of the communication mix, as do persuasion, but the thrust is on **engagement, dialogue, trying to have conversations that will benefit the organization.** In *Up The Organization* (1970) Robert Townsend, former chairman of Avis, observed that people 'don't have to be forced or threatened [to work]. . . . But they'll commit themselves only to the extent they can see ways of satisfying their ego and development needs . . . .'

The original idea that simply making people *feel good* about their employment is *no longer adequate within an unstable operating environment*, where the organization must be quick on its toes, responding to external changes and striving to change itself advantageously. People have needs, which managers must recognize and address if they are to establish and maintain mutually beneficial relationships. Those needs include recognition and tangible appreciation. And managers have to understand what emotional and psychological hurdles may have to be jumped before upward communication becomes possible.

3.5 Organizational structure and environment

The organizational structure and environment and its management style are also fundamentally important to the planning and conduct of public relations, because they **determine the approach to developing communication systems and media.** There are four management theories, or groups of theories, that provide the framework to thinking about this.

Machine theory

In the early part of the 20th century a group of theories, collectively described as **machine theory**, perceived of the organization and its people as being a *machine*:

- A French industrialist, Henri Fayol, developed a classical management theory whose universal principles, mainly related to structure and organization, were based on 'logical' factors, including how formal communication would operate. He saw managers as being *commanders* who gave orders
- Various writers elaborated this, for instance, replacing commanding with *leading* through interpersonal skills and adding *representing* in dealings with other organizations, the ambassadorial PR role
- A manager, F. W. Taylor, advocated 'scientific' principles, notably that work should be organized into its *simplest, smallest actions*, each performed repetitively by one person trained for that task alone.

All of these theories saw humans as *cogs in the machine*, there to labour at their narrow specialisms with minimal autonomy within rigidly structured hierarchies:

- There was tightly held *central management and control*, everyone reporting to only the person most immediate to them up the chain
- Supervision was usually *limited to five people*, because that was thought to be the largest number that a supervisor or foreman could be expected to control.

This approach could be harshly interpreted and when Henry Ford, the car maker, advised by Taylor, began speeding up his moving production lines, first introduced in 1908, the production workers found themselves in growing misery, eventually resulting in riots.

Communication in these structures runs:

1 **vertically**, from superiors to subordinates and vice versa,
2 **horizontally**, from colleagues to colleagues within a unit or between units at the same level and
3 **diagonally**, between units at differing levels.

However, the *main* flow is **downwards**, usually with instructions and exhortations to work harder, quicker.

Human relations theory

In response to the deficiencies of machine theory there emerged **human relations theory**, which focused on *people* and how they might be *motivated* to achieve greater efficiency.

An industrial psychologist, Elton Mayo, argued that *relationships* were the most

Figure 3.1 **Communication flows within the 'machine'**

important factor, and in consequence *teamwork* was the key. He and two colleagues from Harvard University conducted research at the Western Electric Company's plant at Cicero, near Chicago, which became known as the 'Hawthorne Studies'. The team concluded that:

- people should be viewed not in isolation but *as part of a group*
- *informal groups exert powerful influence*
- managers need to *allow for the social needs* of employees to secure commitment.

They had found that *through information, explanation and willingness to listen,* the researchers had inadvertently induced the women to **form a self-governing team** that **co-operated wholeheartedly** with management.

Another contributor to human relations theory was industrialist Chester Barnard, who recognized **communication as the first priority in management** but thought it should be 'expressive', not 'instrumental'. He favoured the machine concept but in addition to giving instructions he saw value in 'feel good' messages that made it all seem somehow better for the workers.

Significantly, followers of this *seemingly softer* approach 'wanted to exchange expressive communication and humane treatment – "human relations" – for compliance with organizational constraints, rather than exchanging money for compliance, as in machine theory' (Grunig and Hunt, 1984).

Here again, *horizontal contacts were discouraged* for fear that inaccurate information, rumours and 'the wrong news' might circulate. Communication up the line was limited by the conditions and was often motivated solely by a *desire for recognition and approval.* Barnard asserted that informal communication systems were irrational, whereas the modern mind might find them reasonable and wholly explicable.

These machine and human relations theories underpin the management approach in more structured organizations;

- instructions come from the centre,
- the emphasis is on close adherence to performance targets and
- the contributions of employees are lauded,

because 'More competition requires more co-operation' (Peters, 1987). Large and numerous awards may be given to honour acts of co-operation: 'The chief issue is attitude, but such awards can help change attitudes, over time.'

Human resources theory

This emerged out of human relations theory:

- In his motivation theories, psychologist Abraham Maslow argued in 1943 that **people have a 'hierarchy of needs'** that start with fundamental requirements of food and shelter and ascend, progressively, through safety to society and affection to self-esteem and finally fulfilment. Each level is dominant until satisfied and *only then* is the next a motivating factor; self-actualization, the top tier, *cannot be satisfied*.
- Many models have been based on Maslow's, usually depicted as a triangle. Cartwright, however, decided to create an extra layer, so creating a blank summit. The model 'cuts off the top of self-actualization to reflect the fact that there are things that will never be totally achieved. Part of human motivation is to strive for the unreachable' (Cartwright, 2001).
- Frederick Herzberg's **motivation–hygiene** theory identified **what causes dissatisfaction and satisfaction at work**. He called these *hygiene*, because they are essentially preventative, or *maintenance* factors. He thought people felt a need to *avoid unpleasantness*, which could be satisfied by hygiene factors, which were

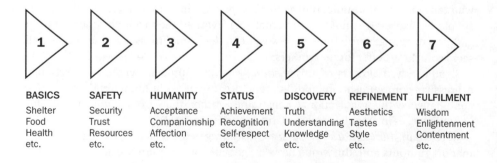

BASICS	SAFETY	HUMANITY	STATUS	DISCOVERY	REFINEMENT	FULFILMENT
Shelter	Security	Acceptance	Achievement	Truth	Aesthetics	Wisdom
Food	Trust	Companionship	Recognition	Understanding	Tastes	Enlightenment
Health	Resources	Affection	Self-respect	Knowledge	Style	Contentment
etc.	etc.	etc.	etc.	etc.	etc.	etc.

Figure 3.2 **Hierarchy of human needs, after Maslow**

short-lived and repeatedly in demand, and for *personal growth*, which could be met by motivator factors. And he specified three typical ways by which work might be altered in order to motivate: *job enrichment, job enlargement* and *job rotation*.

- In examining how managers handle people, Douglas McGregor identified two **extreme sets of assumptions, which determined the styles adopted. Theory X** stated that the average person has an inherent dislike of work and will try to avoid it. There is little ambition and no want of responsibility, but preference for being given direction and a craving of security.
- According to his **Theory Y**, however, the expenditure of physical and mental effort in work is as natural as play or rest. There is no inherent dislike of work; it may be the source of satisfaction or punishment. There is self-direction and control when there is commitment. McGregor intentionally polarized his theories, knowing that in practice managers' assumptions may fall somewhere between the two extremes.
- Robert Blake and Jane Mouton produced a 'management grid' in 1964, known as **Blake's grid**, based on **two dimensions of managers' behaviour in ensuring efficiency and effectiveness**: concern for *the job* in hand and concern for *the people* doing it. They identified five styles:

  - *impoverished* (not much bothered about targets or people),
  - *country club* (satisfying relationships is the priority),
  - *task management* (achieving results is the priority),
  - *middle of the road*, or *the dampened pendulum* (aiming for a balance between productivity and morale) and
  - *team* (high work accomplishment through leadership of committed people who identify with the organizational aims).

- William Ouchi in 1981 combined Japanese and western management techniques in his **Theory Z**, which asserted that **ability to gain the co-operation of people, not technology, increased productivity.** He based his thinking on the concept of 'wa', or harmony, and 'nenko', or lifelong employment.
- Charles Handy's **motivation calculus** was based on **expectancy theory**, by which **people decide on their effort based on what they think is in it for them and how likely that result is**. He argued that there was *more than Effort alone required*, including Energy, Excitement, Enthusiasm, Emotion and Expenditure, his **E-factors**. In the workplace:

  - the *intended results* had to be made clear, so that the person could work out how much 'E' was required, and
  - there had to be *feedback* on performance, for confidence, prevention of hostility and so on.
  - People committed when *the goals were specific*, particularly if they had helped identify them; however,
  - if they were rewarded for performance tied to specific standards people might then *set themselves lower standards*, when the likelihood of success and reward was greater and required less 'E' to be exerted.

Human resources theory perceives **engagement and involvement of employees** as being **central to motivation that will result in co-operation.** This is achieved through

more flexible structures and *greater autonomy for the individual* based upon a degree of **open communication between managers and staff**, open in the sense that the substantive background decisions and their circumstances are explained and discussed. The environment is less about managers giving orders and more about *managers and staff collectively 'taking orders' from their shared situation*.
In this environment:

- *communication is encouraged*, vertically, horizontally and diagonally, and
- there is *less inhibition*;
- ideally, messages flow backwards and forwards *without regard for status* of senders, encouraged in a dynamic atmosphere of collaboration and mutual respect.

But this much looser approach does not have universal appeal. It often works very well in *smaller settings*, with *fewer people involved*, typically where everyone has readily *recognizable symbols of comparable status*, but where one subsystem differs from another in its approach it may not be so practicable. And people have *variable levels of willingness* to participate in these less formal structures; hence much emphasis is placed on **team building**.

Systems theory

Finally, there is **systems theory**, discussed in Chapter 2, which, instead of specifying any one approach, advocates 'horses for courses': **what suits best in the given circumstances, the organization's environment and technologies**. This applies not only to the whole system but also to each and every one subsystem.

Designing for communication

So the design of communication systems has to take into account the variables. Here it may serve a more structured environment, there it may reflect a less structured one; content may be orientated here more around instruction, encouragement and happy families, there more around ideas, opportunities and objective, timely tips. Less specialized people tend to prefer 'keeping it simple' whereas the more specialized may well want more 'bight' and objectivity.

3.6 Communication channels

Owing to the historic emphasis on printed media, such as the 'house journal', there is still a *substantial use of hard copy publications*, but a growing proportion of internal communication uses *other tools*, and benefits from continuing innovations. The media include:

- *magazines*, to tell the human story, explain a complex issue, convey organizational qualities and status

- *newspapers*, tabloid size, with timely news, hard facts, friendly tips, bonding messages
- *newsletters* that provide facts and comment, decisions and deadlines, calls for action, often electronically instead of or as well as hard copy
- *bulletins*, often daily, with a digest of what matters most there and then
- *presentations*, using audiovisual equipment, to treat a larger subject in detail
- *video tapes*, for advice and instruction simultaneously at multiple sites or individual viewing by scattered staff
- *audiotapes*, for much the same but where vision is not needed, to be heard by staff individually off site or at home
- *closed circuit television*, for immediacy across sites in a very popular format
- *displays and exhibitions*, for complex messages, three-dimensional interpretations, opportunities to linger and ready access to answers
- *telephone 'hot lines'*, for enquiries and contributions
- *e-mails*, for short messages and generating immediate interest
- *letters*, particularly for contractual and other messages that require personal attention, and may involve consultation with others
- *brochures and booklets*, for information that may be needed routinely in the future or to address a major current issue involving many people / everyone
- *books*, fictional or non-fictional, for education about the organization, its sector, history, connections, interests
- *notice boards*, for fast rotation of information in arresting displays
- *pay packet notices*, for short messages guaranteed to be read
- *annual reports*, to share the corporate whole and emphasize involvement – these may be the original version or a specially produced adaptation
- *recruitment literature*, to demonstrate how the organization recruits and to encourage recruitment.

This is not a definitive list. For instance, second generation mobile, or cell, telephones, with their facility for sending and receiving text messages, may be used for short calls to action or exchange of information among scattered staff. Technology advances are likely to produce many more such developments; in each instance the public relations practitioner balances the *intended content and purpose* of the communication against the *suitability* of each medium to convey it.

3.7 Managing change

The increase of knowledge and flattening of hierarchies within organizations, resulting in less formality and greater involvement of people in the workplace, is increasing the need to **engage everyone in the processes of change** that have become a commonplace feature of corporate life. This again is of keen relevance to PR practice.

Two initial points about this:

1 The term 'marketing change' has gained currency, but this implies that employees are customers. They are *not* customers, but members of an organization in which they are investing their time and labour, and the planned approach to communicating change and implementing it should fully respect this.

2   Particular emphasis is likely to be given to relatively less structured consultation and to explaining the benefits for both the organization and the individual in terms that are meaningful.

Not everyone is against change, as marketing change implies, far from it. After all, change can be quite comfortable, when it is predictable, more of the same. 'Thirty years ago most people thought that change would mean more of the same, only better. That was incremental change and to be welcomed. Today we know that in many areas of life we cannot guarantee more of the same . . . Change is now more chancy, but also more exciting if we want to see it that way. Change has, of course, always been what we choose to make it, good or bad, trivial or crucial' (Handy, 1989).

Among those who positively welcome change, not only for the variety that it brings but also its new possibilities, are the *corporate entrepreneurs*, people who 'do not start businesses; they improve them. They push the creation of new products, lead the development of new production technology, or experiment with new, more humanly responsive work practices' (Moss Kanter, 1984). These people are categorized as:

- system builders,
- loss cutters,
- socially conscious pioneers, or
- sensitive readers of cues about the need for strategy shifts;

sometimes they become public 'heroes' for their involvement in a successful innovation.

The communication effort has to *harness all the available commitment and goodwill*, and this is unlikely to be achieved within a vacuum, where hitherto the system has not encouraged participation or has 'paid lip service' only to what people say, hearing but not listening.

- Explaining change and managing it through participative dialogue with everyone concerned is a delicate skill that takes time to acquire.
- When the challenge comes, managers need *the right kind of form* in the eyes of their employees; credible track records of having engaged in meaningful dialogue in the past.

Then there should be no need to 'sell' anything but ample scope to share everything.

3.8   Organizational body language

The term organizational body language was conceived by Cartwright and Green in *In Charge of Customer Satisfaction* (1997) and developed in relation to enhancement of customer relations. They argued that organizations, as well as individuals, exhibit a form of body language that sends out messages about the organization. (Cartwright, 2001). 'OBL relates to the whole atmosphere that an organization creates.' This may be said to equally apply *internally* as well as externally, because for the communication loop to work there needs to be feedback, and that can prove much more difficult to provide for someone inside the organization who is taking a living from it than for a customer on the outside.

Commitment, it is often said, only really comes from *a sense of ownership*, that is to say, when people feel that it is really *their* organization, no-one else's. They reach that conclusion slowly, often hesitatingly, only when they are *sure* that it is *safe* to invest the necessary *emotional capital.* So they look for *call signs*, wanting to know:

- if it is dangerous to say anything
- whether there is any risk of retribution should they speak up
- what the managers do with the suggestions after they have them
- whether their eyes glaze over when they are supposed to be concentrating on people's concerns.

People are doing within the organization *what they do anyway elsewhere*, so they are well practised at it. They are **studying the body language**. In the corporate sense, that has many dimensions. Messages go out to the internal publics (there can be more than one) through many channels.

Example

Staffers may not *say* anything but they may *think* plenty, about, for instance: non-action, silence, slow response, all talk and no do, a sense of foreboding, empty senior management floors, endless management meetings behind closed doors and so on.

Employees are *close to the action*: they are **uniquely placed among publics** to climb the ladder through awareness, understanding, support and involvement, but *then* comes the final rung, *commitment.* That is the moment of truth. Is the corporate body language *right?*

The **7S model** that management consultants McKinsey and Co. designed in the 1980s for **understanding ineffective organizations and managing change** puts this in perspective. The seven elements are:

Strategy, Shared values, Skills, Staff, Systems, Style and Structure.

Effectiveness is achieved when the *strategy fits the values* and both are *fully supported* by the other elements. **Mission** can be defined using this model: strategy, shared values and policies and behaviour standards, including all the other 'S' factors, interconnect and reinforce each other (Campbell *et al.*, 1990). **Right in there is** *style*, or 'the way we do things around here'. Communication has to take this factor fully into account for the body language to pass penetrating scrutiny.

Even when all these building blocks are in place, the *quality and nature* of the **feedback** is dependent upon *what exactly* people are paying attention to in the *detail* of their daily experience, whether out of choice or necessity, because they think its what is *expected* of them or *best fits* their interpretation of the culture. And 'If they're paying attention to the wrong things (as judged by the leader), the organization will be unlikely to move in the direction the leader desires' (Davenport and Beck, 2001).

- Corporate vision and mission differ: vision indicates what the organization aims to be and look like within a stated period, the future; mission describes current organizational behavioural standards, which should accord with individual members' experience and perceptions.
- In addition to describing current behaviours, mission statements also address organizational purpose, strategy and values; they are a key communication.
- The learning organization communicates and fosters the enhancement of individual skills through the acquisition, via experience, of knowledge that leads to changed behaviours.
- Creativity and lateral thinking are fundamental internally as well as externally to public relations practice, which is closely identified with enterprise culture.
- Internal communication tools have a strong motivational purpose.
- The internal communication system should accurately reflect and benefit from the nuances of the organizational structure and culture that it serves.
- Each communication method is chosen for its specific suitability to transmit the intended message and the purpose of that communication.
- The communication effort has to harness all the available commitment and goodwill in order to effect beneficial organizational change.
- People look for call signs that assure them it is safe for them to invest their emotional capital in adopting a sense of ownership in their organization.

CASE STUDY
CARLISLE ALIVE AND KICKING

When market leader Carlisle Process Systems embarked upon complete restructuring, which also included a name change under new ownership, this 77-year-old multinational initiated its 'Alive and Kicking' communication programme to explain the transformation to employees and customers; both publics had to be convinced of the need for and the benefit of the changes. Internal communication was built around monthly face-to-face leadership contact sessions, which created great interest and generated many *ad hoc* discussions with individuals and small groups.

Carlisle designs, engineers, fabricates and installs a range of plant required by hygienic liquid processors located in Europe, North America and elsewhere in the temperate climate zones. These industrial products include pasteurizers, separators, homogenizers and cleaning-in-place (CIP) machinery designed to ensure hygiene maintenance to match the requirements of further customers in the supply chain, such as Marks & Spencer, Nestlé and Waitrose.

The UK company was started by the Gate family, of later Cow & Gate fame, which went on to become Unigate. Two mergers later, it is now part of Carlisle Process Systems Inc, part of Carlisle Companies Inc, with 10 subsidiaries that include the three pre-eminent names in the sector: Carlisle in the UK, Damrow in Denmark and Scherping in the USA.

The purpose of 'Alive and Kicking' was to win employees' acceptance and understanding for the re-structuring and to gain improved commitment, productivity and sales. The programme name embodied the intention to demonstrate positively to the world the dynamic and resolve of the newly revitalized company.

Hitherto the company had been known as Wincanton Engineering, and it was decided to make optimum use of the residual strength of the brand by applying it to all products. This would ensure continuity of positive perceptions about the company and would, in turn, support and strengthen the new Carlisle corporate brand. The Wincanton name meant much to employees, who found its retention and extended use reassuring, particularly given the potential for disorientation and divided loyalties brought about by the changes.

From a business hierarchically based on functions, Carlisle had adopted a flatter structure comprising three distinct customer-focused groups: Cheese; Dairy, Food and Beverage; and Manufacturing. This re-structuring marked a return to the company's core strengths and was accompanied by demanding new profit targets. The focus now was on the 'bottom line', not on 'sales at any price'.

The benefits of this radical re-thinking needed to be fully appreciated and grasped by everyone, if the concept of 'selling solutions to process problems' was to be turned into a reality. Staff had lived through a period of turmoil and uncertainty, in which their company had lost some credibility in the market. Now they needed to engage with the idea that through their efforts customers really were enabled to add more value to what they, in turn, sold on to their customers.

'Alive and Kicking' had several specific objectives. These included:

- recognition of the major changes as creating both corporate and personal growth opportunities
- acceptance that core values, relationships and corporate status survived intact
- commitment to 'making it work' by accepting new responsibilities, demonstrating greater flexibility in problem-solving and taking 'ownership' of the outcomes.

Communication centred on the message 'It's *your* business, they're *your* customers.'

Monthly financial indicators on sales and profit were published: actual versus budget, linking every person and every act every day to the results, with the message 'Everyone helps the sales process, it is not just down to the salesman. We all have to be right on customer service, quality, delivery and price, and we have to be right first time!'

The proportion of profit over budget was advised every month; 'it can go up or down, we can add or destroy value.' Whatever was in the 'pool' at the year-end was divided equally, on the basis that 'if the business fails we are all equally out of a job, so we should equally share in the reward.' Monthly indicators were also provided to show current size of the 'pool' and relate this to each person's personal cash take, which proved to be a powerful communication tool.

The programme ran throughout 2002 and produced remarkable results. Within months Carlisle Process Systems moved out of loss and into profit. This was achieved on lower turnover and higher margins. No staff quit and lost customers began to return. Employees demonstrated a new drive and purpose, resulting in major new orders obtained internationally.

Interest remains 'Alive and Kicking', as evidenced by a continuing strong flow of informal communication. The employee profit share scheme has been maintained, with internal profit centres making monthly presentations and taking quarterly presentations from general manager Charles Todd, whose ambition is 'to have all employees knowing instinctively the things that make or lose profit and therefore guiding their everyday actions. This is the only way that the business will have its own natural momentum to take it into a long-term future.'

QUESTIONS

1 Why might it be necessary to disentangle confusion over vision and mission?
2 What factors drive creativity, energy and enthusiasm in PR practice, and why?
3 What are the civil liberties implications of motivational workplace communication?
4 Why might employees misconstrue organizational body language?
5 Should the 'grapevine' be encouraged or suppressed, and why?

■ ⊻ 4 Outside the organization

The operating environment – turbulent times – publics and stakeholders – corporate social responsibility – risk and crisis management

4.1 The operating environment

Internal publics may expect to find out about their organization from within, but, except in the unlikely event that it is a closed system, they *also learn about it from the world outside*.

'It often happens that a message – the content of a communication – reaches the internal public subsequently from the outside world, from an indirect source, rather than directly delivered to the internal public as first addressee. Opinions and judgements of the internal publics interact with those of the external publics, and the combination of the two identifies the frame of the enterprise's communication.' (CERP website, 5.11.02).

In other words, *internal publics also have a life outside*, in the organization's operating environment, where their members may *belong to one or more other publics*, providing ample opportunity for cross-fertilization of attitudes and perceptions, facts and rumours, news and innuendo. **Internal and external publics are therefore closely interrelated**.

Micro and macro environments

The environment in which an organization operates may be broadly divided into:

- The *micro* environment actors, the external publics that affect the organization's ability to operate successfully, particularly the investors, customers, suppliers, distributors, regulators, competitors, opinion formers and relevant media, and
- The *macro* environment forces, the political, legal, economic, social, cultural, technological and environmental factors that set the broad context.

From a *marketing* perspective the environment is primarily of interest for its effect upon *profitability*. A marketing intelligence system is used to identify and follow trends and important developments that are assessed and graded as *opportunities* or *threats*. 'One of the major purposes of environmental scanning is to discern new opportunities.' (Kotler, 1991). 'We define a company marketing opportunity as … an attractive arena for company marketing action in which the company would enjoy a competitive advantage. These opportunities should be classified according to their *attractiveness* and the *success probability* that the company would have with each opportunity.'

Given that the majority of public relations activity is in support of marketing, this emphasis on commercial prospects is likely to be at the forefront of many practitioner's thinking. However, *the environment is of great interest in public relations for further reasons*, not least because some organizations are not companies seeking to make a profit and not everyone engaged in PR-driven environmental scanning is doing it for an organization. The opportunities and threats identified are therefore likely to have broader implications, which may or may not relate to profitability, either directly or indirectly.

Static and dynamic environments

Organizational environments as a whole differ one from another:

- **The more *static* provide a stability that favours routine and prediction** based on extrapolation of past experience. Unfortunately they can also breed complacency, leading to inadequate scanning and insufficient attention to detail. This skimping can in turn impair performance and render the organization vulnerable.
- **The more dynamic are invariably**, but not necessarily, **complex and experiencing frequent change**, probably powered by rapid advances in *knowledge, technology applications* and *demand* for products and services. They demand the closest possible scrutiny and there is no scope for any let up on the job.

Grunig found six characteristics that separate static from dynamic environments. These included variable levels of:

- *technology* change and mechanization,
- *demand* for the organization's products and services,
- *competition* within its markets,
- *social and political support* that it enjoys and
- rate of growth in its use of *knowledge*.

Grunig and Hunt (1984) report the conclusions of Howard Aldrich in *Organizations & Environments* (1979), who identified six characteristics, which may be summarized briefly as:

- *Resources* – the richer the resources in the environment, the greater the opportunities for the organization, and the greater the competition
- *Differences* – the more pronounced these are, whether between organizations or within the environment, the greater the need for flexibility and innovation
- *Stability* – the more frequent the changes, the greater the need to forsake routine
- *Spread* – the wider the geographical spread of resources and key systems, the greater the difficulty of establishing routines relating to them
- *Concord* – the more disagreement between the organization and its publics, the greater the need for flexibility in addressing them

- *Turbulence* – the closer the connections to unpredictably changing inter-penetrating systems, the greater the need to change, to cope with the chaos.

It is not, however, 'the public relations department's responsibility to deal with all of these elements of a complex, dynamic environment. Nevertheless, [it] must deal with key interpenetrating publics and organizations and help other subsystems improve their communication.'

Environmental cultures

The environment may be said to have a number of ingredients comprising a **'cultural web'** (Johnson and Scholes, 1999). These were identified in explaining the culture of organizations for the purpose of developing corporate strategy, but they also apply externally. The organizational environment has within it, for example, various **power structures that need to be accurately identified and understood**, because they are *primary* influences and relate directly to the *relative amount of turbulence*. All these factors are equally deserving of investigation and evaluation.

Three techniques for scrutinizing the environment were mentioned in Chapter 2, where reference was made to there being several more such tools. Among these is SPECTACLES analysis, designed to assist in **coping with the more complex**

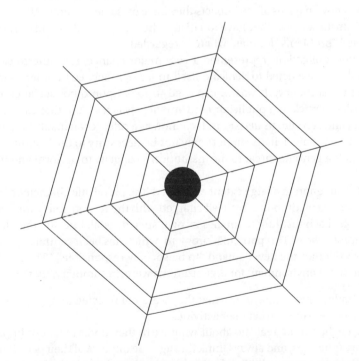

Figure 4.1   **The web of cultural factors in the organizational environment, after Johnson and Scholes**

environment (Cartwright, 2001). This embraces: Social analysis, Political, Economic, Cultural, Technological and Aesthetic factors, Customers, and Legal, Environmental and Sectoral features, the last covering both competitors and collaborators, or partners. This analysis emphasizes the multiplicity of possible interactions between each of these ten elements, their potential complexity and importance to the organization.

4.2 Turbulent times

In the last quarter century the **incidence of turbulence** has greatly increased. In addressing this development, Drucker (1980) observed that all those *many social tasks that used to be undertaken within the family unit had been assumed by institutions* 'organized for perpetuity and dependent on leadership and direction given by managers in a formal structure.' The most 'visible' of these institutions were companies, civil services, universities and bureaucrats generally. This process was worldwide and completed in the developed countries. Meanwhile, he asserted, central government had become increasingly impotent the larger it had become.

In this 'society of institutions', Drucker argued 'The special-purpose institutions have progressively become carriers of social purpose, social values, social effectiveness. Therefore they have become politicized. They cannot justify themselves any longer in terms of their own contribution areas alone; all of them have to justify themselves now in terms of the impacts they have on society overall. All of them have outside "constituencies" they have to satisfy, where formerly they had only restraints that created "problems" for them when disregarded.'

These new obligations represented a very major change, for hitherto each institution had been expected to dedicate itself to a single service in order to serve one public, or constituency; 'It was ... expected to look upon other social concerns as restraints.' To Drucker, a public, or constituency, was a group 'that can impede an institution and can veto its decisions. It cannot, as a rule, get an institution to act, but it can stymie and block it. Its support may not be necessary to the institution; but its opposition is a genuine threat to the institution's capacity to perform and to its very survival.'

The phenomenon to a large extent expressed 'the pluralistic character of a society in which no one institution is by itself charged with the responsibility for the welfare of the whole. Each institution pursues its own specific goal. But who then takes care of the common weal? This particular problem, which has been central to pluralism at any time, underlies the new demand "to be socially responsible".' The implications of this turbulent environment for organizations were, in summary, that

- organizations had to make sure that they were not rejected or opposed by groups that could veto or obstruct their activities
- managers had to be realistic about what extra they undertook, not imperil their primary functions, and always think through the impacts of their decisions
- their tasks and responsibilities had to be more broad and inclusive, and they had to make time to learn at first hand and provide leadership

- they had to be the integrating force, spokesmen for the interests of society in producing, performing and achieving
- corporate policies had to be in the general interest and provide social cohesion before there was a problem or issue
- managers had to create the issues, 'to identify both the social concern and the solution to it', and speak for the producer interest in society as a whole, not just for 'business'.

The process that Drucker described has continued, to the point that it is now probably present in most countries of the world. He set out very clearly **the gathering role of managers as leaders and integrators** as well as people who manage their organizations for optimum performance.

For Ehling *et al.* (1992) he had provided the 'rationale for the existence of a public relations function in an organization that cannot be matched by any that are set forth in college-level public relations textbooks. [He had] provided a clear justification for the establishment and departmentalization of the public relations function and for separating public relations management from marketing management.' Public relations people had been 'mandated' to deal with what Drucker called political problems that were not about marketing. If they did not, they would be rendered ineffectual and, a ringing phrase, the 'losers in the politics of confrontation'.

Drucker's explanation for the growing turbulence was plain. There was an increasing move from the creation of consent, finding the common denominator, seeking compromise, to creating confrontation and adversarial behaviours, identifying the least and most uncommon single cause, favouring 'trial by combat'. The intervening years have proved him correct and provided a compelling explanation for the growth of public relations practice during that period.

Competition is also a primary cause of turbulence. 'The intensity of competition in an industry is neither a matter of coincidence nor bad luck. Rather, competition in an industry is rooted in its underlying economic structure and goes well beyond the behaviour of current competitors' (Porter, 1980). In addition to the rivalry between companies supplying a given market, there were four further sources of competition: *buyers* and *suppliers*, both of whom exert bargaining pressure; *potential entrants* to the market and *potential substitute new products and services*, both of which threaten the existing market.

These **five forces** are key features wherever there is competition, in all three main sectors of the economy, and the turbulence of recent years suggests that this model may be refined by the addition of *five significant additional forces* or pressures:

- *existing players*: scope for rationalization (acquisition, merger, closure, departure or re-entry)
- *customers*: the information available to them (how much or how little they know)
- *suppliers*: the globalization of sources of supply (how practical or impractical)
- *new entrants*: the barriers to entry (how expensive or cheap to get in)
- *substitutes*: the depletion of finite resources (how accessible or inaccessible).

These additions to the original model have grown in importance owing to the intensification of competition; for instance, **organizations that diversify represent a**

Figure 4.2   **Ten competitive forces, after Porter**

threat wherever they may be minded to enter, but so too do the barriers that prevent
entry, because if they are invitingly low they may be *positively encouraging entry* and
thus heightened competition.

Of particular pertinence to public relations practitioners, among these ten forces,
is the question of information supply that empowers customers. They have to assess
continually the likely implications and consequences of information flows with all
these competitive factors in mind.

4.3   Publics and stakeholders

The repeated reference to publics has been accompanied by occasional mention of
stakeholders. But what is the difference? A **stakeholder** has a 'stake' in the organization, an interest that may be direct or indirect, active or passive, known or
unknown, recognized or unrecognized, immediate or removed.

Example

For instance, an individual person may have an interest in the activities of a company that is establishing a new plant some distance from his or her home, yet the factory will be close enough for this person to be affected by air pollutants that will be discharged from it. Little if anything is known of this development or its implications. Then again, that same individual may work for the company and be well informed of the development. In the first instance, the interest is feint, perhaps as yet non-existent, and when interest is aroused perceptions are likely to be negative. In the second, the interest is already strong, and perceptions are likely to be on balance positive: the source provides employment as well as future air pollution.

This stake, however, may be held the other way around: 'An organization has a relationship with stakeholders when the behaviour of the organization or of a stakeholder has a consequence on the other' (Grunig and Repper, 1992).

Stakeholders may comprise *large groups*, even masses, and the language commonly used in describing them is *typically generalized*. There is mention, for example, of whole communities of interest being stakeholders. The concept was developed in the 1960s but did not enter wider usage until the 1990s, in response to rising pluralism, when it presented something of a problem for public relations, which had been ascribing similar characteristics to publics since the 1920s. Could there be any difference, or was an established term simply being 'made over'?

The contribution of public relations to organizational effectiveness substantially depends upon its ability to identify and understand **publics**, which may be elevated to the ranks of 'strategic constituencies' depending upon their relative importance to the organization, that is to say, **the degree to which the organization depends upon them for** *survival*.

Put that way, publics sound more important than stakeholders, and they are probably more closely identifiable. Particularly if they form 'when stakeholders recognize one or more of the consequences as a problem and organize to do something about it or them.' However, pressure and cause-related groups *do not necessarily* form out of, or emerge from, stakeholder mass – they might skip the stakeholder stage – and it is self-evident that *by no means all publics are active*. Nor are they all necessarily *adversarial*, an assumption that fails to take into account the latent goodwill that is often present in publics without any attempt to foster it. Most times a public is benign until it is aroused, either in support or opposition.

It is more likely that the practical differences between a public and a stakeholder are those of *relevance and specificity*, that:

- *publics* have importance attached to them because of their **more specific interest and power, current and potential**, while
- for *stakeholders* the levels of **interest and influence are relatively lower and more generalized**.

This is itself a generalization, but it may help to disentangle the frequent use of the two terms interchangeably.

'A licence to operate'

The role of the stakeholder gained accelerated currency when in 1993 the Royal Society of Arts in London (in full: The Royal Society for the encouragement of Arts, Manufactures and Commerce, founded 1754) initiated an inquiry, *Tomorrow's Company*, in which twenty-five senior managers from leading UK companies participated. The team 'developed, tested and refined a shared vision of Tomorrow's Company, and of its inclusive approach.' It concluded that:

> 'The companies which will sustain competitive success in the future are those which focus less exclusively on financial measures of success – and instead include all their stakeholder relationships, and a broader range of measurements, in the way they think and talk about their purpose and performance.'

The inquiry acknowledged 'companies' growing need to maintain public confidence in their operations and business conduct; in other words, to maintain a strong *licence to operate.*' It identified the external influences that grant this **licence to operate**:

- law and regulation
- industry and market standards
- industry reputation
- political opinion
- public opinion and levels of confidence
- pressure groups
- the media
- individual attitudes of customers, suppliers, consumers, employees, investors and the community.

This represented a significant advance in thinking about **the environmental conditions in which not only companies but also organizations generally operate**. Much of this was not new but it provided a succinct and well-argued case, following extensive research and consultation across a swathe of British commerce, for what it called **the inclusive approach**, by which all external and internal interests are recognized and their mutual relationships are strengthened. Of particular interest to public relations was the *recognition accorded to reputation, opinion and confidence.* Significantly, 'the community' was included among the major publics whose attitudes counted for licensing purposes.

Publics and stakeholders not only have relationships with the organization but *between themselves* and there may be *extensive multiple membership of differing publics or stakeholder groups.* 'There is increasing recognition of the complexity of the web of influence ... an organization is but part of the web of stakeholders' (Varey, 1997b).

This serves to further emphasize the *potential scale and complexity* of stakeholder relationships; accurate interpretation and adaptation to meet the circumstances identified in the organizational environment are *fundamental* to the development of public relations strategy.

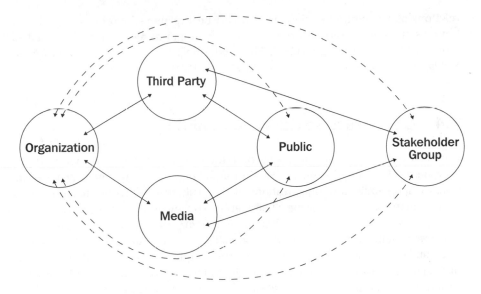

Figure 4.3 **Communication between organizations, publics and stakeholders**

Four types of linkages in the environment

The contacts that any organization may have with its environment can be depicted as:

- *Enabling* – with those outside upon whose authority and resources the organization's very existence depends (shareholders, senior managers, government, local authorities and opinion leaders)
- *Functional* – with those that input to the organization (employees, suppliers, utilities) and those that consume its outputs (customers, consumers, end-users and graduate employers)
- *Normative* – with organizations that have similar problems or share similar values (trade and professional associations and bodies, political parties, cultural and similar groups and societies)
- *Diffused* – with those who have an interest in the organization but no formal links with it (the media and other publics, including minorities and local communities).

These last, the *diffused* linkages, are with publics:

- that *cannot be readily identified* through formal memberships,
- which are **affected by the organization** in some way, or
- consider that **it has transgressed current expectations of appropriate standards of conduct**, a familiar enough contemporary theme.

'Organizations have developed such public relations programs as environmental relations and minority relations to deal with diffused linkages. Although consumer relations and community relations also can be explained by other categories of linkages, the publics served through these two programs also can be described as diffused' (Grunig and Hunt, 1984). The media help here too, in *alerting diffused publics* about the organization's *consequences for them*.

4.4 Corporate social responsibility

If indeed central government has become increasingly impotent the larger it has become, to the cynic this might explain official enthusiasm for the transfer of its **social responsibilities** to organizations, with resultant contraction in the scale of government, presumably leaving it better able to pursue other activities.

The UK government certainly champions this process vigorously. It claims 'real business benefits from being socially responsible', asserts that 'about 80 per cent of [the 100 largest British] companies now provide information about their environmental performance, social impact, or both' and quotes a recent survey of small and medium size enterprises (SMEs) that stated '61 per cent were involved "a great deal" or "a fair amount" in the local community'. (DTI website 9.3.03). In this context, 'environmental' refers to the physical environment; 'SMEs' is European Union (EU) shorthand for any organization employing fewer than 500 people, although this figure may be varied to reflect local conditions in member states.

The UK government is busily supporting this **corporate social responsibility**, commonly called CSR, with various tax incentives, co-funding, brokering of new partnerships, encouraging consensus on UK and international codes of practice, promoting 'effective frameworks for reporting and product labelling', advice on resources and helping to 'promote the business case and celebrate business achievements'. To explain this enthusiasm the government quotes from *Winning with Integrity*, the 2000 report of The Business Impact Task Force of Business in the Community (BITC), a campaigning organization with some 700 corporate members that together employ some 20 per cent of the UK private sector workforce.

The report identified the benefits to companies of engaging in CSR as being:

- '**Reputation** – affected by the costs and benefits of a company's goods and services, how it treats its employees and the environment, its record on human rights, its investment in local communities, and even its prompt payment of bills;
- **Competitiveness** – the advantages of good supplier and customer relationships, workforce diversity and work/life balance, as well as efficient management of environmental issues;
- **Risk management** – better control of risks – financial, regulatory, environmental, or from consumer attitudes.'

The report quoted research in support of these conclusions. Surveys had indicated varying levels of favourability relating to perceptions of CSR involvement by companies, translated in terms of levels of loyalty to employers and willingness to purchase products by reference to the ethical policies and practices of suppliers or their associations with 'good causes', such as charitable donations.

'In 1999 a poll of 25,000 citizens across 23 countries on six continents showed that perceptions of companies around the world are more strongly linked with corporate citizenship (56 per cent) than either brand quality (40 per cent) or the perception of the business management (34 per cent).'

Although it has been variously demonstrated that respondents can be hypocritical, feeling that they *have* to respond by claiming to support CSR because of social pressures, these findings nevertheless have *significant implications*, for companies and *all other* types of organization.

Business in the Community acknowledged the scepticism in its annual report (BITC/FT 2002): the year 2002 had been marked by economic gloom and corporate fraud, scandal and collapse, and according to its chairman:

'The disappearance of a vast and once respected firm such as Andersen has under-lined the importance of reputation, not just with investors and customers but with the public. ... In the US, people lost their reputation once they lost public trust. They were just trash overnight.'

The organization had initiated a Corporate Responsibility Index (CRI) to 'enable large companies to report on and compare their performance on the environment, the workplace, the marketplace, the community and human rights.' BITC already has an annual awards scheme to 'recognize the impact of companies integrating responsible business practices into their mainstream operations – on the environment, marketplace, workplace and community.'

There is growing political interest throughout Europe. The EU's Commission has produced a 'Green Paper' (for discussion) on CSR and a proposal for 'hard' legislation emanated from the EU parliament, although this was later rejected by the Commission. 'Governments are pushing themselves into the act in other parts of Europe. In France, for instance, listed companies [whose shares may be purchased and sold in public stock exchanges] will be required to report extensively on their environmental and social impact with effect from this year.'

However, 'in many cases [CSR] had not been embedded into the core objectives and culture of the company. Its acceptance was shallow and fragmented. It was said that some chief executives who had signed up for particular [BITC] initiatives had not fully taken on board the thought that membership implied acceptance of corporate responsibility throughout their company. The biggest single challenge for most organizations is to find ways of integrating these processes at all levels of the business' (Lambert, 2002).

Yet **expectations about CSR are rising**. An annual attitude survey (by MORI researchers for a group of companies) revealed that three-quarters of UK adults in 2002 thought that industry and commerce **did not pay enough attention to the communities in which they operate** and only two per cent considered that 'the only business of business is business'. Scepticism had risen 15 per cent over six years. 'Surprisingly, almost two out of three business journalists think not enough attention is paid to social responsibility, while nearly two out of every five investors and industry leaders think the same' (*The Guardian*, 25.11.02).

This survey contained some findings of particular relevance to public relations. 'The risk to companies from damage to their reputations is now higher than ever.' **Nearly one in two people claimed 'an ethical dimension' to their purchasing decisions**, the single most compelling point of interest to most managers, and around two in three 'would be influenced if international companies were shown to be associated with environmental harm, unacceptable working conditions, a poor human rights record, unfair discrimination – particularly on race, religion and gender – poverty wages, or bribery and corruption.'

But in reality: 'just one in six has *actively boycotted* a product on ethical grounds and only five per cent of consumers place ethical considerations *at the top* of their list of factors affecting purchasing decisions.' However, one in three *had* bought a product because of its association with a charity and 87 per cent believed that 'companies should make an effort to let us know what their social and environmental programmes are.'

Only 28 per cent of the sample of 2001 adults in that survey could *name a single company* that they thought to be socially, environmentally or ethically responsible.

QUESTION: If organizations are *not* reaping recognition for their 'good works' are they likely to dismiss CSR as an *optional extra*, a desirable add-on only provided it does not impair earnings, and a 'good thing' only when it enhances profits?

According to another survey, of 372 UK managers across all sectors (The Roffey Park Management Agenda 2003), while more than a third of their organizations had CSR policies, many saw this as mere 'window dressing'. Nevertheless, 88 per cent maintained that they wanted more CSR, 'for example, by doing community work, fundraising for charity and through employment diversity' (*The Guardian*, 27.1.03).

The BITC's CRI anticipates UK legislation that will require larger companies to produce **an annual Operating and Financial Review** (OFR). In a survey of companies that would be affected by this, MORI researchers, on behalf of the (UK) Institute of Public Relations, found that 93 per cent 'believed that non-financial reporting enhances a company's reputation' yet 19 per cent had not hitherto heard about the OFR. The institute's president remarked that 'Reputation reporting is important because financial indicators alone are an inadequate means of reflecting true share value' but as he pointed out, 'lack of clear guidelines and the difficulty of establishing objective measurements for intangible issues such as reputation could lead to problems' (*The Times*, 27.9.02).

Reporting to investors about *corporate social and environmental performance* is likely to gain ground, although in 2002 BITC found that only three per cent of financial analysts believed that these matters were important in their work (*Financial Times*, 28.2.03). The Association of British Insurers, whose members are major investors, has developed new guidelines to CSR, which 'bring concerns about social responsibility into the mainstream of investment thinking and practice. We are anxious to avoid unnecessary prescription or the imposition of costly burdens. Our focus is on enhancing value in companies through effective response to risk. Companies and shareholders will of course be able to go further if they wish' (ABI, 23.10.01). The primary aim here is to address risk, which is to say, how to deal with the **commercial implications of rising CSR pressures**.

Socially responsible investment (SRI) is gradually gathering momentum; 'mainstream' investors and analysts are taking more account of social and environmental criteria in their assessments of companies. 'The key thing is not to draw too wide a distinction between what is an SRI issue and what is a financial issue,' [a specialist analyst] says. 'There are grey areas such as EU directives, black empowerment in South Africa and pharmaceuticals prices. This uncharted territory is where the interesting ideas will come from' (*Financial Times*, 28.2.03).

4.5 Risk and crisis management

Upon returning from a mid-winter conference jaunt to the Caribbean, the then British Prime Minister encountered reporters at the airport who were demanding to know what he was going to do about the crisis, to which he memorably replied 'Crisis, what crisis?' It did incalculable damage and soon after the electorate removed him from power. Didn't he *know*, asked Mr and Mrs Sensible-Citizen, wasn't *someone* keeping him informed? How could he go swanning off at our expense and not know what was going on back home? And so on. In reality, the 'crisis' had blown up very quickly and, we were assured, unexpectedly, but then crises have a way of doing that.

Corporate life, just like 'real' life, is **full of risks and potential crises**. That is *why* public relations keeps scanning the horizon, trying to identify and anticipate trouble **before it happens**. There are two distinct kinds of PR crises (Black, 1989):

- **Known unknowns** – these are mishaps and worse that occur *owing to the nature of the activity that the organization undertakes*, or, for that matter, the individual.

  - In most organizations there is risk present that may create crises and each element has to be assessed in order to determine the likelihood of trouble occurring under varying circumstances.
  - The probability rating accorded to each is influenced by any number of external environmental features and 'it is *known* that a catastrophe may occur but it is *unknown* if or when it will take place'.

- **Unknown unknowns** – which are 'sudden calamitous events that cannot be foreseen by anybody'. These are often the result of

  - inconceivable coincidence,
  - some combination of events or circumstances that combine to create a crisis, or
  - aberrant behaviour such as inadvertent pollution and criminal tampering.

'Much of our work as public relations practitioners is predictable and can be planned ahead in an orderly manner. Crisis public relations is a rare requirement and may never affect most of us, but if we are in a field [industry or sector] where disasters may occur it is essential to have a plan to meet sudden emergencies.'

This is probably too complacent. What began as a practice more associated with potentially dangerous occupations, such as oil extraction and nuclear fuel production, has lately gained much greater currency, particularly within more dynamic environments, and prudence suggests that it should be part of *all* public relations practice.

But recognizing a crisis may prove demanding. Physical attack, overnight destruction by fire, failure of computer systems, grounding of transport by bad weather; these are all fairly readily recognizable, because the drama visually unfolds, but what of the many more subtle situations that can occur? For instance:

- What if a pressure group is busily spreading malicious rumours and deceit about some aspect of the organization's operations without its knowledge?
- What if some small adjustment that the organization has made to its processes has inflamed opposition and hostility that is destroying demand without a murmur?
- What if something the chairman said at a recent conference has been completely misconstrued by key opinion leaders and damagingly relayed to others?

Much has been the advice offered on how to recognize and accurately evaluate risk, anticipate crises and handle them competently with minimum damage to image and reputation. However, the reality is seldom as anticipated.

Examples

Bomb explosions are proven sources of crises that are very difficult to anticipate. When oil company Kerr–McGee planned for crises it thought along fairly conventional lines, with small-scale crisis plans for North Sea oil rigs and installation fires. In 1995 it was not expecting a disaffected youth to blow up a government building two blocks from its Oklahoma City headquarters. Then managers realized in the ensuing crisis that they had far too few telephone lines and for hours overlooked where they had plenty in another building, and that they did not have the home telephone numbers of staff, so that they could reach them to discuss arrangements (Dozier, 2002). Invariably 'the devil is in the detail'.

Similarly, Royal Dutch/Shell suddenly found itself at the centre of a serious storm over its decision to sink a redundant North Sea oil platform in a deep part of the Atlantic Ocean. Greenpeace protestors boarded the platform, boycotts of Shell petrol were called, sales across western Europe briefly plummeted and a German petrol station was fire bombed. The 'Brent Spa' had to go another way: dismantled and recycled, in part as elements of a new roll-on, roll-off ship quay in Norway. And when, also in 1995, the Nigerian government executed nine political protestors, Shell 'was accused of different levels of complicity and collusion, or simply failing to use its position in the country to prevent the executions. Whatever the arguments, it left many observers in the West blaming Shell for the executions' (Henderson and Williams, 2002).

It can be very tempting to take the view that it will not, or even cannot, happen to us, as if there is some immunity granted. And seldom is the cost involved in achieving and maintaining favourable images and reputations *fully and adequately linked with the cost of making proper allowance for risks and crisis management.* **Some very valuable relationships can be disrupted**, so why the reluctance to audit the risks, develop contingency plans, learn from past crises (there are bound to have been some), create a positive attitude among managers to thinking about this and prepare a blow-by-blow scheme for handling the *next* crisis under a range of 'what if?' scenarios?

Crisis management planning factors

Five factors have been identified about this (Regester and Larkin, 1997):

- risk is perceived differently by different people
- fundamental attitudes are hard to change
- people expect risk, evaluate risk against benefit and choose accordingly
- not all sources of information about risk are perceived as trustworthy
- emotional symbols can be more believable than hard scientific fact.

'All too often, when bad news does break, the resulting corporate image is full of negative factors. This may frequently result from a misinterpretation of events by the media ... If a company at the centre of a crisis is seen to be unresponsive, uncaring, inconsistent, confused, inept, reluctant or unable to provide reliable information the damage inflicted on its reputation will be lasting – and measurable against the financial bottom-line.'

Some further points to note:

- The *media are often blamed*, but reporters and their editors are as likely to be driven by human instincts and calculations as anyone else; if they do not *know* they are just as prone to making *suppositions*, however reluctantly.
- For 'company' here read 'organization': it can happen *to all types* of outfit.
- And for 'bottom line' read '*financial consequences*': those who live by grant aid, for instance, are not immune.
- And as for being unresponsive and uncaring, that can be a hard one, because the lawyers will never agree to there being any apologies or gestures that offer the merest *hint* of potential liability. The public relations practitioner has to be concerned and humane while not admitting anything.

CHECKLIST

- Static external environments may be distinguished from dynamic ones by reference to: technology and mechanization; demand for products and services; market competition; social and political support; and organizational knowledge.
- Within a complex, dynamic environment, the PR function concentrates on improved communication with the key interpenetrating publics and how these relate one with another.

- The rise of pluralism has fostered turbulence and the need for PR to address non-marketing 'political problems' founded upon demands for social responsibility.
- The growth in competition has also engendered turbulence, with correspondingly greater implications for the direction and control of information flows.
- Stakeholders have an interest, that may be active or passive, direct or indirect, known or unknown, recognized or unrecognized, immediate or removed.
- Publics may have a more specific interest and power, current or potential.
- Strategic constituencies are relatively more important publics upon which the very survival of the organization depends to a greater or lesser extent.
- Corporate social responsibility (CSR) programmes by companies primarily benefit their reputations, competitiveness and risk management.
- The principal relevance of CSR to PR is the growth in consumer claims to there being an ethical dimension to their purchasing decisions, which has a direct bearing on image and reputation.
- Crises arise in consequence of the 'known unknowns' resulting from current operations or the 'unknown unknowns' that cannot have been foreseen.

CASE STUDY
TRANSFORMATION FROM PUBLIC TO PRIVATE SECTOR

When National Savings & Investments (NS&I), a UK government agency with 30 million customers, sought to communicate its new name and corporate identity, designed to reflect its three-year business transformation programme, the £2 million cost equated to just eight pence per customer. This represented a substantial economy for the taxpayer, when compared to the more usual levels of expenditure for similar corporate identity changes undertaken by large companies.

Two factors made this possible. Firstly, the name change was a simple, straightforward extension, from National Savings to National Savings & Investments, so making the most of an established name rather than adopting a complete change. The new name had a ring of familiarity about it and sought to capitalize on the 'heritage factor' benefits of residual understanding and goodwill even as it embodied the agency's new, more commercial, character. A complete change of name, by contrast, would have necessitated a lot more explaining and consequent expenditure.

Secondly, the communication of the change was viewed as a long-term project, to be implemented gradually by informing the customers in the course of routine mailings. This avoided the cost of media advertising, notably on television, where many such changes are heavily advertised, and conformed with the central purpose of building in the future on the foundations of the past.

The UK media has been very critical of what it perceives to be 'money wasted' on re-naming, or re-branding, companies and organizations at substantial expense. There have been some spectacular failures, typically where a completely new name has not been understood or appreciated. The economical emergence of NS&I provoked favourable media comment, especially because it is a government agency, and it continues to escape inclusion in the frequently published critical reminders that castigate the alleged corporate identity 'makeover money wasters'.

The NS&I name change was prompted by research among customers and the media that indicated perceptions of the organization as being old-fashioned. It was seen as an antiquated part of government concerned to persuade people to save through a form of bonds conceived following the Second World War that paid not interest but cash prizes determined by periodic chance selection.

In fact, NS&I's constitution had been radically altered in 1996, with empowerment to compete against other providers of savings and investments products in the private sector, and perceptions had not caught up with reality. In effect, the agency is in the private sector, where it occupies a unique and distinct part of the financial services industry.

The key aim of the UK government in turning this department into an agency and giving it a commercial remit was to reduce the cost to the taxpayer of government borrowing. To achieve this, National Savings & Investments set out to become 'a distinct and valued part of people's savings and investments' and 'an integral and valued component of national debt management'. This called for major changes, including a complete culture change, from a traditional preoccupation with sales and procedures to a marketing orientation focused on customers.

The PR objectives were, firstly, to communicate these changes visibly through the new name, secondly, to counter prevailing negative media coverage and, thirdly, to secure routine favourable coverage for both the agency, its products and services. The key messages included:

- total security for investors: the agency is part of the UK government's Treasury
- large-scale operation, with £62 billion of investor funds
- economic importance, financing about 20 per cent of the UK's national debt
- weight of influence, given that the agency holds around 10 per cent of the cash-based UK deposit market.

Public relations targets reflected the long-term nature of the exercise. One year on, the new name was being used by an estimated 90 per cent of journalists and media coverage had greatly improved. In the previous year (2000–01) the agency scored overall positive on its total media coverage, including television and radio and on-line, in only two of the 12 months. In the first year following the new identity launch (2001–02) coverage had been more positive than negative in 11 of the 12 months.

The only negative month arose through some criticism of the new logo, which incorporates a chestnut, or 'conker', to represent renewal, security and growth, and a crown, to emphasize security through government backing. 'Conkers' are a familiar feature of English culture.

The first-year coverage included 2141 press mentions, compared with 1516 in the preceding year. Four major and positive news items had significantly assisted in this. They included: the appointment of a new chief executive, introduction of a website with an on-line channel, a new product launch and re-invigorated sales of the traditional Premium Bonds product.

This appears to confirm that, however well conceived and executed a new corporate identity and its thorough application, the media relations element of the PR follow-through has to include several truly newsworthy pieces and cannot rely solely on the identity itself or pseudo events. The new identity and the subsequent communication have to be complementary and consistent, and this applies to all publics to which such communication is directed.

QUESTIONS

1 What relevance does chaos theory have to public relations?
2 What are the likely ethical implications of managers creating the issues, in order to identify social concerns and their solutions?
3 Why might research showing support for CSR and demand for more be misleading?
4 What weight should investors attach to non-financial reporting and why?
5 When might risk and issues management be thought irrelevant and why?

░ ⊻ 5 Communication

Communication theory – four types of public relations practice – excellence – conflict resolution – diffusion and effects – attitude formation – attitude and behaviour

5.1 Communication theory

Given that the 'strategic role of public relations is to define and manage stakeholder relationships' (Oliver, 2001), it is fundamentally necessary for the PR practitioner to understand **the processes of communication** upon which such management so heavily depends. For *effective* communication, itself a term open to a variety of interpretations, is not a natural gift, as often supposed, characterized by expressions such as 'the gift of the gab', but a skill based on understanding, observation and practice.

The communication process is described as being circular, linking the sender of the message with its receiver, backwards and forwards between the two. Shannon and Weaver identified the basic structure in 1948 and Schramm refined it in 1953; this is the model commonly referred to as the *communication loop*.

The key components here are:

- the *sender*, who is seeking to communicate information, ideas, attitudes and desires, and
- the *receiver*, who is trying to understand the message, its meaning and its purpose, and *what to do about it*.

The model seeks to answer five questions: (1) who (2) says what (3) in what channel (4) to whom (5) with what effect? The sender starts the process by identifying to whom the message is to be sent and then crafting it as thought most appropriate to fit the requirements of the communication. This all-important initiating phase involves thinking about the proposed recipient; for instance:

- how is the message likely to be received?
- will it be understandable?
- will it be understood?
- what interpretation may be put upon it, and why?

In other words, how is the message likely to be *decoded*, or *deciphered*, what will it *look* and *sound* like to the receiver?

With the *message* content decided, the next stage is to *encode* it so as to make as easy as possible the accurate decoding of it at the other end. This entails deciding how best to *express* the information:

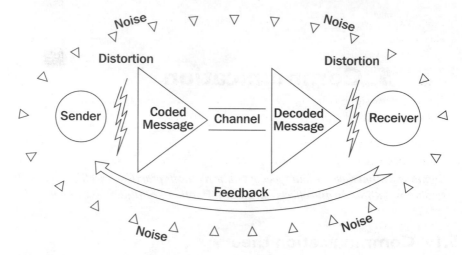

Figure 5.1 **The communication process, after Shannon and Weaver and Schramm**

- there may not be a 'shared vocabulary', whether in the choice of language or symbols,
- or the sender and receiver may *believe* that they are using the same language and common usages when *in fact* there are dialectical or other differences that may affect meaning and understanding,
- or there is *technical* jargon that is either not shared by sender and receiver or is open to differing interpretations,
- or each may use *differing* jargon, technical or otherwise.

In addition to encoding, the sender has to decide about what ***channel*** to use in order to convey the message, and this in turn may influence the encoding. **The choice of means by which a message is received can greatly influence the outcome**. For instance, face-to-face conversation may be most appropriate in some circumstances, an e-mail message in others; generally, the amount of time taken by the sender in making the communication can be perceived by the receiver as indicative of its relative importance.

The next stage in the loop is the receiver's ***decoding*** of the message. This is the critical intellectual exercise that may take seconds or weeks.

- *Has* the message been understood?
- *How* has it been understood?
- Does it change anything?
- Does it require reply? If so, in what form, and when?
- What consequences flow from it?
- What others actions are required, when and how?

The processes of encoding and decoding are further complicated by ***distortion***, barriers relating to the perceptions of both senders and receivers. This distortion may arise in many differing ways; for instance, owing to:

- differences in social, racial or educational backgrounds
- ageism
- mutual distrust
- divided loyalties
- partial or excess information supplied
- contradictory signals, such as visual gestures at variance with speech
- differing priorities or perspectives in a given situation.

Selectivity is also a key factor. 'The target audience [receiver] may not receive the intended message for any of three reasons. The first is *selective attention* in that they will not notice all of the stimuli. The second is *selective distortion* in that they will twist the message to hear what they want to hear. The third is *selective recall* in that they will retain in permanent memory only a small fraction of the messages that reach them' (Kotler, 1991).

This arises in consequence of the *noise* that envelops the communication process. This is the source of many problems, for it is unplanned static or distortion that serves to compound the effects of distortion already present between the sender and receiver. Noise can be literally noise, so that verbal messages are not heard, but the term is more generally used to describe the 'cacophony of sound', all those messages, usually several hundred, with which most people are assailed from the moment they awake until they lose consciousness again.

Receivers have **variable predispositions to receiving messages**, depending upon perceptions of the sources:

- what is potentially in it for them,
- whether reward or punishment, and
- linkages with established memory and memory creation.

The distortion occurs when messages are reconstructed to accord with the receiver's beliefs, a key point in relation to branding. To achieve this congruence the receiver may **add to, or embroider, the message or choose not to notice parts of it**, processes that Kotler describes as amplification and levelling.

Up to this point the flow has been in one direction only, from sender to receiver, but the model indicates *a loop*, in which *messages flow in both directions*. For that to occur there needs to be *feedback*, that is to say, *that part* of the receiver's response that is communicated back. Great indeed is the effort that is exerted by most senders to generate feedback, and, what is more, feedback that can be converted into useful intelligence in order to consider the development of a further message, and the creation of dialogue.

Feedback, however, can be negative as well as positive, useless as well as useful; it can be in a fleeting facial expression or a long memorandum, in action, such as picking up the spade as instructed, or an omission, because in some circumstances even *non-reply* can constitute a response for what it tells the sender.

So the communication model envisages **a circular flow of messages** that is subjected to a welter of hazards that can break the circuit. It has been modified over time to recognize changing conditions, and to allow for the role of the media, but it remains a reliable foundation for trying to understand communication in a world that is burdened with communication failure.

5.2　Four types of public relations practice

Within this framework public relations practitioners set out to communicate effectively, and in the course of time they have developed clearly distinguishable methodologies designed to best serve their various communication purposes. **Four distinct types of practice** have been postulated by Grunig and Hunt (1984) based upon their analysis of the historic development of PR in the USA. These four types have been generally accepted as accurate, although not without criticism. They may be summarized as:

Press agentry, or publicity

This originated in the 1830s, when legends and heroes, such as Daniel Boone, were created. The purpose is described as propaganda, there being little respect for truth. Noted among these agents was Phineas T. Barnum, founder of the Barnum & Bailey Circus, who 'said he didn't care if the newspapers attacked him as long as they spelled his name right'. The credo of these agents was 'There's no such thing as bad publicity', an attitude that has proved remarkably enduring; 'Barnum's famous statement, "There's a sucker born every minute", lives on.'

In a neat turn of phrase, 'Eric Goldman, in a little book on the emergence of the public relations counsel written in 1948, called the era of press agentry the era of "The Public be Fooled".' Publicity, then, is identified as being a **one-way form of communication**, the feedback being 'bums on seats' for entertainment and sport and sales of promoted products, to which may be added hiring of 'celebs'. **Research may well be minimal**.

Public information

This strain of public relations practice is traced back to around 1900, when the first laws were passed to contain the excesses of American big business, which had resulted in one percent of US citizens owning 54 per cent of their country's wealth. This was the era of 'muck raking', the formation of labour unions and the advent of Lee's 'Tell the Truth' dictum. Public information might be said, however, to have earlier origins, of about a century before, when the UK government first thought it should make public announcements in rebuttal of press stories.

The purpose of public information is to disseminate truthful facts, figures and advice on behalf of organizations in all three main sectors of the economy. It is a **one-way process and research may be minimal**. This is the knowledge dissemination that is often characterized as being 'useful to know', particularly in relation to social issues, public administration and so on.

Two-way asymmetric

This is 'scientific persuasion' developed following the US propaganda effort of the First World War by Bernays, Carl Byoir, Rex Harlow and other early public relations counsel. The two-way asymmetric approach involves **messages going in both directions** but **there is an imbalance in favour of the sender**, who is intent upon securing advantage from the exchange. Grunig and Hunt quote one of the early practitioners, John W. Hill, founder of Hill & Knowlton in 1927: he wrote about dissemination of non-controversial information, 'But when controversy exists, public relations may become the advocate before the bar of public opinion, seeking to win support through interpretation of facts and the power of persuasion.'

This rather grandiose interpretation likens public relations to legal advocacy and uses the, then novel, concept of **'public opinion'. Research may well be substantial**, for the purpose is to persuade and change 'organized habits and opinions'. In the late 1920s surveying of public opinion was initiated and was heavily developed in the 1940s and 1950s, to give 'an organization the ability to learn what the public wants and will accept, thus indicating the direction a public relations program should take.'

Two-way symmetric

This is 'mutual understanding' and respect, where **both parties to the dialogue are relatively equal and mutually respectful**, both being able to influence the other and thereby effect change. Cutlip and Center are thought, by Grunig and Hunt, to have first introduced this concept, in 1952, when they wrote about the two-way flow of communication, ideas and opinions 'to bring the two into harmonious adjustment'. However, they concentrated most of their attention on the other three models.

The evaluation of outcomes concentrates not on attitudes but on **levels of understanding** and is therefore most likely to be initiated by regulatory bodies and businesses that are heavily regulated, where there is *greater incentive to develop dialogue*. Bernays advocated this model, in 1923 writing that consultants interpreted the public to the client and vice versa, the purpose being to 'mould the action' of the client and to 'mould public opinion'.

These four types of public relations may not entirely accord with contemporary experience and it is unlikely that a public relations person would confine his or her activities to fit only one or other. Grunig and Hunt, writing in 1984, calculated that:

- publicity accounted for about 15 per cent of US practice, public information 50 per cent, two-way asymmetric 20 per cent and two-way symmetric 15 per cent.

Elsewhere around the world:

- when public relations practice is less prevalent the public information role is more pronounced, and might even account for the vast majority of activity
- where it is more prevalent the other types are more evident.

Critics have argued that the two-way symmetrical model is seldom practiced and effectively it is an *ideal*. Certainly empirical observation suggests that not many organizations readily embrace dialogue that risks (in their interpretation) leading to any more than cosmetic adjustment to their positions. The two-way nature of *the third model* is for purposes of feedback; among companies it *is likely to be the most commonly followed type of public relations.*

5.3 Excellence

Grunig and Grunig (1992) suggested that the most effective public relations practice, which they described as **excellent PR**, would occur in *the two-way symmetrical* model. They and others had found correlations between the two-way asymmetrical and symmetrical models, which led them to represent *'professional'* public relations as embracing both, with **excellence including asymmetrical components**, to take account of *'mixed motives'* such as persuasion and 'managerial bias'.

But what had become of the other two types of public relations practice? Grunig and Grunig identified publicity and public information as belonging to *'craft'* public *relations* and placed them on a continuum that stretched from propaganda to journalism. They argued that 'Practitioners of craft public relations seem to believe that their job consists solely of the application of communication techniques and as an end in itself. To them, the purpose of public relations simply is to get publicity or information into the media or other channels of communication.'

This does not of itself appear to be controversial; publicity is a long-established PR activity and dissemination of 'public information' is a necessary and usually well-intentioned pursuit. But why should it be identified as a *craft* rather than 'professional'? Their explanation is that 'professional' public relations people 'rely on a body of knowledge as well as technique and see public relations as having a strategic purpose for an organization: to manage conflict and build relationships with strategic publics that limit the autonomy of the organization.'

This may require some qualification:

1. It is not the case that all PR technicians are without any knowledge of public relations; more accurately, many have but limited and variable levels of knowledge, as is found in many other occupations.
2. The relegation of craft skills to secondary ranking is a prevalent conceit that ill serves anybody; that public relations practice calls for rather more craft skills than many other occupations might indeed be viewed as commendable.
3. Technicians as well as professionals are capable of understanding that they serve a strategic purpose. Any generalized difference between them about this is likely to be one of emphasis and commitment, probably owing to varying balance between research, planning and implementation.
4. This division of the four models into two continua suggests that practitioners whose work involves one set of models would not use the others, which is not supported by the empirical evidence of practice.

5.4 Conflict resolution

Whenever two people start communicating with one another there is *scope for disagreement* leading to conflict. So many relationships are played out within a predictable life cycle framework that begins with accord and ends in acrimony. The incidence of conflict appears to be growing, not only in international affairs but also domestically and regionally.

Public relations is concerned to **develop and nurture enduring harmonious**

interdependent relationships. Accordingly it has to take account of the *causes* of disharmony and the *degenerative processes* that follow. Grunig and Grunig cite Keltner (1987) as identifying six stages in the long slide downhill:

mild difference, disagreement, dispute, campaign, litigation, fighting and warfare.

There may be some more in between, such as independent self-regulatory arbitration of the kind provided by trade and professional bodies.

In the first three of Keltner's stages communication comprises discussion, moving on to negotiation, then arguing and bargaining. Once the campaigning begins, it is the turn of persuasion and pressure. When litigation occurs, it becomes advocacy and debate. After that communication loses out to violence, all words having failed.

There is a role for public relations *at each of these stages*, particularly *in the early ones*, but Grunig and Grunig complain that organizations that use the asymmetrical approach **usually wait until the campaigning phase has been reached** before they start to practise public relations. This assertion is *supported by widespread readily observable evidence*. So often the question is later asked 'Why didn't we do something about this earlier, instead of waiting until it became serious?'

In the case of cause and issue-related pressure groups, however, the opening phase may be campaigning, the earlier stages having been missed. 'Out of the blue' an organization may find itself under campaigning attack, but L. Grunig found that many such groups, after initially campaigning or seeking litigation or regulation, moved to negotiation as soon as their targets indicated a willingness to talk.

The concept of 'win–win', developed in the 1980s, is concerned to bargain not from positions held by each side but on interests, each party trying to see ways of helping the other to achieve a satisfactory outcome. This is widely recognized among managers to be a sensible way to approach these confrontational situations with external organized groups; pressing on to an outcome where one side wins and the other loses seldom provides enduring resolution, yet 'win–win' negotiation may well provide the basis to a constructive future relationship.

The role of public relations in managing conflict, and thereby avoiding power struggles that intensify into moral crusades by each side, is probably underestimated and underused. It offers **a dimension of excellence** in practice that warrants greater recognition, for excellent PR is a two-way symmetrical collaborative process.

5.5 Diffusion and effects

Of great interest to public relations are the processes that people go through when they are digesting news and information and trying to decided what to make of it. **Diffusion theory** suggests that there are five stages:

awareness, interest, evaluation, trial (trying out the idea on others) and *adoption.*

This interest is keenest in the context of marketing: how do people move from first finding out about something to ending up purchasing it, or something, and to resultant satisfaction? As Kotler (1991) remarked, 'The marketing communicator needs to know how to move the target audience to higher states of readiness to buy.'

There are several **response hierarchy** models, all comprising three stages:

- *cognitive*, when the message content impacts on the receiver, what Kotler calls putting something into the consumer's mind
- *affective*, attempting to affect or change the receiver's attitude
- *behavioural*, prompting the receiver into acting in response.

Probably the best known of these is AIDA: *attention, interest, desire* and *action*. There are several developments of this, including the **Hierarchy of Effects**, in which the stages are: *awareness, knowledge, liking, preference, conviction* and *purchase*.

Kotler describes this as a *'learn, feel, do'* process that obtains:

- when the receiver, or buyer, has **high** involvement with a product category that is perceived to offer **high** differentiation between products.
- However, when there is **high** involvement but **little** perceived difference between products, an alternative *'do, feel, learn'* sequence occurs,
- and when there is **low** involvement and **little** perceived differentiation there is another, *'learn, do, feel'*, sequence.

These cognitive, affective and behavioural stages may be related to *all* branches of public relations communication, not only MPR, and *all apply where specific behavours are sought.*

5.6 Attitude formation

There are two simple structural explanations of attitudes. The **three-component** model states that attitudes comprise:

- The *cognitive*, information-processing element, which includes knowledge, perception and belief, trusted mental images based on objective facts and subjective perceptions
- The *affective*, emotional element, which is evaluative, assigning favourability ratings
- The *conative*, will and intention element, which determines the likelihood of action or the style of behaviour.

The **single-component** model states, by contrast, that attitude is composed of the *affective element alone*. Attitudes therefore are formed on the basis of an overall positive / negative or favourable / unfavourable assessment. This makes no allowance for how the assessment was arrived at, through cognitive factors, or the likely intention to act, so this interpretation has been modified in order to include cognition and conation as *affecting attitude while not actually being part of it*. Attitudes may be preceded by first developing a response to some stimuli or by an action, such as an experiment.

5.7 Attitude and behaviour

Neither of these models that describe the composition of attitudes offer a direct connection between attitude and behaviour, for conation is merely about **forming a tendency to act**. Furthermore, not only attitudes but also specific circumstances affect behaviour.

Cognitive consistency

In the mid 20th century three major theories about attitudes and behaviours were developed. These took as their starting point the concept of **cognitive consistency**: that a person wants *consistency* between:

- the various attitudes held
- attitudes and perceptions held as against real life experience
- behaviours and self-image.

When a person detects inconsistencies resultant *tension* is experienced, and this may only be relieved by changing one or more of the factors that is creating the inconsistency. In other words, something has to give:

- attitude has to change to fit another attitude
- attitude has to be altered to align with behaviour
- behaviour has to be adjusted to tie-up with attitude.

Balance theory

This is concerned with **receipt of information**. Heider argued that a *balance* occurs if a person is *reassured* about his or her (positive or negative) attitude towards an object when another person, towards whom he or she has:

- a *positive* attitude, declares a similar attitude towards the object – the conclusion reached is '*I know I've got this right because we agree about it*'
- a *negative* attitude, declares disagreement about the object; '*I know I've got this right if **he** or **she** disagrees with me*'.

Similarly, an *imbalance* occurs if a person is *unsettled* about his or her (positive or negative) attitude towards 'an object' when another person, towards whom he or she has:

- a *negative* attitude, declares a similar attitude towards the object; '*There's something wrong when **he** or **she** agrees with me*'
- a *positive* attitude, declares disagreement about the object; '*There's something wrong when **he** or **she** disagrees with me*'.

This rather simplistic explanation does not fully explain the complexities and conflicts that occur, because it works on a straight positive or negative perspective without gauging the varying strength of those attitudes, which would indicate how a person might plan to resolve an imbalance. However, some imbalance may be tolerable, resulting in simply agreeing to disagree.

Congruity theory

Osgood and Tannenbaum addressed this problem by adding a measurement of the *strength* or *intensity* of the positive and negative attitudes. Their **congruity theory** is concerned about **what happens when there is a gap** between what a person thinks about an object and his or her attitude towards a person who endorses it or is associated with it. To **achieve congruity, or consistency**, between these attitudes there has to be adjustment of not one but *both* evaluations, until they come into alignment on a scale measured from plus three to minus three.

This adjustment has to be *equal to the total measure of the discrepancy*, but since stronger attitudes are harder to adjust, the evaluation that is rated *further* from the central nought position on the scale will be adjusted *less*.

Examples

Should the conflicting attitudes be rated plus two and minus two respectively, the gap equals four, so to achieve congruity each attitude has to move two points towards the other. In other words, they have to be modified by about 50 per cent, a more or less 50–50 compromise, congruity being reached at the centre of the scale.

If, however, the attitudes, although similarly far apart, are relatively stronger or weaker, so that, for instance, one reads plus three and the other minus one, it is likely that the stronger might need to be adjusted only by one point, to plus two, while the weaker would have to move three points to achieve congruity when they both meet at plus two.

This theory provides a useful tool with which to gauge *relative strength of attitudes* and *likely scope for change* in circumstances that are familiar to public relations people, such as product endorsements by celebrities, corporate sponsorships of sporting events and advice about public health issues. How much discrepancy might there be, for instance, between very positive attitudes towards a television news

Figure 5.2   **Adjusting attitudes to achieve congruity, after Osgood and Tannenbaum**

presenter and mildly negative attitude towards the outdoor event he or she may be going to promote, and what scope would there be for adjusting these?

Cognitive dissonance theory

Festinger considered another very familiar problem, which arises when *new information appears to contradict* an existing attitude or belief. This particularly concerns decision-making, because no-one likes to discover after taking a decision that he or she has *made a mistake*. When new information comes to hand *persistent doubts* may arise about the wisdom of the decision; the rejected options may begin to seem altogether more appealing. Furthermore, on reflection it may appear that the decision constituted behaviour that was *inconsistent* with established attitudes and beliefs. The *degree of discomfort* felt depends upon various factors, including the significance of the decision and the scale and intensity of the attitude or belief that has been contradicted.

This dissonance has to be relieved by **achieving consonance, or consistency**. This may be achieved by:

- revoking the decision
- modifying the attitude or belief that is causing the difficulty
- changing the attitude or belief to 'fit' the new information
- securing supportive evidence of the wisdom of the decision
- securing new information that harmonizes with the attitude or belief.

Consistency theory

Handy developed his **consistency theory** based on this, in relation to the workplace, where *stress* is caused because there are conflicting 'inputs' that create discrepancies between:

- the reality and what a person would like it to be
- actual results and expected results
- attitudes and actions against statements imposed by circumstances.

Again, it is necessary to find a solution that *relieves the discomfort*. For managers the implications were that a person would only change an attitude if the subject matter was either not *that* important to him or her or *very* important and there was no alternative way to reduce the dissonance. The important proviso to this was that a change in an employee's behaviour, meaning in this context compliance, did *not* imply a change in attitude, which would be harder for the manager to achieve but would last much longer.

Fishbein developed a series of models addressing the interaction of the various components of attitude. These also provide a sound basis to public relations practice. These may be briefly summarized as:

Attitude-toward-object : 'The Fishbein model'

An attitude towards an object is based on:

- the strength of belief that the object has certain attributes
- the evaluation of those attributes, for better or for worse
- the number of salient attributes to be taken into account in this way.

Attitude-toward-behaviour: 'The extended Fishbein model'

An attitude towards an act is based on:

- the strength of belief that the act will lead to specific outcomes
- the evaluation of those outcomes, for better or for worse
- the number of salient outcomes to be taken into account in this way.

Reasoned action

An intention to act is based on:

- attitude towards the act
- perceptions of influential subjective social norms.

Figure 5.3 **One-step and two-step communication**

This model was based on the belief that the best key to predicting a person's action or behaviour is his or her *intention to act*, and that was *conditioned by thoughts of what others*, such as colleagues, families, partners and friends, *might think*. Would they approve or disapprove? In other words, intentions are determined by what *people who matter* (to the individual) might think, as well as his or her attitudes towards what is intended.

This touches upon a key aspect of public relations practice: **two-step communication**, by which a message is sent not directly to the intended receiver but to a third party, such as an opinion former, 'reference group' or person who provides a 'role model' to the intended receiver. This third party in turn uses *interpersonal communication*, which can be more persuasive, in order to 'bounce' the message on to its intended recipient. In consequence the message is *likely to reach a wider audience* than might otherwise be the case, and it is *reinforced* in the process.

CHECKLIST

- The communication loop seeks to answer (1) who (2) says what (3) in what channel (4) to whom (5) with what effect?
- The key components of the model are: (1) sender, (2) message, (3) encoding, (4) channel, (5) decoding, (6) receiver, (7) distractions ('noise') and (8) feedback.
- Encoding and decoding of messages is influenced by distortion, owing to any of various factors, and selective attention, selective distortion or selective recall.
- Four types of PR practice have been generally recognized: publicity (or 'press agentry'); public information; two-way asymmetric; two-way symmetric. Excellent practice is said to comprise the two-way symmetrical model plus asymmetrical components when allowance is made for 'mixed motives' such as persuasion and 'managerial bias'.
- An important dimension of excellent PR is the avoidance of conflict and its management and resolution when it arises, based upon an understanding of the causes of disharmony and the degenerative processes that follow in relationships.
- The cognitive (information-processing), affective (emotions) and conative (will and intention to act, style of behaviour) stages of diffusion theory, which describes the processes of receiving, absorbing and deciding what to do about information, are relevant to all public relations communication.
- Attitudes comprise either three components - cognitive, affective and conative – or a single component, affective, influenced by cognition and conation.
- When inconsistencies arise between (1) attitudes and perceptions held, (2) real life experience, (3) behaviours and (4) self-image, tension is relieved through changing one or more of those factors, to restore cognitive consistency.
- Consistency, or balance, is required between an attitude held towards an object and an attitude towards someone whose view of the same object is sought. Inconsistency results in an imbalance, which may be tolerable or intolerable.
- To overcome any misalignment between the attitudes towards the object and the person, consistency, or congruity, may be sought by adjusting both evaluations, which may require greater flexibility in one than in the other.

- When new information appears to contradict an attitude or belief, resulting in discomfort, or cognitive dissonance, consistency is sought in order to relieve this, through revocation, modification, change or seeking reassurance.
- In the workplace, changes in attitude to relieve stress caused by conflicting 'inputs' are most likely to occur when existing attitudes are either strongly held (when there seems no other way to reduce the discomfort) or marginally valued (when change seems of little matter). But behavioural change, compliance, does not imply attitude change, which may take much longer to alter and then last for much longer once changed.
- Attitude towards an object depends upon strength of belief that the object has certain attributes, in their qualities and in the number of them to be counted.
- Attitude towards an act rests on the strength of expectations about the likelihood of specific outcomes, in their quality and in the number of them to be counted.
- Future behaviour depends upon the intention to act, which is conditioned by expectations of what other people whose opinions matter (to that person) might think in consequence, as well as by attitudes towards what is intended.
- In two-step communication a message goes first to an influential intermediary, for that person in turn to use his or her interpersonal communication skills in redirecting the message to its intended final recipient. By this means the message is likely to reach a wider audience and be reinforced in the process.

CASE STUDY
THE DRIVE FOR EXCELLENCE

In civil administration the principal type of public relations followed is public information, telling citizens resident within the authority's area, where it supplies public services, what they need to know and are entitled to know, regardless of any political or other interpretation or construction. It is largely about communicating hard facts and figures on what is happening, where and why, so that the citizen may access services and make informed choices.

At Dorset County Council in southern England the new chief executive decided in 1999 to make effective communication a priority issue and a three-year strategy was prepared with the promise 'We will communicate clearly, openly and regularly with the public, with our professional partners, and with each other, in order to promote a high level of mutual understanding, and facilitate a better service to the people of Dorset' (some 700,000 residents). This was later amended to read 'with our citizens' rather than 'with the public'.

The strategy identified six functions that would be used to maintain the key principles and achieve key aims. These functions were simply stated: public relations – the core function; internal communication – the key that unlocks the door; consultation – the mandate for our actions; media relations – an essential channel; corporate identity – the framework that gives the message strength; and e-communication – the way forward.

Key principles described the quality of communication that was sought and key aims identified the five publics and groups of publics with whom clear and regular channels of communication would be developed. These comprised: external publics;

internal publics; elected political representatives, known as members; other relevant branches of UK government, both national, regional and local; and publics comprising partners, suppliers and stakeholders.

In 2002 there followed a second three-year strategy. Benefiting from experience, the revised key principles contained some significant additions, to: create meaningful dialogue with residents; consult well and act on the results; and concentrate on outcomes, not outputs. The strategy was written within a framework provided by the Improvement and Development Agency, a body advising the Local Government Association, to which UK local authorities, including Dorset, belong.

This framework for communication improvement by local civil administrators contained three tiers. The lowest requirement was to meet the legal duties for dissemination of information. Level two aimed at 'ensuring the [general] public is better informed' and enabled to obtain 'an understanding of the council's policies and priorities.' At the third stage, the highest level, communication had become a 'strategic issue.' It was 'two-way, enabling the authority to listen and learn.'

The Council considered that it had fulfilled the basic level one stage and was 'approaching level two'. The new strategy aimed to take its communication performance to the level three strategic grade within its three-year duration. To this end a substantial and growing department had been assembled, which was implementing an ambitious programme.

The second strategy sought to make a substantial adjustment to the balance between the public information model and the two-way asymmetrical model, by seeking to create meaningful dialogue and measuring performance by effects rather than process. Embarking on this journey towards excellent public relations practice coincided with the official recognition of Dorset as an 'excellent authority' by the Audit Commission, a government body that scrutinizes the performance of the constituent elements of the UK public sector. The citation was for 'a well-managed council and provider of good quality and cost-effective services.'

QUESTIONS

1 Why might some messages suffer more from noise than others?
2 Why might the two-way symmetrical type of PR be seldom practised?
3 How might protagonists view the role of PR in conflict resolution?
4 How might an understanding of balance theory benefit PR practice?
5 What are the likely ethical dimensions to two-way communication?

▾ 6 Research, planning and evaluation

Research and evaluation – effectiveness – strategy and planning – situational theory – segmentation – cost–benefit analysis

6.1 Research and evaluation

Most occupational groups have their traditions, and public relations people are not without one or two of their own, prominent among which is *equivocation about research and evaluation.* For the public relations academics this is the source of much angst. For them research is *fundamental* and they have difficulty in understanding this apparently somewhat mixed attitude among practitioners, which appears to vary from serious commitment to downright dismissal as unnecessary. They have similar problems about the uneven quality and quantity of evaluation. So why the criticism, and is it warranted?

Theaker (2001b), writing about the British experience, traced the first interest of practitioners in research and evaluation way back to the early 1990s, when, coincidentally, public relations was emerging as an academic subject in the UK. 'As recession began to bite and budgets were slashed, public relations practitioners began to talk about whether or not PR could be measured, and so prove its worth. Up to that point, no one had really been concerned about measurement of results.'

For public relations people with memories that stretched back a little longer than the early 1990s this was demonstrable nonsense. From the formative early years of PR in the UK, during the 1950s and 1960s, there had been repeated use made of research and evaluation. True, much research was secondary, that is to say, using published sources, but that was as much a function of limited budgets and ready access to marketing research already done than to any particular reluctance to undertake research.

Nor were early UK writers in any doubt.

Examples

'The first thing to put in hand is research. ... No good Public Relations can be done without sound research. ... Research, planning and action are parts of a continuous never ceasing operation, and what people think about the company plays a vitally important part in planning' (Lloyd, 1963).

'It is important that the public relations man should know the value, potential, and limitations of research ... Research can be an invaluable extra shot in the public relations man's locker. He should review his programme regularly, and if he believes that professionally conducted research can make a contribution, he should not hesitate to advocate its use forcefully' (Bowman and Ellis, 1977).

Evaluation probably received more attention than research, for, from the outset, the PR practitioner was expected to identify and discuss **the value of outcomes**. Much has been written, as well as said, over the years about the difficulty of evaluating public relations owing to its supposed ephemeral qualities. Typical observations included:

'Much of the doubt about the value of public relations arises from the difficulties in assessing the results of public relations activities and the absence of suitable yardsticks by which these results can be measured accurately' (Black, 1989).

And, describing 'self-evident results':

'These are results where nothing has to be spent on a marketing research survey to check, i.e. they are to be seen or experienced. ... sometimes the facts can be so plain that, given clear objectives, PR cannot be intangible and unaccountable. Results can literally stare you in the face' (Jefkins and Yadin, 1998).

The claimed absence of suitable yardsticks is unsustainable; there are more than enough evaluation methods available. So it cannot explain why ' "Gut feeling" was felt to be an acceptable gauge of whether a PR campaign had succeeded' (Theaker, 2001b). Could the explanation for this combination of supposed inability to measure and apparent lack of concern have less to do with not wanting to bother about evaluation and more about *reliance on accumulated knowledge and experience*, on confidence born of practice, as in other occupations; the kind of assurance that comes from familiarity with 'self-evident results'?

Public relations practice is concerned with attitudes and perceptions, based on images and reputations. These may be researched, traced and measured for the purposes of public relations, given an adequate budget. But there is the rub. Could the supposed reluctance among some PR practitioners to commission or undertake primary research for the purpose of evaluation be explained by insufficient funds allocated for the purpose? If so, why should this be? Could *competitiveness* be a root cause, resulting in a reluctance to make an adequate allocation within a competitive consultancy fee quote and to specify research when selling on knowledge and expertise already acquired at the expense of other clients, or previous employers?

Whatever these uncertainties, a few observations may be offered with some confidence:

- Public relations without research is *pure adventure*, and practitioners know it
- *All* public relations outcomes are measurable, by one means or another
- Practitioners most certainly *do* undertake research and measurement, consistent with what they assess to be the requirements of the specific circumstances
- Selling on 'You know when it works' cannot explain the *dramatic growth* of PR, whatever the pressures of rising pluralism

- In the face of *incontrovertible* evidence to the contrary, persistent generalized allegations of immeasurability have to be treated with caution.

Not only outcomes, but also all the variable factors that influence those results need to be carefully scrutinized.

Examples

Public sector media campaign relating to road safety: well, *was* there a reduction in death and injuries caused by dangerous, reckless or just plain stupid driving over the relevant period? If so, to what extent? And what about the weather conditions during that period, the amounts of daylight, holiday and work patterns, and so on?

Private sector exhibition and demonstration programme at selected public events: *was* there an increase in enquiries, invitations to tender, new business opportunities, orders placed or some other yardstick? By how much? And how might those results have been influenced by the choice of venues, seasonal commercial factors, competitor activity and so on?

Voluntary sector lobbying campaign to raise awareness of local homelessness: *was* there an increase in expressions of official interest, invitations to meet with local bureaucrats, offers of help from property landlords, media enquiries or funding donations? What did it all really come down to? And did the lobbying capitalize on government promises, increased social unrest, bad weather, prior media interest, city centre redevelopment plans and so on?

6.2 Effectiveness

Public relations activity contributes to the effectiveness of the organization, but *effectiveness is susceptible to multiple interpretations* and therefore **difficult to define and manage**. Grunig *et al.* (1992) considered effectiveness in terms of four perspectives, starting with systems.

It has been widely asserted, and is readily observable, that the structure and environment of the organization *determines the flow of information* both within it and between it and its external publics. So when an organization seeks to maximize its effectiveness by matching its structure and functions to its external environment its public relations *should* gain in effectiveness. However, this *systems* approach appeared to remain more an ideal than a reality, for otherwise 'the role of public relations practitioners as boundary spanners, mediators, and participants in managerial decision making would be more highly valued.'

The *strategic constituencies* approach also had particular relevance for public relations. It also focuses on interdependencies, but specifically on the most *threatening* elements in the external environment and how well the organization handles them. That in turn depends upon the *detection* of those strategic publics. Successfully responding to them could help reduce uncertainty and conflict by creating stable relationships upon which the organization depends.

Their conclusion was that **public relations could increase the effectiveness of an organization** by two means:

- to 'enact an environment that includes the stakeholders most likely to constrain or enhance the ability of the organization to carry out its mission – to meet its goals'
- by developing communication that built enduring quality relationships with strategic publics.

'These relationships help the organization manage interdependencies, simultaneously limiting and enhancing the autonomy of the organization. The better the organization manages its interdependencies, the more likely it is to succeed in meeting its goals – although factors other than public relations contribute to that success as well.' Note that here the terms public and stakeholder are used interchangeably and that goals may be interpreted as (general) aims and (specific measurable) objectives.

This evaluation of effectiveness in the public relations context is an admirable attempt to lasso a jelly. Most discussion about effectiveness dwells on the minutiae of practice, is generalized and contains little specific explanation much beyond 'it worked'. 'Effective communication' is widely interpreted as asymmetrical persuasion, with or without the dialogue, redolent of quick fixes, but to the experienced practitioner that reveals a fundamental misunderstanding, for public relations is correctly about finding *enduring solutions* through communication.

More specifically, Moloney (2000) complained that 'Modern PR lends itself to manipulative communications ...' and identified common features that by implication are thought necessary in order to achieve effectiveness. Messages:

- frequently fail to declare sources, to 'appear to be free-floating from any originating interest'
- often assert data, rather than reference or argue it
- often use negative emotions, to achieve persuasive effect and downplay reason.

'The removal of these manipulative flaws in the internal construction of PR communications constitutes the case for reform through education and regulation.'

Here 'effectiveness' acquires an entirely different dimension, for it is allegedly sought through non-disclosure of interests, exploitation of data and arousal of emotions to impair reasoning. However, the failure to reveal sources *contradicts the primary aim* of most PR people to *identify the interests* they serve. For the rest, the objection appears to be against rhetoric and advocacy *per se*. Nevertheless, standards of practice are likely to be variable, as in any occupation, and doubtless effectiveness will continue to be the subject of much debate.

6.3   Strategy and planning

Another subject of, at times remarkably deep, equivocation among public relations people is **strategy**. There is *frequent confusion between strategy and tactics*. Repeatedly, tactics are dignified by being described as strategic when in truth they do not satisfy any readily recognized definition of strategy, and frequently the word is slipped into proposal documents, reports and speech as if its mere presence will enhance the sagacity and credibility of whatever it is attached to.

Perhaps the problem lies in making the link between corporate and public relations strategy. The latter serves the former, but what exactly *is* strategy? Oliver (2001) ventured 'the means or process by which an organization aims to fulfil its mission' but this is necessarily general and therefore susceptible to wide interpretation.

Fifield (1992), in addressing marketing rather than public relations strategy, found that 'every author seems to start from his or her own premise and lays down a new set of parameters and definitions ... The one thing that many definitions do is to confuse.' He concluded that marketing strategy 'will mean different things to different organizations. It will fulfil different needs both within the organization and in the marketplace.'

Although it might be objected that Fifield's observations are about marketing, they have a ring of familiarity about them for public relations practitioners. And marketing is itself *probably the major source of confusion*, because MPR, that branch of practice in support of marketing that accounts for so much of overall public relations activity, serves the marketing strategy; however, customers, albeit critically important, are but *one of many* publics that concern public relations.

This heavy involvement with marketing – to the extent that many practitioners specialize solely in MPR – can throw the PR strategic planner off the scent. In reality the public relations and marketing strategies *each* respond *directly* to the corporate strategy, as do all other function strategies. Hence the strong interest of public relations in the organizational vision and mission, because *they* provide the starting point for developing the PR strategy.

Strategy development

Not that deciding the strategy is necessarily left to the experts. Most times the **dominant coalition decides what type of public relations it wants**, and if the public relations function is *not* represented at that exalted level it *may not be heard* and almost certainly will have to *forego any final decision making* about such fundamentals.

This harsh reality could be interpreted favourably, as indicating that PR is considered so important that senior managers dare not let anyone else decide, or unfavourably, that the PR is seen as purely a technical service that is not competent to handle strategic decisions. Public relations people aspire for membership of the dominant coalition not without good cause.

L. A. Grunig (1992) developed a **power-control model of public relations** to depict the factors that *influence which type of public relations is adopted*. She makes several key observations about the power play within the organization:

- *The dominant coalition adopts a worldview, or mind-set, about PR*, which is based upon a broader set of suppositions, the corporate culture and the potential of the public relations department itself. This worldview about PR therefore determines the *scope* of the function to show what it can do.

- *The dominant coalition also adopts a view of the organizational environment*, to the extent that 'the environment is in part at least the subjective perception' of this group of senior managers. They decide what bits are, in their minds, crucial and then 'choose strategic publics for public relations programs from that perceived environment.'
- Other managers, including those in public relations, gain power 'in part because they have knowledge and skills relevant to a crucial problem in the organization's environment.' In other words, *what they have to tell impresses the dominant coalition.*
- 'If organizations choose the most appropriate public relations strategy for communication with strategic publics, then that strategy will help the organization to manage critical environmental interdependencies and make the organization more effective.' In other words, *there is a critical link between strategic management of public relations and organizational effectiveness.*
- *The dominant coalition, particularly the founder, creates the corporate culture,* which is also conditioned by social culture and by the environment. Managers do not gain power if their values and ideology differ substantially from that of the organization.

The parameters within which the public relations strategy is developed are, therefore, subject to a variety of internal influences. And '... if a culture is essentially hierarchical, authoritarian and reactive, the dominant coalition will generally choose an asymmetrical model of public relations. Furthermore, it will choose not to be counselled by the public relations expert who traditionally is not seen as having enough strategic awareness and is therefore of limited value' (Oliver, 2001).

This depressing picture is well within the experience of many talented public relations people, but in the interests of balance some mention is due of those circumstances, increasing in number, where the head of the function *is* a member of the dominant coalition, *does* share in final decision taking and *does* exercise a substantial degree of discretion over the development of public relations strategy. Frustrated talent has a tendency to quit, which may explain, at least in part, the apparent frequency with which most PR people change their jobs.

Figure 6.1 **Strategy and tactic timescales**

A very practical means by which strategy and tactic may be differentiated is that the former deals with the 'bigger picture' and the longer-term, whereas the latter is more concerned with obtaining short-term effects.

The dominance of consultants numerically over in-house people within public relations may be yet another factor contributing to the confusion between strategy and tactics. Invariably consultants are tasked to provide short-term solutions, often through one-off limited period commissions, responding to detailed briefs that fit the strategy. There is no invitation or encouragement to offer a longer-term view, which is the purview of the, numerically far fewer, colleagues within the client organizations. Time was when consultants were usually retained on annual contracts that allowed for a more gradualist approach if that was wanted, but the fashion for haste has changed that.

Strategy development, in contrast to implementation, is a demanding process that is subject to many forces and pressures, not only from within but also without the organization. Grunig and Repper (1992) cited a model developed by Pearce and Robinson, in which they identified the steps that a strategist takes. These provide a useful structure and may be briefly summarized as:

1 *Corporate mission* development
2 *Corporate profile* development, to reflect 'internal condition and capability'
3 *External environment* assessment
4 *Interactive opportunity* analysis, to identify options
5 *Desired options* identification, compatible with the mission
6 *Long-term objectives* and *grand strategies* decided, to meet the options
7 *Annual objectives* and *short-term strategies* decided, compatible with the previous objectives and strategies
8 *Implementation*
9 *Review* and *evaluation*.

The model does not mention vision, so presumably for mission read also vision. The mission is very much linked with the environment, and public relations has a key connecting role here. 'Short-term strategy' may appear to be contradictory, but there is no prescriptive period for a strategy. They are often set long-term, typically for three years, although a duration of one year is common.

6.4   Situational theory and segmentation

Weighing up the situation before plunging in sounds sensible enough. 'The kingpin of the exercise is understanding the situation, i.e. asking: Where are we now? What are their misunderstandings?', according to Jefkins (Jefkins and Yadin, 1998), who clearly anticipated trouble ahead.

To address the 'classic PR situation [which] confronts most PR practitioners' he developed his **PR transfer process**, which describes the conversion of four negative attitudes into four positive ones: hostility to sympathy; prejudice to acceptance; apathy to interest; and ignorance to knowledge. 'Ultimately, knowledge creates understanding: the principal PR objective is *understanding*. Sometimes this may be even of things people dislike or with which they disagree.'

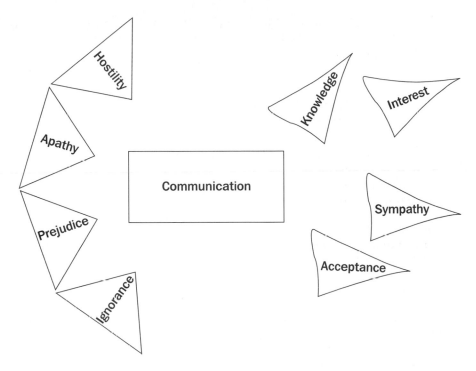

Figure 6.2 **Converting negative attitudes into positive, after Jefkins**

This is familiar indeed to most practitioners and many who undertake public relations on a voluntary basis. So often in the past public relations has been **invoked only when the situation presented problems**, and often then not until some time later, thus making the scale of the task that much greater. Understanding certainly does often allay anxieties, fears, hostility, but in a more pluralistic world situations can be, and often are, more complex.

Grunig's **situational theory of publics** (Grunig and Hunt, 1984) sought to reflect this. 'Publics come and go' and, what is more, organizations *create* them, when what they do have *consequences* for others. Publics form when there is a *shared perceived problem*, but if this is not recognized the public is latent: 'a potential public relations problem waiting to happen. ... Active publics are the only ones that generate consequences for organizations' (Grunig and Repper, 1992).

'The theory states that the communication behaviours of publics can be best understood by measuring how members of publics perceive situations in which they are affected by such organizational consequences as pollution, quality of products, hiring practices, or plant closings.' Three variables helped distinguish people who were:

- members of publics from those who were not in any publics
- prepared to speak up from those who remained quiet about an issue.

These three variables were:

(1) *Problem recognition*, when people communicate most because they seek information to help solve their problem. This process is divisible into *information* *seeking*, or active communication behaviour, and *information processing*, or passive communication behaviour. 'The members of a public exert less effort to understand information they process than information they seek. Thus, processed information has fewer communication effects than information that is sought.'

(2) *Constraint recognition*, when people weigh up the perceived obstacles to their potential actions. The worse this looks to them the less they bother about seeking and processing information.

(3) *Level of involvement*, which reflects the degree to which people identify with the problem: strong involvement is likely to result in high problem recognition and low restraint, leading to active attempts to remove constraints to finding solutions. What constitutes involvement varies, but generally it is about the degree of importance or concern expressed.

Using these three variables, Grunig identified different types of public, from apathetic through latent to aware to active. Later Grunig and Repper described **four kinds of publics**, which may be summarized as:

- *All-issue* – active on all fronts
- *Apathetic* – not interested in any of the issues
- *Single-issue* – active on one issue, or small subset of issues, of minority interest
- *Hot-issue* – active on one issue of widespread concern and big media interest

This is one of many **segmentation theories** but most others are used in marketing. 'As a result, techniques of *market* segmentation are used more widely in public relations than are techniques to segment *publics*.' Which is very true. This is although 'most of [the segmentation] theories are poorly developed' and the situational theory of publics being 'the only segmentation theory that has been researched extensively.'

A most important rider to this is that organizations chose their markets, 'but publics arise on their own and choose the organization for attention.' They 'organize around issues and seek out organizations that create those issues – to gain information, seek redress of grievances, pressure the organizations, or ask governments to regulate them. As publics move from being latent to active, organizations have little choice other than to communicate with them; whereas ... organizations can choose to ignore markets if they wish.'

This may appear overstated, but the point is well made. It is a fundamental difference between public relations and marketing. Some publics do not spring upon the organization, rather as depicted here, but *many do*, and **in turbulent environments the incidence of publics forming and re-forming around issues is ever present.**

Adapting Bonoma and Shapiro's nested model for analyzing industrial markets, Grunig has produced his own version to suit the needs of public relations. In this there are **nests**, arranged similarly to Russian dolls, in which the innermost contains **the variables of** *individual communication behaviour and effects* **that are the more effective in communication planning.** 'Decision makers should begin with the inner nest and work outward only when resources are not available for the research and time needed to work with the inner nests.'

Starting from the centre, the outer nests contain (1) publics, (2) communities, (3) psychographics, lifestyles, cultures and social relationships, (4) geodemographics,

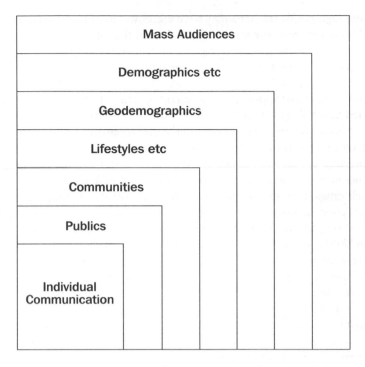

Figure 6.3   **Segmentation, after Bonoma and Shapiro and Grunig**

(5) demographics and social categories and (6) mass audiences. 'The best seg-mentation concepts lie in the second nest, that of publics, but ... the behavior of publics can be understood only by understanding the individual behaviors in the innermost nest.'

6.5   Cost–benefit analysis

The *social* benefits of public relations practice are well rehearsed and often repeated in the context of corporate social responsibility and community relations, but they should not distract from consideration of the *economic* benefits, particularly now that there is growing pressure upon practitioners to demonstrate a satisfactory 'return-on-investment' (ROI) for their activities. Public relations budgets have grown significantly during the past decade. In the UK it is not uncommon to encounter internal departments comprising 35–40 and more people and some consultancies claim annual revenues in the order of £35–40 millions. This underlying growth trend is also observable across Europe and in many other parts of the globe.

   The historic tendency has been to view the cost of public relations as a necessary burden to be bravely borne, an administrative overhead in running the organization, and to waive questions about specific financial returns. Scrutiny of the economic benefits was discouraged by assurances, as we have seen, that PR outcomes were not in any event accurately measurable.

But although public relations may have thereby *evaded more rigorous evaluation* this **did it no service in the longer run**, for it had the effect of *relegating* PR, in the perception of other functions, to *the status of a technical support service* for the primary powers in the corporate hierarchy, such as finance, HRM and marketing. And invariably *they* set PR's agenda accordingly.

This was made most apparent in the marketing context, where public relations was subsumed into a simplistic publicity role, from which it is having great difficulty in extracting itself. So much so that many marketers still consider PR to be no more than a small part of marketing, less expensive, often by far, than the other marketing communications – direct sales, advertising, direct marketing and sales promotion – and something to resort to mainly when budgets are limited.

At such times the popular euphemism used to placate the PR people is 'tight', a word designed to foster their sympathy for the travails of a supposedly under-funded, struggling marketer. Marketers also see some other benefits to them of public relations, for instance, in helping to bolster or 'save' indifferent (and usually far more expensive) advertising, but whatever its immediate purpose, MPR is *primarily* about helping to achieve sales; not surprisingly, therefore, it is often mistaken for sales promotion.

Another well-entrenched perception of public relations also discourages any meaningful analysis of outcomes. It is the preoccupation with 'doing PR' as *both a means and an end in itself*, as though the activity had some therapeutic or similar quality that bears no further inspection. This view is shared by many, including more than a few practitioners who should, and almost certainly do, know better.

It results in many managers approaching their first use of public relations much as they might decide to start going to regular religious worship or taking routine exercise. 'Doing a bit of PR' becomes its own reward, needing no evaluation. While this can serve to postpone discussion of public relations and how it is done, as Ehling (1992) points out, 'it cannot eliminate the question of what should one seek to attain by means of communication.'

Before any **cost–benefit analysis** may be undertaken it is first necessary to dispense with such inhibitions to evaluation and to focus instead on the *core purposes* of public relations, devoid of any substitutions or additions sourced by other functions. Ehling reminds us that in their sixth edition Cutlip and Center (Cutlip *et al.*, 1985) sharpened up their definition of public relations, which we encountered in Chapter 1, away from 'a planned effort to influence opinion' to being about *mutually beneficial relationships* with publics on which *the success or failure* of the organization depends. *That* was the *primary* purpose of public relations.

Compensating variation

Although some outcomes nevertheless may appear to defy rigorous economic analysis, Mishan's concept of **compensating variation** 'theoretically provides an optimal solution to placing dollar value on communication program effects.' **Break-even** is reached where the *cost of communication* designed to maintain a harmonious relationship and avoid conflict *equals the subjective benefits* gained from harmony and co-operation.

At this point there is indifference about continuing with the expenditure and effort. If communication costs rise, disharmony and conflict may seem less costly than the programme designed to reduce them. Should the relationship deteriorate, the compensating variation then required is the amount of cost to be incurred in order to regain the same subjective break-even point, when there is renewed indifference about continuing or ceasing the communication effort.

In using this approach there are two obvious difficulties:

- a monetary value has to be assigned to non-monetary effects, and
- everyone affected by the programme has to be treated fairly or compensated.

Nevertheless, compensating variation probably offers the most satisfactory method, because it is based on how much gainers would pay for their benefits or would be needed to compensate losers. Alternative attempts to assigned monetary values to non-traded goods (outcomes) by reference to traded products and services are based on flawed assumptions about their values being equal to those prices.

Taking positive compensating variations as benefits and negatives ones as costs, it is possible to arrive at the **net benefit** (benefit less cost) and at the **benefit–cost ratio** (benefit divided by cost). Ehling is not prescriptive about their use in deciding upon expenditures; sometimes one or the other is useful, sometimes neither. He recommends benefit–cost ratios, however, for choosing between competing mutually exclusive alternatives, selecting first that with the highest ratio.

He also touches upon **opportunity costs**, where the benefits of *alternatively spending elsewhere* arise. In practice this can occur remarkably often and present difficulties, for the concept is based on *missed* opportunities to obtain better return elsewhere, which in public relations practice may prove particularly demanding to calculate.

CHECKLIST

- All public relations outcomes are measurable, by one means or another, and persistent generalizations of immeasurability have to be treated with caution.
- The effectiveness of an organization is increased by the enduring quality relationships nurtured with strategic publics, which assist in the management of interdependencies, by which PR contributes to organizational success.
- Public relations practice is concerned to achieve enduring solutions through communication, not short-term fixes.
- Factors that influence the overall direction and purpose of the public relations function may depend upon where control of power lies within the organization.
- The dominant coalition of senior managers who run the organization most often decides what type of PR it wants, whether or not PR is represented or consulted.
- The coalition relies on suppositions, corporate culture and the function's perceived potential, in its worldview of PR that then determines the PR scope.
- The coalition also adopts a view of the organizational environment, which parts are crucial and what it considers to be the strategic publics for PR attention.
- PR strategy development is also subject to external as well as internal forces.
- The situational theory of publics measures communication behaviours by reference to problem recognition (information seeking and processing), con-

straint recognition (perceived obstacles) and level of involvement (degree of identification with the problem). From these variables publics may be identified, ranging from apathetic through latent to aware and active.

- Publics may be segmented into: all-issue (active generally); apathetic (inactive); single-issue (active on one issue, or a small subset, that is of limited concern) and hot-issue (active on one 'major' concern attracting wide interest).
- Whereas companies choose or ignore markets, in many cases publics choose companies, and other organizations, and so cannot be chosen or ignored by them.
- The innermost nest of the nested model for analyzing publics contains the variables of individual communication behaviour and effects that are the more effective in communication planning.
- Research and analysis advances progressively from the centre, nest-by-nest, concentrating on the inner nests. The successive nests contain, in turn, (1) publics, (2) communities, (3) psychographics, lifestyles, cultures and social relationships, (4) geodemographics, (5) demographics and social categories and (6) mass audiences.
- Cost–benefit analysis may be applied using compensating variation, when the cost of communication designed to maintain a harmonious relationship is compared with the subjective benefits gained from harmony and co-operation.

CASE STUDY
FIGHTING FIRES

When in the autumn of 2002 the UK full-time firefighters' labour union, the Fire Brigades Union, announced publicly its demand for an across-the-board 30 per cent wage increase, it had a carefully laid public relations strategy and plan for what it anticipated, correctly, would be a major battle ahead for public opinion.

Firefighters are employed by local government authorities, which, in turn, rely on national government for funding. So the union was technically in dispute with a mixed bunch of political representatives scattered around the country, most of whom individually belonged to one or other of three major and two minor political parties. They formed a disparate, large negotiating team in which priorities were mixed, and historically the firemen had experienced little difficulty in obtaining what they wanted from this somewhat ineffectual body, the government meeting the cost of the resultant settlements.

But 30 per cent was bound to take some swallowing, with official economic inflation running at around 2.5 per cent and the government determined to limit public sector pay increases to little more than that. The union employed as its head of policy the domestic partner of a former government public relations 'spin doctor' who had felt obliged to resign as adviser to the Chancellor of the Exchequer, or finance minister, when he found that he 'became the story', rather than remaining out of sight, 'behind the story', where PR people much prefer to be. He denied that he was advising the union, although its leader was a long-standing friend.

The PR strategy called for a rapid insurgence into the national media and public consciousness, with a depiction of the union on terms calculated to best attract public sympathy and support for the pay increase and thereby advance the negotiations to a successful early victory. A 'formidable public relations machine' was assembled and the plan of action was woven around a series of strikes and whistle-stop morale-boosting tours by the leader, using pseudo-events, mainly of men burning wood fires in braziers on the forecourts of fire stations.

'By first threatening to strike and then undertaking a relatively modest two-day walkout, the firefighters have focused attention on their cause and mobilized some sympathy from those who feel that they perform a valuable service for what sounds likely relatively modest money.' On 15 November, in answer to the survey question 'Has the strike this week made you more or less sympathetic to the firefighters, or has it made no difference?' 39 per cent said that it had made them more sympathetic, compared with 23 per cent, who thought it had made them less sympathetic (*The Times*, 16.11.02).

'The employers', as they were repeatedly described, spent a whole night in negotiation, resulting in acceptance of the full increase. But the government had insisted that it was involved, since it had to pay, and when a senior minister was awakened to hear the news he refused to accept it, instead commissioning an enquiry that would take weeks to report. Worse, for the union, it would be looking at the total picture, terms and conditions as well, with a view to identifying some trade-offs for any increase. The government had bought time, designed to slow the pace of events.

It worked: the vital momentum had been stalled, and the union struggled for weeks thereafter, with lessening success, to maintain a grip on the 'news agenda', what interests the mass media day-by-day. Worse, facts began to emerge that damaged its cause. It appeared that, owing to the nature of the occupation, much if not most time spent on duty did not comprise work but mere attendance, waiting for a fire to happen. It was suggested that firefighting accounted for only five per cent of the time.

This in turn left the firefighters with plenty of spare energy, and most of them had second jobs, which was made possible by work timetables negotiated by their leaders. So the seemingly modest wages told only part of the story, and the media soon located men working at their second jobs who were willing to talk about it. This also gave credence to the employers' claim that on average 48 people applied for every vacancy in the service. Nor was the cause assisted by the details that emerged about the rulebook, the various working arrangements and agreements, which, it was argued, collectively increased costs unnecessarily and necessitated a hunt by the employers for economies.

The union's public relations campaign had well fulfilled its purpose, to create an environment that provided the optimum conditions for the negotiators, but it had failed to adequately anticipate and prepare for the government's response. The media began to discover the part-time firefighters, people who provide a service to smaller communities, whose union contested imputations that their members were amateurs and deflected public sympathy away from the full-timers. And attention also turned to the army, tasked to operate 50-year-old 'mothballed' well out-of-date firefighting machines manned by young, hastily trained soldiers, who were denied use of modern publicly purchased equipment by the strikers.

There was an offer of around 15 per cent 'on the table', much as there had been during the previous summer, but now it came attached to various conditions, so instead of 'quitting while ahead' the union leaders campaigned on, with successive strikes further eroding public sympathy. The media largely lost interest, as negotiations continued. A year after they rejected an unconditional deal at around 16 per cent, the leaders recommend to their members acceptance of much the same with strings attached.

QUESTIONS

1   What would prompt expenditure on primary research and why?
2   Why could strategy mean different things to different organizations?
3   How might public relations influence power within the organization?
4   When might publics 'come and go', when might they stay, and why?
5   What might be gained by evading evaluation of public relations effects?

▼ 7 The customers

Relationship objectives – dialogue with privacy – loyalty – lifetime customer value – consumers' decision-making process – the decision-making unit – relationship care

7.1 Relationship objectives

Relationships can develop from the least likely beginnings and some of the most fulfilling may be the least well planned or sought after. People, though, usually allow relationships to develop because they *want something out of them*, and the relationships that organizations cultivate with their customers and they in turn consider that they enjoy with those organizations are no exception. There is *calculation* afoot, often rather deep calculation, and it is *mutual*.

Customers, it has often been remarked, come in all sizes and shapes. The principal division is between those that **consume** the products and services, who account for the vast majority of sales by volume, and those that use them to *in turn add value* in some way that they then offer on to others. This, however, is a fine distinction.

Firstly, the **consumers** are generally thought to be those who *finally* consume, or use, the product or service, but consumers may also buy for others, and quite a lot of people consume but do not purchase, although they had a hand in deciding what they consume.

> ### Example
>
> A woman buys her child's favourite breakfast cereal, which he hungrily devours while mum looks on. She is generally regarded as being a consumer, and she would be if she ate any of the cereal. But in this particular instance technically she is acting as an agent on behalf of the eventual consumer, exercising discretion about her purchase based upon her interpretation of *his* specification. And he is a consumer who did not buy.

Secondly, other **customers,** those aiming to add value by processing, also have much in mind the *consumer* interest. Every product or service must find its ultimate user, so everything done to bring it to this happy outcome is geared to that harsh reality.

Example

A company may purchase raw materials for use in making an 'industrial' product, say cloth, that it then sells on to another company, which in turns uses that to make something else, such as a garment. In this 'supply chain' each customer acquires, adds value and passes on, until eventually a product or service reaches an end-consumer.

Such customers may be referred to as **corporate, trade** or **industrial purchasers**, although many are organizations that are neither businesses nor engaged in industrial processes: they include institutional and government buyers, for instance, as well as manufacturers. The term **business-to-business (B2B)** is widely used to describe these markets.

'The central ideas of marketing are universal and it makes no difference whether we are marketing furnaces, insurance policies or margarine' (McDonald, 1989). What unites all types of customer is that they have **needs and wants which must be satisfied**:

- The consumer is increasingly driven by *personal wants* as well as needs, owing to increasingly sophisticated marketing directed at creating and stimulating consumption, and hopes to be totally *delighted*
- The B2B customer is focused on *specificity* to meet often complex requirements, and expects to be *fully enabled*.

Public relations practice reflects this division, through **consumer relations** and **B2B public relations**. The first is thought by practitioners to be the glamorous, even exciting, 'action', and it accounts for far the greater proportion of expenditure devoted to customers, while the second is usually seen as the opposite, although in reality B2B is often more complex, demanding and professionally fulfilling.

There is a further category of customer; the 'internal customer', as marketing prefers, what public relations people regard as the *internal publics*. The link between employees and sales, however, might be considered tenuous or inappropriate, since it implies that employees are captive targets for being sold at, when in reality they are there to do their jobs. Public relations adopts a rather different perspective on this, not regarding employees as being also customers.

CERP has no doubt about the importance of **consumer relations**: 'People, generally speaking, more and more frequently consider corporate behaviour as a key element to identify and qualify the enterprise, but corporate behaviour itself is first and foremost expressed by the quality of the consumer relations' (CERP website, 5.11.02).

Usefully, given this emphasis, it offers four definitions, starting with:
'Consumer relations is corporate or business activity aiming at:

- matching the corporate and product image as close as possible with that expected by the consumer targets
- ensuring the best quality of products and services, to achieve consumer satisfaction.'

In other words, consumer relations may take the form of *organizational* communication, on-going interaction between the organization and one of its key publics, or *marketing* communication, part of product or service promotion.

This combination is reflected in CERPs' three further definitions, which describe consumer relations as being:

'... planned programmes designed to establish, handle and develop appropriate two-way communication channels with consumers of products and services, with Consumer Groups and Associations and with public Authorities and Bodies whose responsibilities involve consumer protection and information rights.

... a significant asset to a Company or business which recognizes consumer protection and information rights as a fundamental principle to be respected and developed in the Company or business managerial practice.

... planned and permanent pro-active and post-active action addressed to consumers as individuals or groups, aiming at improving consumer confidence in the quality of products or services.'

Here the emphasis is on addressing **consumerism**, developing and maintaining reputation for fair dealing, responsible behaviour, reliable performance, all to create the climate of confidence in both the source and its offerings that provides the optimum environment for marketing of those products and services. It is about **'building brands'** by adding those extra qualities, in the perception of consumers, that give the supplier competitive advantage.

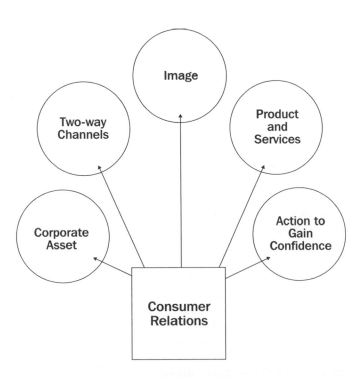

Figure 7.1 **Consumer relations**

And CERP is uncompromising in its strictures about this; for instance, under *Specific Responsibility to Consumers* it includes 'Any attempt to deceive consumer opinion or its representatives is forbidden' – clause 15 of its Code of Conduct.

Public relations in connection with non-consumer customers is similarly centred on relationship building. Accordingly, it takes account of the ***detailed circumstances of each customer*** to a degree that is very unlikely to be matched, or necessary, with a consumer. This gives rise to the development of **specialist knowledge about specific sectors**, to the extent that many public relations practitioners are recognized experts in the fields within which their customers operate.

Their skill sets also tend to differ, to the extent that they are likely to be talking with *very informed and knowledgeable* customers, usually have to *understand technical detail* and frequently need to communicate *complex information and arguments* that are variously encoded to be understood by a variety of receivers.

Customers tend to be **individually more significant** owing to their *purchasing power* and *scale of influence*. There are multiple *business practices* and various *regulatory codes* that apply specifically to different sectors, all of which have to be well understood and observed. Communication is more likely to be ***two-way through opinion formers*** and to include **presentations to key decision-makers**.

7.2 Dialogue with privacy

If customers are to consider that they have a worthwhile relationship with the organization, whether as consumers or organizational purchasers, they must be able to recognize those qualities that they would expect to find in a *valued interpersonal* relationship.

Example

If an airline passenger wants to e-mail his or her preferred airline, the one always chosen to fly 'with', to offer a brilliant tip about passenger comfort, *first* there has to be a feeling that the airline is **really just like a friend** who *deserves* this tip. In other words, that making this generous gesture is going to be *appreciated*. In fact, airlines receive many such communications, perhaps because their passengers are so grateful to be safely carried, and they are skilled at knowing how to respond, sounding really appreciative.

And the same applies, but *more so*, with other customers, where very often there is a formal on-going relationship, probably based on after-sales service, phased delivery or some form of partnership agreement. Routine and regular contact tends to encourage relationship bonding, bringing forth *expectations about interpersonal shared values*, much as occurs between work colleagues. If the customer contact person wants to offer a comment or tip, and many do, he or she needs to be *sure* first that **the relationship is *right***, so that its delicate mechanism may not be put at risk. This is potentially very sensitive; because any disturbance to perceived ability to relate successfully one with another in these situations can result in significant consequences.

There is therefore a *quality dimension* to *successful* consumer and customer communication that can be characterized as **dialogue with privacy**. This is about having the confidence to converse one-to-one with each other *as if old friends*, knowing that each will respect the position of the other and bring to the exchange that level of commitment. Where it occurs, it begins to satisfy the requirements of the *two-way* symmetrical approach to communication; that state of grace described as the **excellence** model of public relations.

7.3   Loyalty and lifetime customer value

The proliferation of **loyalty** schemes is evidence enough of the importance attached to not only attracting consumers but also *keeping* them. And there are also many similar schemes for other types of customer. As marketers never tire of pointing out, it is generally estimated to *cost around five times as much to find a replacement customer as to keep an existing one*. So in customer relations, *loyalty is a core purpose* of communication.

Modern loyalty schemes, however, are about more than mere loyalty. Direct marketers seek **one-to-one relationships for commercial gain**, so loyalty programmes are devised that facilitate this through *segmentation* of customers, to the extent that *each is profiled* and thereby 'known' to the organization. McCorkell (1997) identified seven key ingredients for 'the truly successful scheme', of which two are of particular relevance to public relations:

'4) *Recognize individuality of customer.* Include rewards, benefits and courtesies that recognize the customer as a person.

7) *Use data collected for intelligent marketing.* Schemes can be used to provide data that drive communications recognizing customer shopping patterns, preferences, breaks in continuity and so on. They can also provide useful area data to retailers, improving catchment area definition and permitting accurate targeting of competitive customers.'

The direct marketer's database is therefore a potential cornucopia of valuable information about customers. Although it is preoccupied with sales, and so full of useful nuggets about, for instance, shopping preferences, it should greatly assist the public relations practitioner by providing the quality of information required to assist in initiating relevant and meaningful customer relations programmes.

In most businesses the bulk of profit comes from transactions with *established* customers, which leads to the conclusion that over time specific **values can be assigned** to each one. Some customers say as much themselves, usually when they are dissatisfied, with comments such as 'To think how much I've spent with you'. The concept of **lifetime customer value** (LCV) aims to optimize the *total net revenue that may be obtained from each customer.*

In determining LCV, the *anticipated future worth of each customer* is calculated by forecasting:

- the period over which the customer will remain loyal and
- the customer's *spend within that period,* usually calculated in present-day prices.

'Very often this spend will increase for a while, then reduce before the customer severs the relationship.'

This concept has direct relevance also to the conduct of customer relations programmes, *particularly those with consumers,* many of which include enhancements such as complementary deals, exclusive invitations, memberships, customized magazines, educational leaflets and information access.

7.4 Consumers' decision-making process

To marketers, consumer behaviour is of eternal fascination. The term is used to describe how people act not only when they are searching for and buying products and services but also *how* they use, evaluate and dispose of products, services and ideas that they expect will satisfy their needs. Three major *comprehensive* models of consumer decision-making help explain what happens.

Nicosia model

This model is **interactive,** portraying a cycle of communication in which the organization influences the consumer's reactions, which in turn, as feedback, affect the organization's further conduct. It is an elaborate flow chart comprising four 'fields', of which the first indicates the consumer's attitude towards the product, based on:

(1) the attributes of the *company* communicated in its message and
(2) the attributes of the *consumer* that affect his or her perception of the message – such as personality, motives, experience, and thus knowledge and beliefs.

The remaining 'fields' describe:

- '*pre-action*' search and evaluation, leading to motivation to purchase,
- the '*action*' of purchase and
- '*feedback*' comprising sales data and consumer experience, the latter determining predisposition toward further messages.

This model is known to happen in reality, but it describes and does not explain or predict.

Howard–Sheth model

This is more complex and distinguishes between

- *extensive problem-solving,* starting with limited knowledge and either no preferences and/or perceived high risk of making a mistaken purchase

- *limited problem-solving*, starting with limited and insufficient knowledge and searching within fairly well-defined criteria for choice
- *routine responses*, where there is already a strong preference or brand loyalty.

The basic model includes:

- *Inputs* – information stimuli
- *Intervening variables* – (a) hypotheses based on learning and experience and (b) external variables, those personal and circumstantial factors that affect perception and learning in various ways, such as the importance of the decision, personality, social environment and culture
- *Outputs* – buying behaviour, including attitudes, intention, brand comprehension, purchasing decisions and further decision-making.

This model identifies many of the variables that influence consumers and explains how they interact one with another. It simplifies but not so far as to ignore the unpredictable impact of the external variables. However, it is suited to choosing between what is available *within a specific product or service category*, for example competing makes of kettle, rather than deciding between two or more *unrelated alternatives*, say, to buy education for a child or a second family home.

Engel–Kollat–Minniard model

This consists of four basic stages:

- *Search for information*
- *Evaluation of alternatives*
- *Choice*, including an extra 'loop' for extensive problem-solving
- *Outcomes*, influences on the decision, both motivational and environmental.

The model emphasizes the conscious decision-making process and is both easy to understand and relatively flexible, capable of describing what occurs in varying degrees of complexity. It includes a number of relevant variables, such as memory, but their effect on behaviour is not precisely explained.

Relevance to public relations

For public relations people engaged on customer relations programmes, these three models provide a particularly useful **broad frame of reference**. Like all models, they provide *simplified* representations of reality and they may indicate gaps in knowledge and understanding that might need filling.

Sheth model

Sheth also produced a model that describes **how families make decisions**. It lists seven factors that influence whether a decision to purchase will be shared or taken independently of others. These factors are:

social class; lifestyle; role orientation; family life cycle; perceived risk; product or service importance; and time pressure.

A 'family' may comprise:

two adults living together

- who have **no children**, either because they have not produced any or the children have grown up and left home
- with **one or more children**, all living together ('the nuclear family')
- with **one or more children** and **one or more other relatives**, such as grandparents ('the extended family').

The family can be viewed as a

social unit,
network of relationships or
reference group,

the latter exerting critical influences during the *formative years* of life in relation to, for instance, social standards and behaviours, self-awareness and perceptions and interpretation of environment.

Within the family *various roles are adopted* in relation to decisions about purchases:

Influencer – introduces information, starts up the interest
Gatekeeper – controls the flow of information in the following search
Decider – has the power, 'final say', on what is to be purchased
Buyer – executes purchase decisions
Preparer – converts the purchase for family use, for example, 'flat pack' assembly
User – consumes or uses the product or service purchased
Maintainer – keeps the product fit for purpose
Disposer – prompts and implements disposal of the product or termination of the service.

These roles, and the number and type of persons who adopt them, vary according to circumstances, such as the *type of family structure* and *how roles are assigned by reference to gender*. Often one person fulfils several roles; sometimes the decider and the buyer are two different people. Often users are neither deciders nor buyers; children are said to exert great 'pester power' as influencers and potential users.

The *family life cycle* (FLC) reflects the evolution of families over successive generations. There are common stages of development, which are reflected in changing economic circumstances. This has been variously described, including this commonly used seven stage version:

- *Young*
- *Young single* without children
- *Young couple*, whose youngest child is *under age six*
- *Young couple*, whose youngest child is *aged six or older*
- *Older couple*, whose children are *aged 18+* and still living at home

Figure 7.2 **The family decision-making team**

- *Older couple*, whose children have all *left home*
- *Older single*, living alone

While all this is of abiding concern to the searcher after consumption variables, it also has great relevance to customer relations programmes. For instance, much has been said and written lately about the part played by children in how families run themselves and in particular their influence over consumption of products and services.

Example

Children love chocolate bars, but their consumption contributes to obesity, about which the UK government is becoming increasingly concerned. Obesity is a common problem throughout the developed countries, so how to reconcile a child's 'sweet tooth' with its need for fitness? Global chocolate manufacturer Cadbury found its answer in 'Cadbury Get Active', a campaign linking chocolate consumption to acquiring sports equipment, the idea being that the children could eat the products and then exercise away the consequences. And the scheme was UK government-approved.

There was no difficulty in seeking to explain the weight of demand. 'Almost from birth, children are bombarded with advertisements. And it's never too young to start learning how to be a good consumer. Supermarket aisles are filled with brightly packaged food with pictures of pre-schoolers' favourite television characters. ... Once children reach school age, "pester power" is established as an important factor in marketing strategy' (*The Guardian*, 30.4.03).

The idea seemed fine as well, but the campaign was welcomed by a storm of media derision, because of how many products had to be purchased to obtain one piece of equipment. For instance, it was reported that 5440 bars of chocolate were needed to pay for a set of posts and nets to play volleyball. Put another way, for instance, £1000 worth of chocolate had to be purchased to obtain 'cricket gear' and £40 worth of chocolate was needed to acquire a basketball that 'usually costs £5 in the shops'. That latter amount of chocolate was said to equal 20,000 calories, and a typical 10 year old would need to play basketball for 90 hours to work them off.

'If there is such a thing as bad publicity, Cadbury has scored a winning goal,' commented one television reporter (*Channel Four News*, 29.4.03). 'Linking exercise to consumption of chocolate is nothing short of a scandal. While it is fine to indulge once in a while, this type of corporate exploitation of children has to stop. This isn't social responsibility – it is social negligence,' trumpeted a prominent consumer representative. 'If Cadbury genuinely cares about the health of children, it should donate the sports equipment rather than using it as an excuse to encourage children to shovel chocolate down their throats' (*The Guardian*, 30.4.03). The UK government's Sports Minister retorted 'They are going to eat it anyway' (*Channel Four News*, 29.4.03).

7.5   The decision-making unit

The **decision-making unit** within any organization comprises 'all those individuals and groups who participate in the purchasing decision-making process, who share some common goals and the risks arising from those decisions', according to Webster and Wind, cited by Kotler (1991). Accordingly it can be *much larger than* that of a family, and the processes may be *very much longer, more detailed and complex,* with *greater risk attached to outcomes.*

However, the roles are similar:

Influencer – often contributes to the preparation of the specification, as well as providing information; typically a technical expert

Gatekeeper – frequently interprets the role as being to keep out sales, other contacts and information, possibly to doubtful advantage

Decider – sometimes well removed from 'the action' and not readily identifiable from the outside

Buyer – selects the supplier and negotiates the deal, may also contribute to preparation of the specification

Approver – authorizes the proposed actions of deciders and buyers

User – often initiates the process by identifying a need and contributes to the preparation of the specification.

Figure 7.3 The organizational Decision Making Unit

'When a buying center includes many participants, the seller will not have the time or resources to reach them all. Smaller sellers concentrate on reaching the *key buying influences*. Large sellers go for *multilevel in-depth selling* to reach as many buying participants as possible. Their salespeople virtually "live" with their high-volume customers.'

For many public relations people, this tends to translate into generating communication with *specifiers*, who may appear in various guises and at one or more remove from where the products or services are required. Architects provide an obvious example. They seldom finance or construct anything, but they design, and to do *that* they have to specify. There are numerous similar examples.

7.6 Relationship care

In the Second World War the UK government advised its citizens to restrict their conversation in public places, for fear that enemy agents overhead something to the country's potential disadvantage. The slogan: *Loose talk costs lives*. Judging by the lengths to which some people go to obtain valuable marketing intelligence, loose talk still has its dangers, a fact that many public relations people recognize very well. The experienced practitioner historically preferred to say little and hear plenty, and to weigh every word, however seemingly casual its presentation. This, despite the much increased inclination to 'come forward', remains a sound precept and seldom more so than in customer relations.

The consequences for lapses can be serious, particularly if the words come from the lips of senior managers, whether of their own devising or placed there for them to utter. In fostering and maintaining customer relationships, the PR person should be *acutely aware* of the importance that must be attached to *all interactions* with customers, whether through customer magazines, chief executive comments or any other communication.

The organizations that really do *not* appear to care much about this, those who seem to fly in the face of the conventional wisdom about corporate reputation, seldom mince their words. But surprisingly often those that clearly *do* care nevertheless manage to commit some startlingly clumsy gaffs.

Examples

- Gerald Ratner famously declared the products his large UK jewellery retail chain sold to be 'crap', in the middle of a televised speech to the cream of British senior managers. His business collapsed. It was a stunning moment; what *could* have got into his head?
- Dianne Thompson, CEO of Camelot, which runs the National Lottery in Britain, talking about the odds against winning, declared that in all likelihood 'it won't be you,' an allusion to the long-running sales slogan *It Could Be You*. Her remark was reported in the media (*PR Week*, 4.10.02). The National Lottery is being repeatedly re-launched and continues its heavy sales decline.
- Marjorie Scardino, chief executive of Pearson, owner of the *Financial Times*, in an interview with the journal of the Royal Society of Arts, said that financial journalists had not worked hard enough to 'ferret out' big stories such as the Enron and WorldCom scandals. 'We could have done a lot more digging. But business journalists often don't know a lot about business.' Sales of the *FT* are in decline, even though the paper is competing with the *Wall Street Journal* to become 'the first truly global business newspaper'. It has had to make savage cuts to remain in profit (*The Guardian*, 6.1.03).

Such stories are legion, but *why*? Scardino immediately apologized, saying her comments were taken out of context and not directed at FT staff alone, and they were 'the best in the world'. Words and comments so often *are* claimed to be 'out of context', but after the event that is probably of little consequence, and in any event context can be variously interpreted, by both sender and receiver.

The *reality* is that communication with customers, whether direct or mediated, *has* to be Handled With Care, increasingly so given deteriorating perceptions of poor 'customer care' and the reputational damage that it is doing undeservedly to many organizations. The customer relations programme has a heavy responsibility to bear.

CHECKLIST

- Customers may be consumers or business-to-business (or industrial) purchasers with needs and wants which must be satisfied. The first hope to be totally delighted, the second to be fully enabled.
- There are substantial and significant differences between the two types of customer. Consumer relations accounts for far the greater PR spend on customers;

B2B public relations is often more complex, demanding and professionally fulfilling.

- All customer communication benefits from achievement of a quality 'dialogue with privacy' similar to that attainable within a valued interpersonal relationship.
- Gaining customer loyalty is a core purpose of communication and is sought by reference to customer lifetime value (LCV), the forecast future worth of the customer based on duration of loyalty and estimated spend during that period.
- The interactive Nicosia model of consumer decision-making depicts a communication cycle comprising four fields: (1) consumer attitude towards the product, (2) pre-action search and evaluation, leading to motivation, (3) the act of purchase and (4) feedback, indicating predisposition towards further messages.
- The Howard–Sheth model distinguishes between extensive problem-solving, limited problem-solving and routine responses. The basic version includes inputs, intervening variables and outputs.
- This model identifies many of the variables that influence consumers but is suited to choosing within a specific product or service category, not between two or more related alternatives.
- The Engel–Kollat–Minniard model has four basic stages: (1) search for information, (2) evaluation of alternatives, (3) choice and (4) outcomes. It describes what occurs in varying degrees of complexity.
- Sheth listed seven factors that influence family purchase decision-making: social class, lifestyle, role orientation, family life cycle (FLC), perceived risk, product or service importance and time pressure.
- Eight purchasing roles are adopted within the family: influencer, gatekeeper, decider, buyer, preparer, user, maintainer and disposer. Often one person fulfils several roles, which vary according to circumstances.
- The family life cycle (FLC) describes the evolution of families over successive generations. A commonly used seven-stage version includes: young, young single, young couple with young children, young children with older children, older couple with adult children, older couple and older single.
- Six purchasing roles, comprising the Decision-Making Unit, are adopted within the organization: influencer, gatekeeper, decider, buyer, approver and user. One person may fulfil more than one role.
- PR communication is often with specifiers, who may appear in various guises and at one or more remove from where the products or services are required.
- In fostering and maintaining customer relationships, it is necessary to be acutely aware of the importance of all interactions with customers, without exception.

CASE STUDY
PRINCE CHARLES'S CHRISTMAS PUDDINGS

When the delightfully named Puddings & Pies, a privately owned 'Country Fresh Food Company', embarked upon a PR-led brand awareness programme it little supposed that one outcome would be to become a supplier of Christmas puddings to His Royal Highness Prince Charles, The Prince of Wales, the next British monarch.

Puddings & Pies, located at Sherborne in the English rural southwest, produces a wide range of high-quality foods, which are sold mainly into the catering trade and to food retailers, including delicatessen shops, traditional English teashops and farm shops, within approximately 50 miles' radius of its kitchens. Everything is made to order by hand.

The company's policy statement states simply: 'We only use free range eggs, local farmhouse cheese, butter, milk and cream. All our flour is traditionally ground at a local watermill or a family miller's in the Cotswolds. All our meat is supplied by local farms. We do not use any flavourings, any additives, any colourings, any genetically modified products.'

The company uses a friendly Grandma symbol, to imply that all the food is prepared 'just like granny does'. With only a very limited budget, Puddings & Pies embarked on an intensive round of exhibiting at agricultural and other country shows and at UK catering trade exhibitions. This led to invitations to participate in local farmers' markets and, at its peak, the programme included an average of 10 shows each month, which represented a major commitment for this micro-sized business.

Apart from selling retail every product it displayed at these events, confirming that it had accurately identified an attractive niche market for 'proper food that looks home made', the principal objective was to attract trade enquiries. These came in abundance, from a wide variety of sources, some 'out of area', searching for premium-priced quality.

This was achieved for a fraction of the cost of advertising and has contributed substantially to a trebling of annual turnover and more than trebling of profit. That in turn has led to investment in additional plant and premises designed to maintain hand-made production while expanding capacity. The exhibition programme has been adapted over time and is now complemented by marketing activities that include point-of-purchase displays, very successful retail product sampling and some advertising.

The Christmas puddings tasted so good at Prince Charles's country estate that, from being a private customer, he became also a trade customer, through his quality foods company, Duchy Originals, for which Puddings & Pies is developing an exclusive range of products, for sale under the Duchy Originals brand. This 'royal endorsement' is also leading Puddings & Pies into invitations to supply direct some of the leading London food halls. The Puddings & Pies experience demonstrates the remarkable brand awareness impact that can be achieved by diligent use of low-cost PR techniques with very limited financial and labour resources.

QUESTIONS

1 When might dialogue with privacy be more attainable, and why?
2 How might LCV influence the design of a customer relations programme?
3 How might intervening external variables in decision-making determine the choice of communication channels in customer relations?
4 How relevant is the FLC likely to be in framing customer relations communication?
5 What measures might the PR person take to avoid quotation 'out of context'?

▪ Ṿ 8 Within marketing

The promotional mix – marketing public relations – areas of support – brands – integrated marketing communication – Cause-Related Marketing – the relationship between MPR and marketing

8.1 The promotional mix

To briefly recap: much public relations activity is directed at supporting marketing, where it is assigned to that part of the 'marketing mix' called *promotion*. There it works alongside other forms of marketing communication, which is one of the three categories of corporate communication, the others being management and organization communication. Public relations in this guise, together with all other marketing communication, contributes to the creation of shareholder value, which is about building sustainable competitive advantage.

Marketing is a disposal subsystem, tasked to market and distribute products and services. The public relations function may be located alongside, in the disposal subsystems. More probably it will be found in the management subsystems, although it may be alternatively located among the adaptive or maintenance subsystems. Where it goes is a reflection of how the dominant coalition of senior managers views the role of public relations within the specific context of their particular organization. Where *exactly* it is located in the organization is of no *great* consequence, for PR is **boundary spanning**: it operates across boundaries, both within the organization and between the organization and its external environment.

The **'marketing mix'** is also known as the **seven Ps**. These comprise:

- *product,*
- *price,*
- *place* (distribution) and
- *promotion,*

all of which relate directly to the offering, plus

- *people* (because everyone who has a customer interface influences purchase decision-making),
- *process* (reflecting the involvement of the customer in the production processes) and
- *physical evidence* (since less tangible services often need to be made more apparent). So *promotion* is but *one of seven* components of the marketing mix.

The various forms of marketing communication in turn comprise the '**promotion mix**'. This comprises:

- *direct sales* or personal selling,
- *advertising*,
- *sales promotion*,
- *direct marketing* and
- *public relations*.

Of these marketing communications, direct sales continue to account for the greatest expenditure; many companies have substantial sales forces. In 2000 estimated total UK expenditure was: sales £20 billion, sales promotion £14 billion, advertising £13 billion, direct marketing £5 billion and public relations £2 billion (Doyle, 2000).

This puts the PR contribution to marketing *by expenditure* well into perspective, although the relative differences indicated reflect UK conditions and cannot be readily assumed elsewhere. For instance, sales promotion in the UK is heavily used; it is calculated that over 60 per cent of the population participates in at least one sales

Figure 8.1 **The marketing and promotional mix**

promotion on average every month. Yet in Germany use of sales promotion is very limited indeed.

Moloney (2000) points to a growing use of public relations by marketers (which is observable in many countries) and suggests that this is 'because they believe that advertising alone is not persuasive enough, when the consumer is better educated, is seen as "active" and "ethical", and is considered to be "compassionate".'

Certainly all the indications are that the *hunt for more persuasiveness* lies at the heart of marketing's growing interest in public relations, but there are several other, more mundane, factors that, where they apply, also explain the take-up. These include:

the availability of appropriate advertising media,
rising costs of advertising production,
inapplicability of sales promotion,
sales force reductions and
smaller audiences to reach.

Compared to other marketing communications, however, this 'tool', as marketers call it, is judged primarily on 'physical economics': put bluntly, both research and practice confirm that for most marketers using public relations is a cheap alternative to what they generally prefer. 'Quite literally, marketers are being forced to consider PR's applicability to marketing products, brands and services' (Kitchen, 1997).

But there is another factor at work as well. *the rise in importance of corporate reputation.* How customers think *about the organization itself* is having a big impact on how they decide to view its products and services. *That* makes public relations seem rather more interesting from a marketing standpoint.

8.2   Marketing public relations

Time was when public relations in support of marketing used to be known simply as publicity and its purpose was to support sales through media coverage. The term stuck until the 1980s, when it was superseded by this conflation of marketing and public relations to produce MPR.

But what *is* MPR? Kotler (1991) defines this 'tool' as

- 'A variety of programs designed to improve, maintain, or protect a company or product image.'

This represents a substantial advance, adding *images*, including their *protection*, both those that apply to organizations *and* to what they have to offer.

This important point is now widely accepted and understood: MPR adds up to more than its predecessor. Hart, for one, took it further:

'Overall, one may say that public relations is concerned with creating a favourable image, or, to use a less emotive word, a favourable reputation. ... The emergence of reputation as a factor in the marketing mix leads onto the extension of the classical 4 P's into Five. The fourth P of promotion (which more properly anyway should be 'perception') now has to be considered as those activities which are involved with the product (brand image) and those concerned with the company (corporate image). It can be said that whether or not a product is purchased is dependent on five factors – the product, its price, its availability, the brand image and the corporate image. ... In so far as PR is the function which builds reputation or corporate image it can be seen then to have a direct correlation to sales and hence to profit' (Hart, 1995).

This represents a quantum leap in the argument for deploying public relation skills in the service of marketing. MPR is not only about adding to the battery of techniques and tactics, it is gaining in *marketing consequence*. To reinforce his point, Hart quotes Levitt's identification of 'sixteen areas in which a good reputation can be shown to have a positive benefit' in B2B markets. In practice reputation factors have always greatly influenced commercial and institutional purchasers, but the point is well made, and such factors are also of growing interest and concern to consumers.

Various definitions of MPR abound, and a prosaic summary such as **'the marketing component of public relations'** is probably entirely adequate for all practical purposes. *However*, among marketers it is still often seen as 'free advertising', an impression that not a few public relations practitioners encourage by seeking to 'value' the published editorial coverage that they have secured by reference to the alternative cost of advertising in the same space or time. The problem with this is that

- the space or time may not be buyable,
- receivers attach markedly more credibility to editorial than to advertising

and in any event

- public relations is not without its own costs.

So whatever else MPR is, clearly it is *not* free advertising.

8.3 Areas of support

From a marketing perspective, public relations is part of the marketing communications mix, but if that is so, what *exactly* is it doing there? Marketers talk about **exchange theory**, as well as communication theory, so whatever PR contributes is likely to be judged within that commercial framework. Kotler (1991) argues that MPR can contribute to four marketing objectives:

- awareness,
- credibility,
- stimulation of the sales force and dealers and
- holding down promotion costs.

'The smaller the company's promotion budget, the stronger the case for using PR to gain share of mind.'

That memorable last phrase, 'share of mind', may be compared with the commonplace and less subtle 'share of shout' allusion to noise. MPR, then, has a *cerebral* contribution to make to marketing, and is not entirely, or necessarily, about publicity. But nevertheless that sits alongside its *cheapness* as one of MPR's contributions. It appears that no matter how subtle MPR may become at influencing customers to purchase, if it is not downright inexpensive, relatively, most marketers are not *that much* interested.

How, then, may this low-cost marketing communication tool contribute in practice to the marketing tasks? Kotler offers six suggestions 'beyond simple publicity':

- assist in the launch of new products
- assist in re-positioning a mature product
- build up interest in a product category
- influence specific target groups
- defend products that have encountered public problems
- build the corporate image in a way that projects favourably on its products.

Here too the corporate image obtains a mention, as being part of MPR's workload, as also is *defence* as well as promotion. Nevertheless, most marketers prefer a simpler view of MPR as being *the delivery of successive good news*, faithfully reproduced by the mass media with extra credibility attached. And *that* creates a problem for them in valuing MPR, a problem that is neatly summed up by Doyle (2000), for whom MPR's main features are:

- *Credibility*, because 'news stories and features are more credible sources of information to buyers than ads and promotions that are obviously biased and paid for'
- *Imprecise*, being more difficult to control the message and target it accurately than with 'conventional commercial communications'
- *Low cost*, owing to 'free media exposure'
- *Difficult*, because 'it depends upon the perceived importance and interest of the message.'

In other words, in his view, on the one hand MPR is cheap and effective, but on the other it is less controllable and certain, because its very strength, the 'free' mass media 'exposure', is *also* its very weakness: mediated communication has to be *subjected to the filtering process* of the mediators, usually journalists.

Marketers recognize the practitioners' skills – for instance, Kotler observed that 'PR practitioners are able to find or create stories on behalf of even mundane products', and indeed they do – but worry that messages have to satisfy media criteria first. They assume that all messages have to jump this hurdle, although in practice MPR very often communicates *direct* to customers and consumers, for instance, through exhibitions, literature and events. This, therefore, is a *defective element in marketers' perceptions of public relations*, one that is now being reinforced by the introduction of instruction in the art and mystery of writing press releases as part of marketing training.

PR people are in no doubt about this media challenge. They spend very many hours trying, sometimes with growing desperation, to dredge interest for the reader, viewer or listener out of information and other material that holds fascination for only a limited circle of people within the organization. Then often only to find that the message source insists on filleting the facts that create the media interest, out of anxiety about control, sometimes extending to rampant 'control freakery'.

In a 1994 speech, Peter Gummer, who established the world's largest public relations consultancy, asserted that PR contributes topicality, credibility and involvement, the latter by 'creating interactive opportunities' (Stone, 1995). Top of his

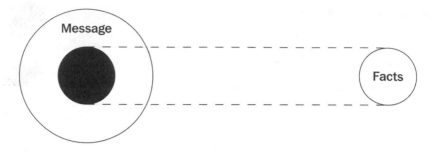

Figure 8.2 **Extracting, or 'filleting', the facts from the message to leave a hole**

list was this imperative, of 'linking the product with real-time news events'. It is a requirement that many non-PR managers find difficult to understand, much less accept. As Oliver (2001) remarked, 'Public relations can only be effective if it has a credible story to tell.' And *some* managers find that to be too great a challenge for them, typically concluding that it is better to 'keep it simple some other way.' Furthermore, for them talk of 'the broader and more strategic function of public relations [that] is concerned with corporate image' (Hart, 1995) usually falls on deaf ears.

Example

To launch the new version of the Range Rover motorcar, what the British motor industry calls a 'four-by-four' that is designed to travel across difficult terrain as well as roads, the MPR effort entailed persuading motoring writers from a variety of media to travel to Scotland in mid-winter in order to 'test run' the new product. A 'plane was chartered and repainted, part of a military airfield was rented, as was a country estate in the Highlands, an expensive castle-turned-hotel was fully booked, a special 'off-road' course was built, a famous explorer was hired to give an 'adventurous' after-dinner speech and several senior managers were assigned to act as hosts.

Some five hundred journalists were flown to the venue over a period of five weeks, where one hundred attendant staff engaged in 'being nice, cleaning cars and repairing the inevitable prangs'. So reported one of the journalists, who remarked that in three years as a professional road tester it was the most sumptuous launch he had experienced. 'Almost every car maker will mount a similar PR offensive to mark the arrival of a new model. Exotic locations, excellent food and Grand Luxe hotels. The free bars never shut, the room service is paid for, and there's almost always a gift … to help you remember it all.'

'My best estimate of £2 million for the extravaganza works out at a cool £4000 per journalist. Still, compared to the Range Rover's £1.5 billion engineering costs, it's a drop in the ocean. … So does this multi-million-pound niceness campaign work? … With my hand on my heart, resting over a Land Rover fleece, Skoda wallet and Mercedes watch I can tell you that it has absolutely no effect on my impartiality whatsoever.'
(*Financial Times*, 5.2.02)

8.4 Brands

Now that corporate brands are being brought to the attention of consumers alongside product brands, those broader public relations responsibilities are adding to MPR's potential contribution, for 'Corporate and brand images interact to enhance overall ambience and [PR in respect of both types] influence the bottom line [profitability]' (Kitchen, 1997). Accordingly corporate brands are being brought to the consumer's notice, even where the product or service has sold very well for many years without it.

Example

The Nestlé identity now appears on the UK's largest selling biscuit, or cookie, KitKat, a chocolate-coated wafer. The product is approaching its half-century but who made it was not an ingredient of the marketing, or presumably a concern of purchasers, before Nestlé acquired the brand. Now the consumer is reminded on every wrapper, and the Nestlé name and familiar symbol presumably provide reassurance and confidence in the product, lest it be needed after all this time.

The term 'brand' is so generously used, but what *exactly* is a brand? At its most prosaic, a brand is simply a name and all the qualities that are perceived to attach to it. But that needs qualifying. According to Doyle (2000), brands:

'reduce perceived risk, simplify the choice process and save time. This relationship [of trust] is based on the image customers have of the brand. A *brand image* is a set of beliefs about a brand's attributes and associations. A customer's image of a brand is built up from four types of sources: experience ... personal [endorsements and tips] ... public [mass media coverage and consumer report analysis and] ... commercial [marketing and sales].'

The third of these indicates where MPR fits into the picture.

Doyle goes on to place brands and brand images into three categories:

- an *attribute* brand – the image generates confidence through beliefs about functional attributes
- an *aspirational* brand – the image indicates who buys the brand and their enviable lifestyles
- an *experience* brand – the image shares emotions and associations with the consumer.

In B2B markets the emphasis is on *attributes*, more down-to-earth about function and performance, whereas consumers are more interested in *lifestyle* and *experience*. 'Experience brands have a number of advantages over attribute and aspirational brands. ... Consumers are becoming more individualistic ... Experience brands are more robust because they do not depend on a product or a "look". ... The archetype of an experience brand is Richard Branson's Virgin brand, which stands for an unstuffy, irreverent, us-against-them attitude.'

The role of MPR in enhancing brands was addressed by Houtman in Harris (1998), cited by DeSanto and Petherbridge (2002). Houtman, whose title at Chrysler was manager of corporate image and brand, identified five rules for building brands through public relations:

1 Know what the product, and the campaign that surrounds it, stands for.
2 Target those buyers who have a passion for your product.
3 Understand how the industry to which your product belongs has evolved.
4 Integrate the timeless qualities that have helped make the brand successful.
5 Reduce cross-considerations by targeting an exclusive market and audience.

Viewed this way, where there is already a successful brand with 'timeless qualities', MPR is primarily about **filling any gaps of uncertainty about purchase that are resulting in hesitation and hovering over the corporate elements of the product surround.** But the brand does not have to be long established for MPR to bring these 'extra' dimensions to the marketing effort. Just as public relations is the eyes and ears of the organization, so too it can bring the bigger picture to bear on brand promotion and defence, trying to make sure that marketing is wholly consistent with all other messages.

Example

'Harley-Davidson began with one motorcycle in a shed way back in 1903,' according to the company's chairman and CEO. 'But our anniversary is not just about a machine. It's truly a celebration of family and friends who have been touched by the Harley-Davidson experience and want to share it with the world. We promise that we will continue to fulfil the dream of our customers for the next 100 years!'

To mark the occasion the company embarked upon a 14-month open road tour to celebrate 'the most significant birthday celebration in the history of motorcycling'. The tour, starting in July 2002, visited 10 cities – Atlanta, Jersey Shore, Los Angeles, Toronto, Dallas, Mexico City, Sydney, Tokyo, Barcelona and Munich. The finale comprised 'The Ride Home', a series of organized rides for enthusiasts through North America, returning to the company's Milwaukee headquarters, for four days of celebrations and special events culminating in the official birthday party on 31 August 2003.

The 'world's largest rolling birthday party' brought 'the Harley-Davidson experience to everyone, riders and non-riders alike', with musical entertainment, activities for children and families, movies, parades, biker fashion shows and rare exhibits from Harley-Davidson's history. It also marked the 23rd year of the company's support for a charity, the Muscular Dystrophy Association. During that time customers, dealers and employees had raised over $27 million to fund research and services for patients. All the anniversary events raised more money to help find a cure for neuromuscular disease.
(*Yeovil Express*, 6.3.02)

8.5 Integrated marketing communication

This matter of *integration* is critical, on which PR practitioners place great emphasis; they know how destructive can be inconsistencies, in generating perceptions of confusion, incompetence, even deceit. One of the earliest, and often hardest, communication lessons that any organization learns is to make sure that there is a controlled and co-ordinated approach, as Tesco, one of the UK's largest groceries retailers, discovered in the 1970s, a time when any director who happened to be available came to the 'phone to answer business media enquiries. There is need of 'a consistent corporate message and tone that appropriately reflects the organization in the way that the organization wishes it to be reflected ...' (Oliver, 2001).

This public relations priority is shared with marketing. 'At its most basic level, integrated marketing communications [IMC] means integrating all the promotional tools so that they work together in harmony. ... Their sum is greater than their parts – providing they speak consistently with one voice all the time, every time.' In addition to 'the basic communications tools', integration may be horizontal, vertical, internal, external and in relation to data (Smith, 1999).
These may be summarized as:

- *horizontal*, across the marketing mix and subsystems, so that different functions send out consistent messages through their various decisions and actions
- *vertical*, so that both marketing and communication objectives are consistent with the corporate mission and objectives
- *internal*, keeping everyone relevantly informed and motivated
- *external*, providing a single, cohesive message through the close collaboration of external partners such as advertising and public relations agencies
- *data*, to ensure a marketing information system which collects and shares relevant data across subsystems.

Much importance is attached by marketers to this simple precept. Smith asserts that 'It can create competitive advantage and boost sales and profits, while saving money, time and stress.' That is certainly borne out by experience, as is the prospect of the alternative:

'... disjointed messages which dilute the impact of the message [and may] confuse, frustrate and arouse anxiety in customers.'

Example

As anyone who has received inconsistent and inefficient messages from insurance companies holding their precious pension savings will readily attest.

The most relevant benefit of IMC from the public relations standpoint is its *effectiveness*. 'At its most basic level, a unified message has more impact than a disjointed myriad of messages [and] a better chance of cutting through the "noise" of over 500 commercial messages that bombard customers each and every day.'

Kitchen (1997) asked seven marketing and seven public relations executives, drawn from seven companies on average each employing 17,000 people, what IMC meant to them. The conclusion was that IMC 'extends beyond marketing to corporate activities too. For many FMCG [fast-moving consumer goods] firms, there is a significant need to *market the corporate brand*. Thus while PR can be utilized by marketing, marketing can also be utilized by PR.'

8.6 Cause Related Marketing

The BITC's annual Awards for Excellence scheme includes an award for 'Marketplace Impact' called the **Cause Related Marketing** Award, 'for using the power of the brands in partnership with charities or causes to address key social issues.' Moloney (2000) quotes BITC's definition of CRM as being 'a "commercial activity" to "market an image, product or service for mutual benefit. It is an additional tool for addressing social issues of the day." It emphasizes goals such as "enhanced reputation", "awareness, improved loyalty." '

He cites by way of example the supply of 29,000 computers to UK schools by Tesco. In fact the scheme is said to have supplied £77 million-worth of computers, yet it still has its detractors. A consumer organization calculated that it took 21,990 vouchers, acquired by buying groceries, to provide a single computer worth £1000.

A similar scheme introduced vending machines containing packets of Walkers potato crisps, or chips, into school hallways by offering free books in exchange. This was met with substantial dietary criticism; it also resulted in 93 per cent of 15 and 16 year olds ranking the brand as their highest 'top of mind' food snack (*The Guardian*, 30.4.03).

Donations, in cash or in kind, are tied to purchases, which it is intended will be stimulated by the seller's association with a 'good cause'. But the causes have to be 'right' and the linkages have to be 'real'. For example, the UK National Lottery is promoted heavily by reference to the many good causes it 'supports' (the government requires that a proportion of proceeds is given to a wide variety of social purposes) but repeatedly research has demonstrated that only a small minority of the customers, or gambling 'punters', take any account of this; *the vast majority simply want to win.*

CRM should not be confused with **social marketing**, which describes what charities and other not-for-profit organizations – many of which are beneficiaries of CRM – undertake for themselves. Social marketing describes communication with members, donors and other *non-consumer* publics with a view to developing and maintaining beneficial relationships. It is, in effect, an alternative term for public relations in the voluntary sector.

8.7 The relationship between MPR and marketing

The relationship between public relations and marketing can be sensitive territory. Many writers on marketing over the years have asserted the dominance of marketing, interpreting MPR as simply part of 'promotion management', a minor role within a much more significant and senior function. It is a view that has been assiduously inculcated into successive generations of marketing students, and only lately has there been much of a let up, owing to the rise of pluralism and resultant knock-on effects for marketing.

Those effects (Seitel, cited by Kitchen and Papasolomou, 1997) include:

- consumer protests about value and safety
- government scrutiny of marketing claims
- product recalls, giving rise to media coverage
- food ingredient scares
- advertising claims being questioned, in social and civil dimensions
- rumours about companies
- media criticism of companies and 'business'.

'Following Kitchen and Papasolomou (1997), managers increasingly recognize that in the 1990s PR programmes and techniques can add another dimension to marketing campaigns.'

Writers on public relations have been less certain, some, often practitioners specializing in MPR, happily concurring, while others preferring to assert the 'independence' of public relations as a separate discipline that has plenty more to offer than the limited role commonly defined for it by marketing. Given PR's assumed responsibility for reputation, some practitioners perceive MPR as having a *corrective job* to do, protecting marketing from *the consequences of its actions* where these appear to contradict overall corporate well being. They often mention by way of illustration controversies relating to **environmental issues**, where marketing has brought embarrassment or worse upon the organization.

So are marketing and public relations:

- Separate but equal?
- Or equal but overlapping?
- Are they the *same*?
- Or is PR simply part of marketing?
- And could marketing be part of PR?

There are sound arguments to be advanced for all of these possibilities, which only serves to render the whole 'debate' all the more arid. The dispassionate empirical view is likely to be that both are *equally important and separate*, similarly to all other functions, such as finance, law, human resources, production and so on. The fact

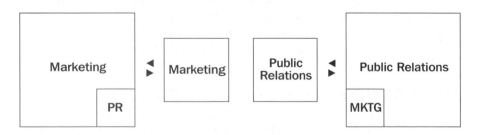

Figure 8.3 **The relationship between public relations and marketing**

that PR spends more of its time, in aggregate, with marketing than with any of the others does not, of itself, make the case for subsuming it into the marketing function, which in any event, should that occur, would eliminate much of the *value and purpose* of public relations.

This is an argument borne of rivalry that doubtless will persist interminably. In the meantime, assuredly, marketing will continue to concentrate on attending to customer needs and wants of its products and services by way of exchanges, while MPR will persist in its focus on meeting customers' expectations, through fostering understanding and goodwill towards the company and, in consequence, its products and services.

CHECKLIST

- MPR is part of the 'marketing mix' called promotion, one of several tools of marketing communication, in turn a category of corporate communication.
- Wherever it is formally located internally, the PR function spans boundaries, both within the organization and between it and the external environment.
- For Kotler MPR is about: publicity, new products, product re-positioning and defence, product category awareness, publics and corporate image.
- For Doyle MPR's main features are: added credibility, weaker delivery control ('imprecision'), lower cost and news/topicality imperative.
- In its essence MPR is primarily about filling any gaps of uncertainty about purchase that are resulting in hesitation and hovering over the corporate elements of the product surround, all the many additional factors perceived by the buyer.
- Integrated Marketing Communication (IMC) describes, at its simplest, the integration of all promotional tools to optimize harmony and therefore impact.
- In many markets there is a significant need to promote the corporate brand as well as product brands; the IMC concept may be extended therefore to include corporate activities, for marketing purposes.
- From an overall PR perspective, all messages must be wholly consistent one with another; this applies universally to all corporate communication, including marketing, and extends also to tone and style of delivery.
- Cause Related Marketing (CRM) is designed to address and remedy social issues and ills while generating product sales through achieving enhanced reputation, awareness and customer loyalty.
- Social Marketing is communication by third sector organizations with their members, donors and various non-consumer publics.
- Marketing concentrates on customer needs and wants by way of exchanges; MPR on meeting customers' total corporate, product and service expectations.

CASE STUDY
AEROSYSTEMS COMMUNICATES ITS OWN MESSAGE

For 15 years Aerosystems International, which manufactures computer software-intensive systems for a variety of military and civilian transport, was to all intents and purposes an invisible company. Then in 2000 it decided to change all that. At the time it had but four customers, and all of them built aircraft. The time had come to find more customers and to enter new markets; first it had to generate awareness.

The company had been formed in 1985 by IT company Cap Scientific and the long-established Westland Helicopters at Yeovil in the English southwest. The company was established to provide real-time-embedded command and control solutions, primarily for Westland, and its identity therefore was unclear to the market, its products being largely credited to the parent companies. Three ownership changes resulted in BAE Systems becoming both a new parent company, alongside GKN Aerospace Services, and a new customer. This in turn led to work for Boeing and Lockheed Martin, resulting in there being four OEM, or mainframe, manufacturing customers.

In 2000 the first move was to create a public relations function; the second to instigate a thorough review of the corporate identity, starting with that most fundamental detail, its name. Most people in the defence community perceived Aerosystems as being 'part of the OEMs' and when they did recognize any difference they called the company Ael for short. The review resulted in a decision to keep both the 'proper' name and the logo design too.

Then attention turned to making sure that all ID applications were mutually consistent, itself a major advance, since until then the logo and typography had been interpreted very loosely by each department and unit, scattered across five separate locations, with no overall policing to enforce consistency. The task of establishing a uniform, satisfactory corporate identity extended to a newly built office building, opened in 2001 to house all company personnel, apart from one outstation located some 80 miles away.

The accompanying brand awareness campaign focused on three publics: ground maintenance staff, pilots and specifiers within the decision-making units. Two primary communication channels were identified: technical journalists writing for a host of, often, arcane publications, primarily serving the defence industries; and exhibitions such as public flying demonstrations by the Royal Air Force and the Fleet Air Arm of the Royal Navy, which, apart from attracting large general public audiences, are attended by key military and civilian personnel who exercise purchasing influence.

Owing to the nature of its business, Aerosystems has been able to mount highly engaging interactive exhibitions, both on-site for visiting journalists and at shows, which are seen not as sales platforms but valuable networking opportunities. Two PR-specific results have been identified: quality relationships with key journalists, resulting in substantial press coverage of the company and its developments; and greatly increased awareness and favourable recognition of the company in its key markets.

These PR outcomes have served the corporate strategy well. The company has entered new markets, in army, naval, rail and automotive applications, and achieved sales in the USA and several European countries, while strengthening its position with its four core customers. PR has also materially assisted internally. Employee loyalty is high, with an annual 'attrition', or loss, rate of 10 per cent, a particularly significant factor in a knowledge-based company where recruitment and retention are key factors. Some 70 per cent of staff members are graduates and one-third hold doctorates.

The PR effort has been widened to embrace CSR and corporate community involvement, or CCI. This is focused on three further publics: civic opinion formers, local schools and environmentalists. A variety of educational projects designed to assist recruitment include work experience placements, funding, and instruction in website construction and graphic design. The company has gained civic recognition as a major local employer. And it is committed to tree planting schemes following the 'Year of Promise' in 2000, when the company undertook to plant sufficient trees to offset its annual paper consumption.

It could be fairly argued that, since previously Aerosystems had not undertaken any promotion, the results were bound to be substantial. Equally, given the circumstances, it seems reasonable to suppose that even modest budgets would provide the means to generate significant results. However, the company's grasp of the scale of the challenge and what was needed, working on a relative 'shoestring', might well have been rejected as impractical by another organization that was more accustomed to working with substantial marketing budgets and advertising expenditure.

At Aerosystems it is argued that every £6000 that could be spent on a whole page corporate advertisement is better spent where it can complement the company's existing resources. So it is, for example, that aircraft maintenance personnel and pilots are invited to experience hands-on simulated use of the company's products at show stands, senior military personnel are encouraged to ask searching questions about practical applications and journalists are welcome to spend a day at the company's premises, checking up on what's new at first hand. This skilful MPR is closely interlinked with corporate PR, starting with identity awareness and extending to CSR and community relations.

QUESTIONS

1 Why should interest in corporate reputation make MPR more valuable to marketers?
2 How might MPR protect a product's image and why?
3 Why might MPR 'never sell a bad product'?
4 When could marketing be utilized by public relations, and why?
5 What could make PR and marketing look one and the same?

▪ Ⅴ 9 Public affairs

The public sphere – government public relations – propaganda – lobbying - issues management

9.1 The public sphere

'Let's start with image. In politics it is everything. And if you want to get on you need a good head of hair. And the simple fact is that baldness is a political loser. Since the early days of television the only bald [UK] prime minister … was 40 years ago and he wasn't even elected. He inherited his job …' Thus explained Kelvin MacKenzie, a former national newspaper editor, describing the leader of the largest opposition party as 'the loser in waiting' owing to his premature and pronounced baldness. (*Kelvin saves the Tories*, Channel Four, 7.6.03).

It is nearly 45 years ago that President John Kennedy reputedly won power in the USA by a narrow margin after he had appeared live on television, sporting a suntan, to point-score against an opponent, the (later) President Richard Nixon, who looked as if he needed a shave. The radio audience thought that the latter won the argument, but the majority of *viewers* opted for the better-looking candidate; appearances counted more.

Examples

- When Prime Minister Tony Blair stood for leadership of his party, paid-up members explained on UK television that they were going to choose him because he would, they thought, *look good on television*.
- In a closely fought German general election in 2002, a news agency quoted an *image expert* saying that Chancellor Gerhard Schroder would be more convincing 'if he did not dye the grey from his temples.'
- During his presidential campaign, the Mexican media flatteringly portrayed President Vicente Fox as a charming, straight-talking cowboy; in fact he is a former executive of a multinational.

This degeneration of political debate to mere *spectator entertainment* appears far removed from the earnest arguments in the assembly rooms and coffee houses of 18th century London, where first the 'public sphere' took root. There, and increasingly elsewhere, 'men of affairs' gathered to discuss the issues, gossip and rumour of the day, encouraged by the appearance of the early newspapers and magazines. They formed opinions, began to organize around issues of concern to them, sought to influence the government, established the early commercial and intellectual societies and generally began the slow process that led to universal suffrage, the vote for all adults, which continues to this day.

The public places where this occurred were in aggregate small, not many people participated at first, and those that did were rich and privileged, or at the very least intent on becoming so. But they laid the foundations to modern interpretations of democratic free speech and representative government that were to spread rapidly and for which both men and women have laid down their lives. In 1929 every UK adult finally won the right to vote, so what has gone wrong? Why *do* so great a proportion of voters now consider that their only means of influence is to *abstain from voting*, to throw away that long-fought-for right? In the last UK general election, for example, less than 60 per cent of voters bothered, and how many of *them* were deciding on looks, not content?

It is the agreement of the vast majority of people to exercise their right to vote that gives legitimacy to the political class. Without that, the public sphere is at serious risk of being reduced to illegitimate assertion of authority by a tiny minority. The mass involvement necessary for democracy evaporates, and politics becomes a spectacle, the source of prime-time satire and gossip, in which promises are greeted with ridicule, announcements are generally mistrusted and motives are deeply distrusted. In short, democracy becomes for the vast majority of people, those who are not paid-up members of one or other faction, a hoax, a sham designed to give a few people a very good living indeed and also, in the UK and some other countries, self-awarded honours and titles in abundance.

This degeneration has its origins long before the advent of widespread television. In *The Century of the Self* (RDF Television/BBC, 2002) Ewen observed '[Edward] Bernays's and [Walter] Lippmann's concept of managing the masses takes the idea of democracy and it turns it into a palliative. It turns it into giving people some feel good medication that will respond to an immediate pain or an immediate yearning but will not alter the objective circumstances one iota. I mean … the idea of democracy at its heart was about changing the relations of power that had governed the world for so long and Bernays's concept of democracy was one of maintaining the relations of power, even if it meant that one needed to sort of stimulate the psychological lives of the public, and in fact in his mind that was what was necessary. But if you can keep stimulating the irrational self then leadership can basically go on doing what it wants to do.' Later in the four-part documentary series Ewen observed that Bernays has thought 'the man in the street' was 'driven by the spinal cords.' Lippmann, who had declared 'Democracy has to be changed', had fascinated him.

Habermas described the public sphere in simple terms as being where private people gather as a public. This transformation from a venue for rational debate between concerned and interested citizens to the current circus was, he thought, the consequence of the burgeoning mass media and public relations. Somewhere along the line, certainly, politicians changed from being sober men and women, earnestly debating the issues of the day, often at such length as to challenge all but the most ardent and committed to stay listening, into performers who attach more importance to being on television than to speaking in parliament, assiduously court the glitterati of café society and industriously copy the lifestyles of the celebrities their electors adore. They have become a specialized branch of show business, with whose members they enthusiastically mix.

McNair (1996) identified the first political public relations consultancy as having been established in Los Angeles in 1933, 'since which time the industry has expanded throughout America and the rest of the democratic capitalist world. Now … it is axiomatic that no serious contender for public office can afford to do without the services of his or her 'spin doctor' or media adviser. Once the politician is in government, the role of the political public relations specialist becomes even more important …'.

According to Moloney (2000), in 1999, as the UK prime minister was about to 're-shuffle' his government, 'one minister's promotion prospects were reported to be diminished because his team of press officers was not as good as others'. Indeed, the British press frequently discusses the relative merits of this or that government department's public relations performance, as if tipping runners and riders in horse races.

While public relations clearly has become a, possibly *the*, most important component of modern politics, attention to any passing political utterances quickly indicates that the probable causes for this degradation lie in **consumerism**. Why otherwise should baldness be a bar to office, or 'five o'clock shadow' and any other alleged or implied presentational failing? Why otherwise are policies advocated primarily or wholly on the basis that they serve the results of opinion research? And if consumerism *is* the source, should it be allowed free rein in a 'market' where, ostensibly, nothing is bought or sold, in that votes are cast as of right and not for, at least direct, payment? Is the contemporary 'telling people what they want to hear', which is serving the current generation of politicians so well, a new version of buying votes, a practice that in the UK supposedly ended in 1832?

9.2 Government public relations

This modern condition of the 'public sphere' is not confined to the UK. There is, however, probably a greater *intensity* of political PR activity in the UK than in most other countries. The advent of '24 hour news' has been accompanied by the emergence of *round-the-clock government news output*, seeking to continually 'set the news agenda'.

In the UK as in many other countries there has been a **government information service** provided by civil servants for many decades. 'Public relations in a government department has two main tasks: to give regular information on policy, plans and achievements of the department; and to inform and educate the public on legislation, regulations and all matters that affect the daily life of citizens. It must also advise Ministers and senior officials of reaction and potential reaction to current and proposed policies' (Black, 1989). It is essentially non-political, a position that, as expected of civil servants, is jealously guarded. Or at least, it *should* be, for in the past decade or so there has been significant change.

Job rotating civil servants, who did a turn at PR as part of their careers, working in about 30 government departments, have given way to a much expanded dedicated

Figure 9.1 **The role of special advisers**

PR **information management** operation. This has been accompanied by a quantum leap in resourcing, resulting in some 1200 press officers and an estimated £200 million aggregate annual budget, according to Budge *et al.* (1998), quoted by Somerville (2001). All this to run the delivery of what the UK government and its agencies wish the public at large to know about, and, by the same token, to withhold what is *not* intended 'for public consumption'.

Greater interest, however, has been focused by the media on the **'special advisers'**, most of whom have at least a partial public relations role. We are told that they are relatively few, less than one hundred, although their number has trebled under the present government, and most if not all of them are *former employees of the governing party.*

Their activities are the source of much controversy, since they appear to be primarily employed to promote favourable images of government ministers and their wives, but are paid out of taxation, and to this end they are involved in media output. A committee of members of parliament has declared that they perform a valuable function but that 'the boundaries between their work and those of career civil servants do not appear to be well understood.' Their work can come to explicit public notice in unfortunate circumstances.

Example

On 11 September 2001, an hour after the first terrorist-controlled civilian passenger airliner had been flown into the World Trade Center in New York, a special adviser, Jo Moore, e-mailed colleagues advising 'Media handling. It's now a very good day to get out anything we want to bury. Councillors' expenses?' The reference to 'councillors' expenses' related to a minor 'U-turn' on pension rights for local government politicians.

A former governing party official, Moore kept her job, confessing an 'error of judgement' but, it was widely thought, showing little contrition. According to at least one national newspaper, her chief error had been in getting caught. Subsequently, however, she was again embarrassed and was dismissed. The civil

The '**spin machine**', as the media describes it, has provoked many public rebukes, with headlines such as 'When the spinning had to stop' and 'Spinners are now out of control'.

' "No spin is the new spin" has become this year's brittle joke. There is some truth in it, though it is hard to be a spokesman in such an adversarial climate,' wrote one political editor. ' "You lot are much harder on the spokesmen than we are in Berlin," a German reporter told me the other day after attending a briefing' (*The Guardian*, 16.12.02).

Nor is the criticism confined to editorial output. The government has become its country's largest spending *advertiser*, having spent £136.5 million promoting its policies in 2000–01, over three times the level of expenditure of its predecessors in their last year in power (1996–97). The second largest opposition party's spokesman, who researched the data, commented 'These figures show the huge price tag for [government] spin. Whilst it is important that departments communicate effectively, it cannot be right that [the government] is spending this much more. The government should be spending public money on public services, not on yet more spin. It should invest less in public relations and more in public services' (*The Daily Mail*, 30.3.02).

Government is not alone in its heavy use of PR. The **political parties** are individually engaged, nationally, regionally and locally, in seeking to communicate with voters. 'The proactive public relations pursued by parties as they campaign for election (or re-election) represent the visible, truly *public* dimension of political communication. Much political public relations work remains hidden from public view, however. Aware that information, and access to it, is a power resource, parties in government have become enthusiastic custodians of a vast machinery for suppressing, censoring and at times falsifying information which, it might be thought, the citizenry of a democratic state has a right to receive in relatively unadulterated form' (McNair, 1996).

This is often most apparent, to the thoughtful and persistently enquiring citizen, at the *local level*, where manipulation of facts and figures may be more readily identifiable from local and personal knowledge.

Example

Leaflets soliciting votes often seek to deceive quite clumsily, as where a percentage increase in annual local taxes is compared with increases of only those other authorities where the increase is greater, carefully not mentioning those where the increase is lower. And the proposed increase may be favourably compared with that of the previous year using only partial figures, even though the *full levels* of tax are applied by the *same* political party through its control of not one but two tiers of local and/or regional government.

Similarly, it is often observable that statutory notices have not been displayed or sent as required by law, because the (politicized) authority *does not wish to inform* people who might exercise their democratic right to object to a proposal for which the authority intends to give formal approval or which it may propose to undertake. Manipulation of regulations dealing with local planning and other matters that have a social impact is commonplace and often the spur to the formation of new cause and special interest publics.

(A thoughtful and persistently enquiring citizen)

Stone (1995) pointed out that in the UK **local government** is usually the largest local employer, and certainly this is so in the outer regions, further removed from the seat of national power. In a small administrative area that is predominantly rural this is highly likely; in another such 'county' with a larger population and broader mix of commercial activity, local government is typically one of the three largest employers. Stone asserted that the typical (higher tier) county council employed 35,000 people; there are also lower tier authorities within the same 'patch'. This weighty and expensive local government, or government locally, is familiar throughout many countries, some more so, as in France.

This civil administration is further increased by the presence of **regional government**, which, as in the UK, may constitute a further upper tier. Federalist states such as Germany are all too familiar with the costly burden of democracy when it spawns *multiple layers* of government. And in Europe there is the *additional layer* represented by the **European Union's institutions**. None of this, however, appears to do much to overcome widespread public mistrust and resentment of the political class, which is viewed as being wholly self-serving, as its members are seen to scramble for these multi-layered job opportunities. Nor does the laboured intrusion of government into daily life appear to most electors to result in any *commensurate* benefits for society.

This is of the *greatest relevance to public relations*, which is a burgeoning on-cost for every elector to help bear, for each bureaucracy seeks to promote itself and its activities and to protect its interests. The size and intensity of public relations activity at the *national* level should not obscure the very substantial activity that also occurs at *regional* and *local* levels, and, within the EU, at the *continental* level.

9.3 Propaganda

It has been argued, in Chapter 1, that propaganda is not public relations, a position that is generally asserted by PR practitioners, not so much from an ethical standpoint but more on practical grounds: propaganda can be very effective, but if it 'goes wrong' its consequences have been observed to be dire for the propagandist. For many of them it recalls the saying *those who live by the sword usually die by the sword*, the meaning of which may be also interpreted from an ethical standpoint.

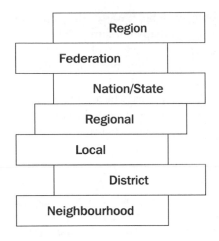

Figure 9.2　**Multiple layers of government**

Critics assert that propaganda is the dark secret in the public relations cupboard, the embarrassing Bernays inheritance PR people must always deny. However, propaganda can be well intentioned and used for benign purposes, for instance the 'New Deal' in 1930s USA. But the *collective European memory* is of the hideous German, Italian, Spanish and Portuguese dictatorships' use of propaganda for their own mostly ill-intentioned purposes in the middle decades of the 20th century. They have left the stronger legacy, making propaganda synonymous in many contemporary minds with the most profound abuse of humanity.

That public relations practice is *not* propaganda may be argued in the context of the **excellence concept**, which has at its core the communication loop, two-way communication. This may be, probably is, *asymmetrical*, that is, between unequal correspondents, the sender seeking to exert its superior power over the other in order to benefit from the dialogue, using the feedback simply in order to strengthen the effectiveness of its effort.

It may be, sometimes is, *symmetrical*, the two parties exercising *relatively equal power* and therefore having *relatively equal capacity* to benefit from the exchange. In order to achieve such outcomes one or other party may resort to 'win–win' and similar negotiating stratagems, in order to achieve a lasting mutually acceptable result. The painful 'peace process' road to reconciliation of political, economic, cultural and social differences in Northern Ireland provides an example.

Where this loop is missing, the possibility of propaganda being present arises, and Grunig and Hunt (1984) argue that this is the case with *publicity*, when the sender feels free to be 'economical with the truth' in the pursuit of desired outcomes. That may have a relatively benign intention, such as creating an 'impromptu' reception party, or a commercial exchange, such as selling concert tickets. In government, publicity is widely used, at all levels, and to that extent propaganda is present, but it is usually for obviously benign purposes.

The phrase 'economical with the truth', significantly, emanated during the 1980s from the highest level of the British civil service, where propaganda is seen as having more uses than for publicity alone. It was during a trial relating to 'official secrets' that the phrase was used; perhaps not surprisingly, since the UK government is among the most secretive. A Freedom of Information Act has been deferred repeatedly and indefinitely despite mounting demands for greater democratic access (*Financial Times*, 10.11.01). Nor is the British government alone in wanting to limit access to information; it just happens to be among the worst offenders.

In the UK the use of propaganda appears to be concentrated in politics; it has been long used by governments, for instance, to justify warfare.

Example

The British public was overwhelmingly opposed to military invasion of Iraq in February 2003. Only 16 per cent supported the government, but 62 per cent said that it would come round *provided* there was first a UN Security Council resolution in favour. To combat this opposition the government published a supportive 'dodgy dossier' that included plagiarized sections of a doctoral thesis. 'The dodgy dossier was a public relations disaster for the Prime Minister,' claimed an opposition politician who was a former Defence Secretary. The chairman of the all-party parliamentary committee on public policy, a government supporter, said of the dossier 'It breaks every rule of integrity in public life.'

And when the government found that it could not secure an affirmative vote in the UN Security Council, having previously advanced several differing arguments in favour, it reverted to claiming that Iraq not only had weapons of mass destruction but the *capacity and intention to use them at 45 minutes' notice on a British military base.* That *imminent threat* persuaded parliament in March to endorse the government's position, the widespread supposition being, among politicians and citizens, that the prime minister had secret intelligence to justify his claim.

Subsequently it became self-evident that this had not been so. The government sought to expunge the claim, but television footage provided the evidence. Under the military occupation of Iraq no such weapons could be found, much less any that could attack the British at 45 minutes' notice.

(Information sources: the entire UK national media, in particular *Channel 4 News*, 7.2.03 and 11.2.03)

Public relations people are engaged on disseminating this propaganda, but nevertheless it remains the case that public relations itself is not propaganda, which relies on deceit and trickery in pursuit of a following. Being 'economical with the truth' is taken by propagandists far beyond prudent use of facts, figures and arguments in order to engage in dialogue and reasoned persuasion.

It may be argued that this is really a matter of *degree*; that propaganda is a *natural development* of public relations, just the greater use of hyperbole and better-calculated advocacy (many politicians are lawyers) in order to be more effective, that is, achieve greater beneficial outcomes for the message sender. But, quite apart from any ethical considerations, in an increasingly pluralistic age such an amoral position is unlikely to be sustainable, as is observable in politics, where politicians and their supporters concentrate on the shortest of short-term outcomes and effects, giving the impression that they are engaged in some 'snatch and grab' operation and will not be around for long to deal with the consequences. They think within *timeframes dictated by political convenience*, such as the periods between one election and the next, yet they deal in matters that have *major long-term implications*, such as public health and education standards. And the economy.

Example

By the Treaty of Maastricht in 1992 the member states of the European Union committed themselves to impose whatever economic rigours they considered necessary upon their peoples in order to meet various demanding 'convergence criteria' deemed necessary for the introduction of an EU-wide common currency. The UK government implemented the treaty, and in due course the country met the criteria.

However, the political will was missing, so when in 1997 the time came to commit, the UK government invented five new 'economic tests' that the British economy would first have to satisfy before it could join the 'euro zone'. Meanwhile all but two countries signed-up, even though four of them did not satisfy the original convergence criteria.

Six years later the UK government continued to say that its five tests had not been met and spoke in terms of several more years passing before they would be satisfied. In the meantime it equivocated over holding a referendum, used widely among other European nations. The opponents of the UK being in the zone formed a majority of public opinion; a substantial minority did not wish the UK to be in the EU either. Owing to this interminable delay, the rate of inward investment into the UK by global and multinational companies collapsed and many that had established themselves in the UK, in order to be in an English-speaking country within the EU, questioned how much longer they could wait for entry to the zone, which would significantly reduce their currency exchange costs.

Both the UK proponents and opponents of British membership of the euro zone, and of the EU, repeatedly asserted that *the decision to enter the zone was irrevocable.* Opponents were particularly vehement on this point, as were their media supporters. Both sides however presented a defective case, for the new draft constitution of the EU stated, clearly and categorically in article I/59, that any member state could quit, 'setting out the arrangements for its withdrawal, taking account of the framework for its future relationship with the Union.'
(*The Guardian*, 9.6.03)

The conceptual thinking about public relations in its formative early years kept reverting to its *applicability to democratic government.* If, as McNair (1996) asserted, 'the public relations function is a necessary dimension of the modern political process,' the heavy *use of propaganda appears contradictory.* Given the 'enhanced tendency' of politicians 'to seek to "manufacture our consent" ' within a 'media-assisted mass democratic participation', public relations people employed in the service of such masters might be expected to concentrate on trying to achieve two-way communication that effected mutually rewarding exchanges. And brought voters back to the polling booths. Or is all the talk by politicians about public debate and dialogue a reflection of the degree of their aversion to any such 'infringements' of their 'licence to operate'?

9.4 Lobbying

Anyone can **lobby**, according to the politicians. By 'lobby' they mean make representations, aimed at *influencing decisions of government* about laws and regulations, and many encourage their electors to suppose that their doors are always open, waiting to receive their contributions to the democratic process. This portrayal of lobbying is, however, at variance with much of what *actually happens.*

Most lobbying is *not* undertaken by concerned individuals, usually constituents of the person being lobbied, but, particularly in the UK and USA, by organizations or their paid representatives, an activity called **public affairs**, which is that part of public relations which embraces **relations with government** at all levels. The terms 'lobbying' and 'public affairs' are often used interchangeably.

CERP says public affairs are 'the planned and formalized efforts of a company to exercise its rights and duties as a corporate citizen in the community, the nation and the society and to encourage employees to discharge their rights and duties as individual citizens' (CERP website, 5.11.02). This definition involves the employees as well as the organization they work for; although in practice lobbying is *primarily an organizational activity*, as CERP acknowledges in one of its three further definitions. This spells out more precisely the purpose of public affairs as:
'a corporate activity designed towards

- Improving the business climate surrounding corporate operations to the extent by which that climate may be influenced by government, thought leaders, and the general public, and
- Minimizing the adverse effect of government's involvement in matters of economic and social concern to the corporation in question.'

CERP also seeks to widen the net, to allow for the European, non-British, perception of lobbying as being **a mechanism for achieving greater social cohesion**. Lobbying is about:

matters of 'significant and substantial concern' to 'individuals, business, labour, foundations, private institutions and government'

and also:

'relations between an organization and government, parliament, civil servants and special interests and pressure groups at both national and trans-European levels.'

So, one way or another, lobbying seems to involve all manner of organized interests, whether governmental, bureaucratic, corporate, institutional or representational of causes that arise outside those structures.

Lobbying has been developed over the past several decades primarily as a means, according to Moloney (2000), to enable ' "insider" groups to maintain public policy in their favour.' It is widespread throughout the world and recognized as a legitimate part of democracy, although the legitimacy of such claims depends upon the *level of accessibility* available to the less advantaged, poorer funded interests. One way around this is through *association*; typically companies rely upon trade bodies representing their industries to lobby on their collective behalf, much as labour union members employ their officials to represent their aggregate interests.

This mechanism 'to rebalance the contest between interests of different power and influence' has been credited by lobbyists with some highly principled social contributions. Certainly, in so far as it *unsettles the political class* to the extent that it **exposes its policies to external scrutiny and adjustment**, such supposedly altruistic mediation is entirely consistent with excellence in communication. The reality, though, is rather less about altruistic lubrication to improve the operation of democratic machinery and much more about self-interested pouring of cans of oil into well-targeted engine parts, otherwise known as 'pressure points', for purpose of competitive advantage.

Lobbying is a lucrative expertise; hence the large number of public relations people who are specialist lobbyists, or public affairs advisers and consultants. And as pluralism flourishes, so demand for their services grows. It requires a thorough understanding of the relevant political system and the critical interrelationships between differing elements. Information flows, the sources of policy initiatives, the parts played by various officials and advisers, the differing decision-making structures and procedures: all the arcane detail of government is the stock-in-trade of the lobbyist.

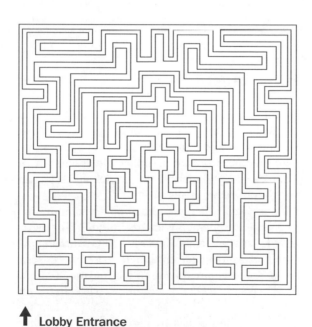

↑ Lobby Entrance

Figure 9.3 **The lobbying maze**

Outsiders of 'the system', including many senior managers, often mistakenly assign *far too much importance to the politicians*, the 'front line-up', and fail to appreciate the importance of the 'back office personnel' who deal in the detail, where so often lie the nuances that can make all the difference. Similarly, they may *underestimate the need to prepare* the case as thoroughly as they would for litigation, and that includes taking into account how 'the other side' is likely to respond and why, given its circumstances and existing pressures.

So the skilled lobbyist, in seeking to make **private, one-to-one representations**, is more likely to tread the back corridors of the less obvious offices that lead to bureaucrats than the well-presented main 'corridors of power' that lead to politicians. But companies that employ lobbyists as consultants are more likely to seek their *advice* than to send them forth as *advocates*. That role is more usually performed by in-house people employed within specialist public affairs units, who are well versed in corporate culture and adept advocates of their causes.

This trend by public affairs advisers towards giving strategic advice rather than taking lobbying action reflects the growing *scale, complexity and fragmentation* of government. Lobbyists identify seats of power and encamp there, from which multiple vantage points they may provide perspectives denied to their corporate clients. This geographical spread also better equips them to become informed of 'grass roots' developments, particularly the emergence of locally based pressure groups.

A further trend is the *greater integration of public affairs with public relations consultancy*. Public affairs advisers are seeking to **exert more pressure** on behalf of their clients **through media relations**, for they are finding that as governments become ever more driven by public relations considerations they are also becoming more **sensitive to media coverage and comment**, which can be as influential, or more so, than representations by lobbyists.

9.5 Issues management

Lobbying is a prominent feature of **issues management**. This is 'the process of identifying issues, analyzing those issues, setting priorities, selecting programme strategy options, implementing a programme of action and evaluating effectiveness' (Cutlip *et al.*, 1985). In other words, it describes the attempt by organizations, but particularly companies, to try to **identify and anticipate issues and do something about them before they turn into crises**.

As Bland (1995) observed, *issues and crisis management are similar* in that they broadly involve the same considerations and techniques. 'The biggest differences are the time scale and the sense of panic.' Generally, issues develop over months, crises over minutes. Issues management ideally therefore prevents crises.

→ But identifying the issues requires practised skill and **much careful scanning of the environment**. It has been argued that issues only 'go live' in the public imagination when someone chooses to 'make an issue' out of a problem that they perceive. And opinions differ as to where issues are most likely to arise: **pressure and cause-related groups** are often cited, but so too are organizations themselves, who, so often portrayed as 'sitting ducks' just waiting for someone to shoot at them, are, on the contrary, thought by some to be the *major* source. And many people think *government* is the prime originator of issues.

Grunig and Repper (1992) cite Chase's three strategies:

- reactive (oppose change),
- adaptive (try to satisfy outside demands) and
- dynamic.

This last is 'clearly asymmetrical: "This strategy anticipates and attempts to shape the direction of public policy decisions by determining the theater of war, the weapons to be used, and the timing of the battle itself".' The military imagery accords with how issues management is often perceived: Chase was 'a veteran public relations practitioner' who coined the term issues management in 1977. However, avoiding war is less expensive, distracting and potentially ruinous to reputation. After all, issues are primarily disagreements that need to be resolved to the mutual satisfaction of all concerned.

'Issues management, in practice, essentially is another name for the external component of strategic management.' Chase later argued that issues management was the culmination of an historical process that began with press relations and led on to first public relations and then public affairs, but others contested this. Not surprisingly, since public relations people have been paying particular attention to issues since the earliest days. The more pertinent point is: *what can they do about them?*

Issues come and go; their incubation periods vary and, rather like products, they can hang around a long time. If they are adequately anticipated and properly addressed, issues *can* be positively helpful. Whether they represent potential opportunities or threats, for sure rhetoric is not enough, and nor is neglect, however well intentioned.

CHECKLIST

- Habermas defined the 'public sphere' as where private people gather as a public.
- The degeneration of democratic politics into media entertainment has coincided with the rise in the use of mass psychology and in consumerism.
- PR has become a, or possibly the, most important component of modern politics, at all levels (federal, state, regional, local and district).
- Impartial government information sources have become politically partisan.
- In the UK the use of propaganda appears to be concentrated in politics.
- Public affairs describes PR-driven relations with government at all levels.
- Lobbying is making one-to-one representations to politicians, civil servants, bureaucrats and other public policy planners by concerned individuals, organizations or their paid representatives, who are lobbying experts, mostly PR consultants described as public affairs advisers.
- The term 'lobbying' is often used to describe all public affairs activities, although these may include other PR activities, notably media relations.
- Issues management is the monitoring of the operating environment in order to identify and anticipate relevant issues in order for the organization to address them in a timely and effective manner. It is 'another name for the external component of strategic management.'

- Crisis management is planning in anticipation of foreseeable crises, the implementation of those plans in the event of crises and the evaluation and addressing of resulting consequences.
- Issues and crisis management are complementary and share some similar characteristics; the former should reduce risk of crises but does not obviate the need for planning in anticipation of various crises scenarios.

CASE STUDY
COMMUNICATING IN A CRISIS

In 2001 Foot-and-Mouth Disease (FMD) swept through British livestock. It was probably the most serious animal disease epidemic in the UK in modern times; the virus is likely to have been imported in a contaminated food product. The impact of FMD was particularly pronounced in some regions, being all pervasive, catastrophically destructive and traumatic for those concerned.

It occurred at a low point for livestock farmers, who were recovering from the economic consequences of the recent BSE disaster, which had set in train a reduction in UK consumer demand and the loss of European markets. For some farmers, the arrival of FMD indicated that it was time to quit the industry. Their representative body, the National Farmers' Union (NFU), said it was difficult to overstate the overriding profound sense of loss and waste, emotional as well as financial, and that many farmers were also angry.

Across the world's media the story was graphically depicted, as piles of cattle were burnt in order to eliminate the disease, not without criticism from some farmers in other countries. The carnage continued for many weeks, during which time farmers and their families were confined to their homes, large parts of the countryside were shut off to visitors and the UK's tourism trade collapsed. Who would want to visit a countryside enveloped in foul black smoke and stench, even if they could be allowed in?

In its evidence to the subsequent government enquiry the NFU included communications among the matters it addressed. It complained of inadequate liaison and co-ordination of activity between the veterinary experts and the administrators in the agricultural government ministry and between government departments and agencies. This had led to inadequate management and resource response, some misapplication of resources and 'in some regions no effective involvement of stakeholders'. Only over time had matters improved, with the involvement of the army 'after a serious delay of nearly a month', the appointment of two regional operations directors and the establishment of the Cabinet Office Briefing Room (COBR) to co-ordinate activities among government ministers. A Joint Co-ordination Committee (JCC) had as its mission 'to create and maintain an accurate ground picture, to create an all-informed network and to facilitate passage of information flows, information management and dissemination of instructions.'

Communications had been patchy and inconsistent and 'delays in tackling problems and obstacles were rooted in failures in communications. ... With a wide number and variety of actors involved in a complex and evolving disease outbreak and control programme, it was inevitable that there would be gaps and lapses in communication from time to time. Much was very successfully implemented and achieved. But, in our view, there were still too many failures of communication.'

Examples of failures cited included:

- Considerable confusion in the (general) public's mind about the animal health and welfare consequences of FMD. 'This lack of understanding in turn led many people to question the need to slaughter infected animals since "they will recover". This belief distorted their view of [the government department] and of farmers.'
- Confusing and apparently conflicting statements issued at various times, giving rise to rumour and speculation, for instance as to future slaughter plans.
- Poor maintenance of the ministry's information website.
- Guidance to cattle valuers, contractors and government field staff inconsistently distributed, interpreted and applied.
- Reliance on trade associations to communicate guidance and other messages, but 'some operators were not always members of these trade associations.'
- Telephone help lines frequently jammed and inaccessible. 'In some instances, the advice given was frequently incomplete or inaccurate.'
- A video film explaining biosecurity (provision of washing and disinfection points) distributed to farmers as the general ban on public access to the countryside was lifted, which had 'to some extent undermined the message' on the need for farmers to observe appropriate care.

The lessons to be learned were:

1 In civil emergencies, government information websites should be constantly updated.
2 Easily accessible and authoritative help lines should be established at an early stage.
3 Clear, consistent guidance to government field staff, farmers and other operators on operational and environmental procedures should be widely disseminated.

The NFU's evidence to the enquiry concluded that 'the overriding message is that government communications with farmers was very patchy at best and poor and unreliable most of the time.' It quoted the comments of a farmer in Cumbria, where the outbreak was severe. These included: 'From my work I know how bad communications were at the start of the outbreak, how families were left on their farms without help or information, often surrounded by carcases. This should never have happened and it must never be allowed to happen again.'

QUESTIONS

1 Is the conduct of 'public life' attributable to public relations, and if so why?
2 Should government 'invest less in public relations and more in public services'?
3 How appropriate is the use of public relations in delivering local public services?
4 How may lobbying rebalance the contest between interests of differing power and influence?
5 Is 'making an issue' the cause or consequence of pluralism?

◼ ̌ **10 Community relations**

Corporate community involvement – objectives – the environment – community action – valuing donations – the voluntary sector

10.1 Corporate community involvement

When talk of **corporate social responsibility** (CSR) turns to specifics, a number of differing areas of activity are mentioned. For its Corporate Responsibility Index, for instance, Business in the Community (BITC) identifies:

- the physical environment,
- the workplace,
- the marketplace,
- the community and
- human rights.

Its annual awards scheme also covers the first four of these. Beyond that there is widespread and frequent reference made also, by companies, respondents to surveys and others, to matters such as:

- charity donations,
- ethical practices among suppliers,
- workforce diversity and
- corporate risk control.

So CSR has multiple dimensions, and each organization places the emphasis where most appropriate for its purposes.

The **community** is high on most CSR priority lists, because it is largely about the practicalities of corporate life; it can seem an obvious choice, particularly to the organization that operates among many neighbours in a highly populous, not to say overcrowded, city or region, a circumstance familiar enough in many parts of Europe and Asia. What used to be known as *community relations*, about corporate getting-on-with-the-locals, has acquired greater importance since the 1970s, not least owing to some very well reported disasters that might have been avoided. And it has acquired a new name to match: **corporate community involvement** (CCI).

The new name denotes a new level of interest and concern. CCI is 'the face of corporate social responsibility in practice,' (Theaker 2001a), one that is plainly more visible than most other CSR activities. And CCI touches upon a number of *practical aspects of operations* that apply to *all types and size* of organization, including:

- workforce recruitment and retention,
- physical expansion,
- operational parameters and
- consultation on local issues.

How an organization relates to its community, the people around its operational site, has been likened to ripples on a pond: it can opt to do the minimum, 'paying taxes, observing the law and dealing fairly', thereby making little disturbance, or it can determine to make more impact. Ripples on ponds, however, are poor indicators of what is going on beneath the surface, so the appropriate imagery for a more *proactive* participant in local life might be better drawn from the animal kingdom.

The organization might be seen, for instance, as:

- A large, friendly, somewhat benign herbivore, grazing gently and wishing only the best for everyone around, always approachable provided not too much effort is called for.
- Or it might be a lean, hungry-looking hunter, always on the lookout for the next opportunity to leap in and take an initiative, in the hope of recognition and reward.
- Again, it *might* be a very large, avuncular creature, very much a local fixture on the skyline, with a substantial track record for defending smaller fry and worrying about the whole neighbouring herd.

In other words, **companies set their own *scale* of agenda** to reflect their circumstances as they perceive them.

Examples

Small start-ups want 'early wins' at *marginal cost*, so they are looking around for opportunities to win credit for doing things that are *really relevant*. That might be funding a community toddlers' crèche for local young mothers, because they have a few working with them, but equally it might be low-maintenance landscaping, with a lawn, scrubs and trees, of an unsightly frontage that residents living opposite will see every day and the local council will applaud.

An established business with a knowledge-based workforce may opt for supporting local schools, with an eye to future recruitment. A company that attracts heavy road traffic to and form its site may want to offer the local authority funding for traffic engineering and road improvement schemes. A professional practice may want to volunteer to help with local schemes that would benefit from its particular knowledge and skills.

Indeed, once the decision has been taken to treat CCI seriously the options can seem almost limitless, particularly when it becomes known locally that the organization is open to suggestions. Typical activities include:

- funding landscaped local roundabouts
- decorating old people's homes
- reading aloud to young children

Figure 10.1 **Varying perceptions of the organization as neighbour**

- secondment of staff to work with local organizations
- raising funds for local causes through sponsored activities
- open days with hospitality and entertainment
- sponsorship of local events
- seed funding for local community activities
- providing a venue for local organizations to meet regularly
- contributing trees to local landscaping schemes
- offering work experience to young people
- creating bursaries and scholarships at schools and colleges.

10.2 Objectives

Being known locally as an organization that is open to suggestions for its CCI programme can bring hazardous exposure to the vagaries of human nature and the enthusiasms of the few, if there is no forethought about objectives, just what they are and how they are to be measured. **Clear, concise objectives** make possible the identification of the *particular* potential CCI areas of activity that are **of interest *to the organization*** and to prioritize them accordingly. *Then* the approaches that are received may be assessed within a structured framework, much as a person may refuse one charity a donation because he or she has already selected and committed to another.

Community needs are, understandably, open to interpretation: that is to say, some are obviously more pressing, have wider applicability or will benefit greater numbers of people than others; some address long overdue improvements, while others are opportunistic and marginal; some are properly the responsibility of the civil authorities, others are rightly within the compass of community action. And 'evidently some things are beyond any company to provide. Business can only pay its local and national taxes and rely on government to supply such things as law and order; schools; healthcare and social services' (Newman, 1995).

CCI, it seems, is 'perhaps one of the "softest" and most intangible of CSR activities' but it 'can be used as a strategic business tool in managing a company's relationship with the community' (Portway, 1995). Her CCI objectives at the UK operation of IBM in central southern England were to:

1 contribute towards a favourable social and economic environment for IBM's business,
2 be recognized by selected target audiences as a leader in corporate community involvement, and
3 promote the morale and motivation of employees.

These objectives were met through:

- education and training in schools
- 'voluntary sector empowerment' with training, consultancy projects and employee support in voluntary work
- support for the disabled via 'The Computability Centre', established with two partners as a national UK charity in 1992 to give advice and information
- support for good environmental practices, awareness and research.

Portway's ' "manage and measure" approach', using objectives to report to relevant 'audiences' on progress, should ensure that CCI evades the risk of falling into a potential quagmire of tendentious pleading and sentimentality. To assist in this, Cutlip *et al.* (1985) advocated **segmentation**, both of the locals as a whole, according to their relative importance to the organization, and of the 'prime movers', the people that *really* matter.

The *first* such analysis should indicate **how, and perhaps *why*, power is distributed**. Predictably, the landowners and big business head the list and SME managers follow-up in the rear, but in between these they suggest people like public relations executives and journalists, as well as local administrators and bureaucrats, that is to say, people who are supposedly in *positions of influence for a living.*

But this has to be a generalization. There are plenty of people who exert influence that might not be *that* obvious, and local power structures can be remarkably deceptive, particularly in areas where traditional forms and values have been swept aside by modern changes in demography and culture.

The *second* analysis is probably closer to most CCI planning, for it identifies and confirms **the people that any programme *should* address**, starting with the employees, or members, and their families and friends. These people have always been at the centre of community relations priorities. Then there is, inevitably perhaps, the local media, and the various local cause-related and pressure groups and individuals who, for one reason or another, are the 'crusaders', a potentially unflattering term for a variety of local residents that ranges from the well-intentioned proactive citizen to the scurrilous rumour-monger.

The prime movers that interest many companies are the key politicians and local officials who run the most relevant parts of local government, such as urban and transport planning, and the various welfare and similar unincorporated groups, typically connected to military, religious, cultural and social interests; the list can be long and varied.

This intensity of interest is likely to be *reciprocated* by local government, and government locally, for any company with a substantial presence is a source of wealth generation: it pays local taxes, provides local employment and indirectly stimulates the whole economy. In consequence it is welcome to participate through memberships of various advisory and other bodies. 'It has become common practice for senior members of the firm to take an interest in local politics, and it is good policy to make it equally possible for workers to serve on local councils or boards' (Black, 1989).

This involvement with local people is depicted by Stone (1995) as a 'three-cornered tug-of-war ... between self-esteem, altruism and commercial advantage. Get any one of these wrong and you are in trouble. It is only when *feeling good, doing good* and *doing well* are in balance ... that community relations can be truly effective ... .'

Example

'We haven't jumped on the bandwagon – we are the bandwagon,' declares the Co-operative Group, emphasizing its support for local communities. The group has its origins in co-operative retailing founded on principles of self-help and self-responsibility. It embraces several substantial national UK businesses, notably grocery retailing, retail banking, insurance and funeral services.

Its Community Dividend is 'the flagship of our community investment policy and it is the primary way in which we support self-help groups in the communities where we trade. ... Since being launched in 1998 the scheme has raised more than £3.8 million [from customers who are Dividend Cardholders] and over 800 local community groups have been supported each year, from credit unions to playgroups. Grants of between £100 and £5000 are given to groups who are providing a lasting benefit to the community and addressing society's ills such as poor health or poverty.'

The Group's Co-operative Action scheme supports the development of 'new forms of co-operative and mutual enterprise in the UK. It is funded by numerous retail co-ops as well as the Co-operative Group, CIS and The Co-operative Bank.' And the Community Food scheme, 'to further develop mutually beneficial relationships with the community', offers 10 per cent discounts on purchases at its 1000 plus food stores by self-help community groups that spend an average of over £50 per week in-store. 'A broad range of community self-help food initiatives, such as community cafes, breakfast clubs and not-for-profit village stores, are invited to apply for a Community Food Discount Card.'
(Co-operative Group website, 2.3.03)

10.3   The environment

A substantial amount of CCI time and effort is accounted for by concerns relating to the **physical environment**, and with good reason. Environmentalism, that is to say, interest in the world ecosystems and mankind's treatment of the planet, 'came of age' with the landmark United Nations conference on environment and development held in Rio de Janeiro in 1992, the 'Earth Summit' that was attended by politicians and civil servants from 178 nations, very nearly *every* nation. More significantly, no fewer than 118 heads of state attended.

The ensuing UN conferences and EU 'green directives' have generated much talk and some do at the 'supersonic' level of human affairs, but probably the greater impact has been more *localized*, not only in the worried advanced countries but also in other states, where there may be some scope for learning from the mistakes of others in matters of industrialization, infrastructure, food production and so on. Throughout Europe there is ample evidence of **widespread public awareness, interest and concern about environmental issues.**

'On the whole, the environmental issues are seen as real "values", identified and accepted by the public opinion all over Europe, even though to a different extent and with a different impact, because they represent the search of quality to every society in all European countries' (CERP website, 5.11.02). 'Today, all enterprises must consider the environmental issues in their communication processes owing to the impact that these issues have in each community, involving public opinion, prompting judgements and views.'

This **'environmental relations'** relates to both internal and external publics, 'both carrying "concerns" on environmental issues,' albeit expressed differently. Of internal publics, CERP observes that 'employees, workers and their families show concerns mainly linked to the environmental safeguard at their working places, to "noise", to manufacturing processes of harmful substances and so on. But, at the same time, the internal publics are part of a community, they perceive judgements and opinions on the company and the environment from the external publics, and thereafter establish "values".'

In addition to all the many other arguments in support of corporate concern for the environment locally, there is a *commercial dimension*. In short, doing something positive about the local environment can **benefit brands**; it all depends upon the detailed circumstances.

Example

When the Australian wine producer BRL Hardy purchased 1700 hectares (4250 acres) in South Australia's Riverland it became involved in wetland conservation with Australian Wetland Care, a conservation organization already on site, which includes over 12 kilometres of mainly wetland river frontage. This link largely 'shaped' the Banrock Station brand when it was launched in 1995. The environmental theme was carried through to cardboard tags impregnated with the seeds of a local flowering shrub, attached to the bottles, and part of the sales revenue donated to Landcare Australia and Wetland Care Australia. In the UK this wetlands association has led BRL Hardy to support the UK's Wildfowl and Wetlands Trust, to mutual benefit: the charity has secured substantial extra funds and Banrock Station has become the UK's fifth largest wine brand and sixth fastest growing grocery brand.
(BITC/FT guide 2002)

10.4   Community action

As part of its Better Britain Campaign, Shell UK sought to assess the **'community sector'**, prompted by the World Summit on Sustainable Development in Johannesburg in 2002. The company calculated that in the ten years since the initial conference at Rio de Janeiro there had been a two to three fold increase in activity in the UK (alone), although the absence of baseline data defied certainty. Shell's own scheme, however, had grown from some 10,000 projects in 1992 to 26,000 in 2002.

Its report 'describes a strong and growing movement, locally based and focused but working in a global context. Thousands of organizations and hundreds of thousands of people who are stepping forward and doing what they can for their neighbourhood, for their friends and neighbours and, ultimately, for all of us across the planet. ... The next step must be to consider how the sector can be supported and developed' *The Quiet Revolution*, (2002).

Schemes described in the report include:

- *A car sharing scheme*, whose 50 members aim to reduce traffic by sharing journeys by road. 'The group hope to have the same success that Europe has had with similar schemes – that five car club members reduce the need for one privately-owned car, bringing less reliance on private cars, fewer parking problems, an increased incentive to walk and cycle and a better quality of life all round!'
- *A furniture recycling scheme*, one of some 300 supported by Shell. Household items and electrical appliances are collected, restored or renovated and 'recycled' to young, disadvantaged people aged 16–25 years. There are also training schemes associated with the work and its administration.
- *A bicycle recycling scheme*, that rescues discarded bikes from public refuse tips and elsewhere, then cleans, repairs and resells them. The scheme also runs a bicycle taxi service.
- *An environmental improvement scheme*, run by Bangladeshi women, who have created an organic vegetable garden in part of a public park. The scheme also has a social dimension linked to environmental issues and horticulture.

Shell supports a variety of schemes elsewhere around the world.

Example

One such Shell scheme is The Flower Valley Conservation Trust in the Cape Floral Kingdom, South Africa. This is said to be one of the world's richest but most threatened botanical regions, containing some 7000 species, of which 70 per cent are not found anywhere else. Only four per cent of the area is formally protected.

The Trust has acquired 550 hectares, with help from Shell and a UK conservation body, Fauna and Flora International. The management project includes conservation of endangered flora, known as 'fynbos', in ways that benefit the local Cape community, where there is 50 per cent unemployment. This is done through harvesting flowers and wood for papermaking and other related microenterprises.

(Meeting the energy challenge: The Shell Report 2002)

10.5 Valuing donations

In 1998 BITC initiated the **PerCent Club**, whose initial 38 UK member companies pledged to *donate at least one per cent of their annual pre-tax profits to the com-*

munity. In 2002 148 organizations indicated their intent to fulfil this commitment, either to good causes or **some form of community involvement**. Giving at least one per cent is *not mandatory* on members but the 92 that did so in 2002 are entitled to display a specially designed logo to proclaim their benevolence. Of the qualifying 92 there are 22 companies that are listed among the *Financial Times* list of 'Top 100' companies.

At the beginning of the 1990s 'leading companies were contributing 0.42 per cent of their pre-tax profits to the community, much of it in cash. These were the days before business gave a monetary value to gifts in kind and staff time.' Owing to more accurate measurement 'you would expect contributions to be considerably higher. While this is true in money terms, the £499 millions contributed in 2000–01 is exactly the same percentage of pre-tax profits as the £225 millions contributed in 1990–91' (*The Guardian*, 25.11.02).

In an annual attitude survey, mentioned in Chapter 4, respondents were asked to select from three statements that which they thought *best described* their view of the *balance between programmes and communications*. Respondents replied:

- 72 per cent: companies should make an effort to tell us but should not spend significant amounts
- 15 per cent: It is important to know about companies' programmes, they should spend significant amounts
- 7 per cent: Not important to know, no money should be spent on communications
- 5 per cent: Don't know.

10.6 The voluntary sector

The **voluntary sector** in the UK employs 563,000 people, or two per cent of the workforce, and in 2001 it accounted for £5.4 billion of the country's gross domestic product, or economic output. Total income was £15.6 billion, of which 4.9 per cent was received from business, *less in real terms than ten years earlier.* 'Research by the National Council for Voluntary Organisations (NCVO) shows that support from companies is in fact the only source of charitable income that has declined in real terms in the past decade.'

The British people, by contrast, donated £5.41 billion (34.7 per cent) and the UK government was worth another £4.52 billion (29 per cent). The charities managed to raise £3.53 billion (22.6 per cent) by their own efforts and received another £1.37 billion (8.8 per cent) from charitable trusts.

NCVO wants government to force companies to give more, but there is evidence from another body, the Charities Aid Foundation, that the value of *gifts in kind* nevertheless rose by 25.4 per cent between 1999 and 2000. This raises the question of whether it is worthier for companies to hand over the money and 'have done with it' or use their other assets to help. The latter route may be more economical and controllable to the donor, but that does not mean it is any the less, or more, beneficial to the recipient. Furthermore, it may be a means to being able to 'do more' in real terms.

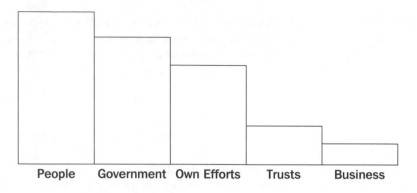

| People | Government | Own Efforts | Trusts | Business |

Figure 10.2 **The voluntary sector's sources of income**

During 2002, its 20th year, BITC consulted with over 500 businesses in an attempt to review its role and responsibilities and to see where it might enhance its effectiveness. This exercise occurred in the wake of the September 2001 terrorist attacks in the USA, a period in which 'an increasingly disappointing performance in all the major economies of the world started to push the argument [for CSR] in the opposite direction' (Lambert, 2002). 'With profits and budgets under pressure just about everywhere, the question was how far companies would be able to sustain, let alone increase, efforts to support their different communities.'

The dialogues that BITC had with these companies' senior managers, who included over 300 chief executive officers, indicated that there was plenty of scope for improvement in the relationships between the voluntary and private sectors. 'People from the private sector complained about the complex political relationships within the voluntary sector; there were too many agencies doing roughly the same thing, and there was a need for consolidation and takeovers. Their counterparts in the voluntary sector tended to regard business people as innocents abroad, who spent their time trying to reinvent the wheel. To this observer, at least, it seemed that both sides were missing a number of opportunities by going down their separate tracks.'

This conclusion entirely coincides with the commonplace experience of most managers in both sectors, in their dealings with the other over the past two decades and more:

- Company managers can find the complex, often Byzantine, decision-making structures frustrating and daunting and the duplications of effort frankly tedious. When they also encounter the amateurish vagaries and occasional outbreaks of internecine warfare that characterize not a few charitable bodies the temptation is for them to run.
- Voluntary sector managers for their part can become thoroughly rattled by the apparent ignorance of their daily realities, particularly where managers from a large corporate culture fail to understand, much less appreciate, that results have to be achieved by different means when most of the time everything is done on a 'shoestring' budget and/or with dependence upon volunteers, who may, or may not, quite feel like it on the day.

The one side thinks 'What's *wrong* with these people?' while the other asks itself 'How do these people *ever* manage to tie their shoe laces?' It is a chasm to cross.

CHECKLIST

- Corporate community involvement (CCI) is CSR in relation to local communities, a development of community relations 'good neighbourliness'.
- Companies set their own scale of agenda to reflect their perceived circumstances.
- Community needs are open to wide and self-interested interpretation and some are properly the responsibility of civil institutions, not companies.
- Corporate CCI objectives provide the framework for using CCI as a strategic business tool, with proactive, not reactive, programmes to match.
- Effective CCI is said to result from achieving a balance between managerial self-esteem, corporate altruism and commercial advantage.
- Local communities are segmented to identify (1) the distribution of power and influence and (2) the publics, starting with employees, their families and friends.
- Issues relating to the physical environment account for much CCI activity, which is then called environmental relations. Positive action can substantially enhance corporate brand recognition, image and reputation.
- The BITC's PerCent Club corporate members donate at least one per cent of their annual pre-tax profits to the community.
- The differing cultures of the private and voluntary sectors give rise to differences in perceptions of each other that may result in lost opportunities to collaborate.

CASE STUDY
MAKING UP FOR LOST GROUND

The Prince's Trust was founded by HRH The Prince of Wales in 1976 and is the leading UK youth charity, offering 14–30 year olds opportunities to develop confidence, learn new skills, obtain employment and start businesses. The Trust targets people who are unemployed or facing barriers in life, and over 450,000 have participated in its programmes.

In 2002 the communication team developed a strategy to position the Trust more clearly as a leader and solutions provider on the key issues that affect socially excluded young people, the client group that the charity aims to help. One of the Prince's Trust's key target groups is young people with no or few qualifications, so educational under-achievement was identified as a priority topic for a communication campaign.

Every year over 30,000 young people in England leave school without any qualifications at all. They are at increased risk of unemployment, homelessness and crime, unless they are able to get their lives back on track with support. The team's aim was to bring the facts to public attention, highlighting the social and economic impact and the potential solutions that the Trust and its partners could offer young people in these circumstances.

It was decided to capitalize on the existing 'news agenda' by mounting an awareness campaign that coincided with the next annual August announcement by the government of the results of the main secondary education public examinations (GCSE). The focus of the campaign would be to counter the traditional media treatment of these results, which concentrated on over-achievers. This campaign would offer a message of hope for the 30,000 without any examination passes, reassuring them that they could still succeed in life, and explaining the Trust's volunteers' programme.

The programme provides a 12 week training course for 16–25 year olds, most of whom are unemployed, which is designed to develop their confidence, motivation and skills through teamwork in the community. The various activities include a community project, a fund-raising activity and a residential outward-bound week (rugged outdoor adventure). Further elements include work placement experience and support with employment interviews and writing personal profiles for job applications.

The Trust compiled a media briefing paper on educational under-achievers, drawing on its existing research and external data relating to under-achievement, truancy and exclusion. The paper considered the impact of a lack of qualifications on life chances and the potential social and economic costs. It summarized the Trust's £5 millions three-year programme and what various government agencies were also doing about the problem; these included the Connexions Service, the Learning and Skills Council and the Basic Skills Agency. The briefing paper and an accompanying press statement was forwarded to journalists specializing on education and social affairs ahead of the announcement of the examination results.

Next the Trust's team drew on its resource of 'celebrity ambassadors' to help promote the campaign to young people. The boxer Prince Naseem participated in a radio feature, produced for national distribution to radio stations, which included a case study of a young person who had failed all his examinations the previous year and then undertaken the Trust's course and commentary by a Trust representative. The footballer Rio Ferdinand, then currently high profile in the media owing to his recent transfer to play for Manchester United, gave an exclusive interview to BBC Radio One, a mainly pop music national station for young people.

The Trust's website was amended to include a pop-up page signposting the Trust and other support for anyone who had failed the examinations. And the Trust's local offices were briefed on how to respond to a potential influx of telephone calls.

The overall campaign reached over 12.5 million people. Coverage included news on both BBC terrestrial television channels, live and taped interviews on not only Radio One but also 52 regional radio stations, features in two national newspapers and reports in 25 regional newspapers, over 41,000 website visits during August (up 350 per cent on the same month of the previous year) and a high volume of direct enquiries into both free phone services and local offices. Two months later the BBC sourced from the Trust case studies on truancy and both the Trust's policy and fundraising departments received approaches from several potential partners, keen to collaborate. The campaign had increased recognition of the Trust as a specialist on educational under-achievement and had been deemed an all-round success.

QUESTIONS

1 What might be common sources of friction in CCI?
2 Why might CCI be one of the softest and most intangible CSR activities?
3 To what extent might segmentation of the local community assist CCI, and why?
4 How might 'environmental relations' impact on employee relations?
5 Should companies have to give a higher percentage of their pre-tax profits?

▾ 11 The media

Serious media and entertainment media – media values – mediated communication – on-line media – the relationship between public relations and the media

11.1 Serious media and entertainment media

'[He] switched on the television news. An important decision by the government was to be reached in twenty-four hours, but until this time – nothing. So nearly all the news was about this nothing. Special planes had been chartered so that reporters could land in distant places and talk about this nothing. Men spoke about it from Paris and Washington. There were expensive and complicated nothing interviews. Never had more been done for nothing. "You don't want this nonsense, do you?" he asked Hazel. "Of course not. I'll turn it off".'

Seldom has the banality and contrivance of television news been so well captured as in this depiction, by J. B. Priestley in *The Image Men*, of what has become an all-too-familiar wearying routine for viewers the world over. This is **'news' as entertainment**, thinly disguised as being serious. *Strangely unnecessary at weekends*, when it might interfere with the observance of rest and play, yet *in abundance on weekdays*, morning, noon and night, round the clock: all the news fit to print, shout, look deeply significant about, illustrate with computerized graphics; in short, attach to reality like some life-enhancing ritual observance.

Mass communication is probably nowhere more prevalent than in the UK, where approaching 60 million people read more newspapers per head of population than any other nation on earth and:

- two out of three are said to have a mobile, or cell, telephone
- 99 per cent of all households have a colour television
- going on for 50 per cent of homes have at least one computer
- mobile text messaging is thought to be more prevalent than anywhere else and
- there is certainly no lack of interest in radio, particularly popular music interrupted on the hour, every hour, by news
- television news output on the five main channels has increased by 80 per cent in less than a decade.

Not to mention the satellite television stations, the cable television stations, the thousands of magazines and umpteen radio stations. The British, it seems, cannot have enough of mass communication, all carefully contrived, packaged and presented for their edification, but *why*? Nor is the UK alone in this; around the world there is an 'explosion' of media.

The modern media have five characteristics (McQuail, cited by Oliver, 2001) that offer some perspective on this. They may be summarized as:

- The media are, collectively, *the main source of information*. In consequence they exert **power**, for 'knowledge is power'.
- The media provide the venues of the modern **public sphere**, where the issues of the day are presented and debated, argued and explained, in studio discussion, documentaries, political advertising and speeches.
- The media '*tell it how it is*' about contemporary mores, changing values and cultural influences, so what they have to say about this or that **social reality** provides the framework within which people think about people, places, organizations, issues.
- The media are the major delivery systems for **projecting images** that entertain and inform, giving rise to *fame and subsequent fortune*.
- The media **represent 'normality'**, which is of particular consequence in matters touching upon morals and ethics. People *use as points-of-reference* for determining their own attitudes and beliefs what the media represent to them as being currently socially acceptable.

It is in the depiction of news that these characteristics are most clearly discerned. For instance, the main nightly television news bulletins are relied upon by countless millions of people as their main source of information from beyond their immediate life experience. And 'the normality' represented there can determine how *whole nations* of people *think about this or that*, from the great issues of the day to minor trivialities.

Television news is supposedly impartial, unbiased and therefore trustworthy, differentiating it from newspapers, but '… impartiality helps to explain why TV news is so predictable and unadventurous and, more importantly, why TV news is growing less and less attractive to large cross-sections of the viewing audience', according to a senior UK television executive (Shaw, 2002). 'Television news should be accurate, fair, honest and respectful of privacy but that should not stop it from campaigning or pushing a particular agenda that concerns its audience. … Why shouldn't there be a news programme slanted to one or other particular point of view?' This is known in the USA as **advocacy journalism**, 'in effect, taking sides or a particular point of view, and it is proving popular, if controversial.'

This is nothing novel in newspaper journalism, where particular, often self-serving, interpretations of social reality and normality are energetically advanced. The 'Daily Wind-up' style of so many newspapers may account in good measure for the **'grumble culture'** that, in the UK at least, particularly afflicts people aged 35–54: the deepening dissatisfactions and discontents that relentless 'bad news' can foster in even the most resilient and purposeful readers. The 'grumpy generation' cites 'the sterility of popular culture' as one of three main causes of their dissatisfaction (*The Daily Telegraph*, 26.8.02).

A satirical comment on this 'wind-up' editorial style depicted a fictitious Daily Mail lead front-page report. The headline contrived to combine falling stock market prices with crippling national strikes and air traffic chaos awaiting holidaymakers. A subsidiary headline asked 'Why not pack it all in?' and the story that followed predicted that readers would all become bankrupt or would be murdered, starved to death or killed in a plane crash. It was exaggeration, but by how much?
(*Private Eye*, 26.7.02)

The media have **three basic 'duties', to inform, educate and entertain**, so when they are not being serious they are trying to be entertaining, even frivolous. This particularly exercises public relations people. They contribute both *serious* material, about, for instance, matters relating to the environment, company results, politics, redundancies and so on, *and* they are the source of much *lighter* content, relating to, say, show business, celebrities, readers' competitions and pseudo-events. They *also* provide plenty of the **information that fills the middle ground**, usually about products and services, such as travel features, fashion stories, lifestyle depictions, explanations of how things work, guides on where to go for what and interesting facts and figures on all manner of subjects. In short, **content and its sourcing is multi-dimensional** and **reflects the culture it serves**.

11.2 Media values

'More than half of [UK] TV viewers believe television programmes are getting worse. The annual report by the Independent Television Commission and the Broadcasting Standards Commission said 55 per cent of viewers felt standards had declined. ... Most with only four or five channels said they did not want any more' (BBC *Ceefax*, 12.3.03).

If this applied solely to news and current affairs, the cynical and shallow collaboration between politicians and broadcasters to fabricate news to their mutual satisfaction would provide explanation enough, but the criticism extends across *all television* broadcasting.

The then Director General of the state-owned BBC argued against reliance on 'the economic marketplace' or allowing advertisers 'to make the total running'. In March 2003 he criticized 'tame, flag-waving coverage of the Iraq War on American television and radio', which had happened 'because the US became obsessed with regulating the economics rather than the content of broadcasting; it is not meant to be the British way of doing things. "If you allow economic factors to weigh heavily you would never have had the British television system anyway. ... We spend more money per head in this country on original television production than any other country in the world, even America" ' (*The Guardian*, 11.6.03).

Given this overall level of expenditure, could the *content* and *production standards* be the source of so much dissatisfaction?

The BBC is also not without criticism of its handling of the military invasion of Iraq, despite its very extensive reporting of it, in the UK and in the Middle East. In a confidential internal memorandum dated 6 February 2003, its senior management had cautioned 'to "be careful" about broadcasting dissent', wrote a media researcher (*The Guardian*, 22.4.03). 'A study of coverage in five countries for the *Frankfurter Allgemeine Zeitung* shows that the BBC featured the lowest level of dissent of all. Its two per cent total was even lower than the seven per cent found on the US channel ABC ... As Baghdad fell on April 9, BBC reporters could hardly contain themselves in their haste to endorse the victors. ... Here the BBC enunciated a version of events very similar to that of the [UK] government.'

In matters of popular entertainment, the UK television output is often unfavourably compared with that of 25 years ago, so much so that many old shows are repeatedly shown, usually at peak viewing times, and there are multiple cheap-to-produce compilations of clips from popular bygones. Contemporary reliance on amateur participation by members of the general public and 'C list celebs' to fill hours of television time is viewed by many as inferior and unworthy.

All such matters so central to popular culture arouse much debate in every country, but they are of *particular interest* to public relations practitioners. If, as critics assert, PR provides an 'information subsidy' (Gandy, cited by Moloney, 2000), it is **empowered to exert some influence**, for better or for worse, and, like advertisers, it has a need to be *associated with successful output*, that is to say, broadcasting of a standard that appeals to the audiences it seeks. Mass disaffection is emphatically not in the interests of public relations, which, *given its involvement*, must accept some *responsibility* for media values.

The *visual imperative* of television has long been a significant factor, giving rise over the years to ever-greater compression of messages, through devices such as

Figure 11.1   **The all-pervasive media**

the 'nine second sound bite', flashing imagery and sound and monosyllabic two sentence drama scenes. This has laid fresh demands upon the skills of the public relations practitioner as well as the screenwriter and script editor.

And this use of vision to contrive urgency and pace has extended to radio, using sound instead, and to the printed media, where photography has become cinematic in its proportions and treatment. Overall design and layout of the printed page is undergoing a transformation as well, to present the content in compellingly attractive formats that find favour with advertisers as well as readers.

Media values are highly pervasive. Newspapers and magazines have to decide what is *ethically* **appropriate for them**, which is translated into *editorial policy*. The quality of *self-regulation* by the newspaper industry varies from country to country, culture to culture.

Example

An American war photographer in Iraq promptly, and very publicly, lost his job when he 'used his computer to combine elements of two photographs, taken moments apart, in order to improve the composition', against his newspaper's editorial policy, which forbade the alteration of news photographs.
(*Los Angeles Times*, 2.4.03)

Yet writers may expect to *keep* their jobs if they **refuse to disclose their sources**, for this is widely considered to be a fundamental principle of journalism that may only be breached in extreme circumstances. This principle appears to extend well beyond protecting sources of 'leaks' and other valuable information. Nor do most journalists reveal the entertainment and gifts that they receive, the 'freebie' travel and holidays, the unreturned motorcars and other products lent for purposes of review. Occasionally one is dismissed, when it becomes 'too embarrassing' for the employer.

'A very big corruption in all British journalism is the network of friendship and obligation between people who write and the people about whom they write. We have no codes and we make no declaration and we leave our readers in the dark,' admitted a prominent *Times* feature writer and former member of parliament.
(*Writers' News*, 2.03)

Ethical questions also arise over such devices as the **infomercial**, television advertisements that are presented in a programme format, usually comprising two presenters introducing and talking about products in a studio setting. Does their pretence to be just like other programmes represent a true deception upon the viewing audience or merely a congenial device for distraction? Are infomercials an incursion into 'editorial' airtime that could be filled with a 'real' programme, and, if so, what of their production quality?

Product placement also raises questions about what is appropriate. And questions arise also concerning **advertising features**, editorial that promotes products and services, and **advertorials**, paid-for advertising in editorial format, often in the form of a flattering report, offer of free samples or reader competition. All three are routinely used by public relations in support of marketing. Any deception about their purposes is likely to be relatively innocuous, and readers' competitions are very popular. But to the extent that they risk *corrosion of editorial values* they are questionable practices of which both the media and public relations should be wary.

11.3 Mediated communication

These practicalities are but the small detail of daily **media relations** when compared with the 'spin policy' of each media player, those 'agendas' that they pursue, often with a political intent and always with an eye to a market for their product. How the media interpret events, any events, can be most instructive for discerning how they are likely to perform their role in **two-step communication** between the organization and its publics. The use of hyperbole, or gross exaggeration, is common, and sometimes the consequences *can* be most unwelcome and damaging.

Example

When two ten-year-old girls were abducted and murdered, then discarded in a field, on 4 August 2002, the UK press responded with saturation coverage. Typical of content were these headlines and observations: 'There is still more light than darkness in Soham … A terrible thing happened in Soham, but the dark is not invincible. … There is not one candle flickering in this darkness, but hundreds. … The community of Soham itself is another powerful candle in the darkness. … The police are another light in the darkness. … Helpline receives calls from around the world. … A special service for use in schools.'
(*The Times*, 20.8.02)

Then came the public response. 'Soham has become a day trip destination for some visitors attracted by its association with a heinous crime. The streets have been jammed with traffic … . Coaches taking tourists to visit nearby [sites] have made detours to the fenland town. A couple were seen sitting in deckchairs in the churchyard of St Andrew's eating fish and chips [a traditional English dish]. … [The vicar, or priest] urged the public to follow the example of the media, which had withdrawn from the town. … A [local] woman … said "… it is time for the circus to leave town.".'
(*The Daily Telegraph*, 26.8.02)

The **two-step flow** concept of communication has been modified to depict what happens when the third party is *a journalist or similar 'gatekeeper'*, the person who is to pass on the message to its intended recipients. This person also has access to information from other sources, which he or she may care to exercise, and in practice often does, in search of an **'angle'**, that is to say, an interpretation that will be **distinctive to him or her** when compared with that of rivals elsewhere in the media who are in possession of the same original information. The journalist may also have *contact with the receivers*, and *they directly with the original public relations source*, so in effect the gatekeeper may not be the *sole* means by which the message may reach its destination, and nor may the gatekeeper *solely rely* on the originating public relations source.

Once the media become involved in the communication process, there is ample scope for *variation* to the original message. That is why public relations people endeavour to supply messages that are so well conceived and timed for the purposes of the media involved that they *will be passed on with minimal alteration*, by which means a **greater degree of control** is retained by the sender but with the *added-value endorsement* of the media attached. The *greater the confidence* that journalists repose in their sources, the less likely their probable inclination to alter the 'copy' before 'filing' it for use.

How receivers approach receipt of mass media messages may be at variance with what the media intend. Thus:

- news that is intended to be serious may be considered risible
- intended humour may be thought distinctly unfunny
- educational facts and figures may be met with grave suspicion.

Although the very source imparts status to the message, as it is seen, heard or read, that does not mean that it is *necessarily that well* received or accepted. Letters to the Editor provide ample evidence of that.

People condition how they receive media messages by how they *use* the media. They select from the vast choice before them by reference to what they want out of it. The **uses and gratifications theory** identifies five use classifications (Baskin *et al.*, cited by Harrison, 2000). In summary, the media may be:

- a source of entertainment
- the place to find items that are of particular personal interest
- a diversion
- a substitute for social relationships
- a check on personal identity and values.

If the 'telly' or radio is only on for *background companionship*, for example, there is **little prospect of much attention being given to content**, and there is heavy use made of these media for this purpose. Similarly, skimming for specifics or types of content serves to filter out much else, as where, for instance a newspaper is 'read' but not a single advertisement is seen. The public relations practitioner is, therefore, always at pains to assess the likely *effectiveness* of his or her output, and to use this in considering beforehand the likely value of intended effort. A common temptation is to mistake the placing of a message with the media as an end in itself, when it is *how* the end-receiver will receive that message and its *effect* that is the primary consideration.

This, together with agenda setting, whereby the media seek to identify the current topics and tastes that drive contemporary discussion and interaction, are key elements of mass communication. In other words, the media are very active in *constructing how receivers see the world*, and therefore they can not only filter but also *distort* messages in the process of communication, and this may be intentional as well as accidental. Public relations seeks to counter this through **repetition of key**

Figure 11.2   **Repetition of key words and phrases, images, sounds and symbols**

words and phrases, images, sounds and symbols, offering **rewards for** the receivers' **attention** and providing *credible representatives* on behalf of the organization to present the message.

McQuail (cited by Oliver, 2001) developed a framework for taking into account two independent dimensions that determine differing views of both the media and society:

- The first separated the media that seek to be significant players in *achieving social change* from those that tend to be more *reflective of the contemporary* economic, political and social *conditions*
- The second distinguished between *culture and ideas* on the one hand and *material forces and factors* on the other.

This assists the media relations planner to **plot a position for a strategy that best fits the media**; whether:

- more campaigning and focused, or reserved and wider in its perspective
- more orientated toward *societal influences* on the content and effect of communication or on the *technological advances* in the means of communication.

The original **process of communication**, discussed in Chapter 5, conceived of a simple exchange between two people, but when the media become involved *in reality* much more is going on: the mass media are *not* the source, as so often supposed, but rather the providers of their *selective interpretation* taken from the originating sources. Those sources intend that their messages will have effects and, as we have seen, take measures, with varying degrees of certainty and efficiency, to optimize their intended outcomes. There is, therefore, *something of a gamble about communication via the media*, and **it is the elimination of this hazard that drives media relations practice**.

The desired outcomes vary, however, in the *levels of change*, whether in attitudes, perceptions or behaviours, that they seek. For instance, in MPR it is likely that a communication will intend that the recipient *acts purposefully in response*, probably by buying something. But that may not be always the case. Often, for instance, 'mere' *making known* is intended, as in publicity. And frequently communication is designed to communicate *shared values*. In other words, the effect sought is **mental**

and emotional agreement, the purpose being to gain or renew commitments that may of themselves in the short-run result require only the most minimal adjustments.

This shared values approach is widely used in advertising, where the receiver is driven to discontent until he or she has acquired the missing product or service that completes the three-cornered picture presented: the product or service, the shared values and the purchaser. In public relations shared values are often communicated in the context of *memberships*, whether commercial or social, educational or cultural, religious or political, the *primary* purpose being 'bonding' rather than expenditure. Such messages benefit from universally felt human need of companionship, fellowship, association and faith, of identification with a purpose or cause, of belonging, unity of purpose.

Nor is communication composed simply of words, pictures and sounds alone. There is much *signalling* in communication, both inter-personally and in corporate and cultural contexts. That is why so much care and attention is given to corporate identity signs and symbols, colours and typographies. For how the sender intends these to be perceived may differ from how the receiver regards them after decoding, and the intervention of the media further exposes the communication to the risk of interpretation that is at variance with what the sender intends.

11.4   On-line media

The development in electronic media continues apace, but, to adapt a famous remark, reports of the death of traditional media have been exaggerated. The use and abuse of the new media is controversial, as we shall see, but without doubt they have brought many potential efficiencies.

The cracking pace and enthusiastic hype of the 1990s appears to be at last giving way to greater realism among the **'new media industry'**; for instance, 'The past five years ... can be neatly summed up by three key words – boom, bust, boredom. ... [It is proving difficult] to convince the population at large that it can afford £30 a month for faster web access [broadband] unless [there are] more compelling reasons to do so. ... The six billion dollar question is whether this will finally, finally be the year when paid-for content takes off. The billing mechanisms are slowly slotting into place, but whether consumers are prepared to pay is another matter' (*The Guardian*, 16.12.02).

Nor are such concerns confined to the UK. The online manager of the *Contra Costa Times* in the San Francisco Bay area of California, for instance, bemoaned the 'failure' of newspapers in cyberspace (*The Guardian*, 31.1.00). 'In 1995 and 1996,' he wrote, 'newspaper leaders unveiled a bold vision in which cyberspace would release us from the earthly bonds and the enormous costs of newspaper production and distribution, while building a bridge to a vibrant hi-tech journalism of the next century. It hasn't worked out that way. There are some darn good online newspapers. But the major newspaper companies have not succeeded in building anything close to a Yahoo, eBay or Amazon.com.'

Interestingly, of the six explanations proffered for this, he lists 'Journalism, as defined by highbrow traditionalists and communications school professors, no longer seems to carry the weight it once did.' However, there is plenty of evidence that quality journalism most certainly *does* attract readers to the electronic text, but whether they still value it when they have to *pay* for it is in doubt. Publishers that have successful free sites have yet to start charging or are in the early stages of doing so but have yet to establish a market for paid-for access, even though everyone expects to pay for their traditional hardcopy versions.

Many specialist publications are including **electronic access without extra charge** within their annual subscriptions. Publishers of business-to-business (B2B) titles 'say they are now in a much better position to make it pay. "... there has been a realization and recognition of fundamentals again. What is it that motivates a reader to read, what is the must-have information and what are the things people really do value in the working life." ... market-specific news appears to be a key element. ... The key question is whether readers will buy. ... "There is a lot of stuff in trade magazines that historically people like to think of as must-have content. But it might actually turn out to be 'nice to have' or even 'not that bothered about having." ' (*The Guardian*, 9.12.02).

Some people obtain their news and information solely on-line, and presumably their numbers will increase with time. They usually have a *strong predisposition* to the new media already, perhaps because they work in the sector. This is reflected in the experience of MPR specialists, who find those products that have a closer relevance to the new electronic media, such as computer consoles and games and mobile telephone messaging, are more likely to achieve the greater flow of **website visits** and resultant response.

Video streaming is also being used extensively and this is capable of sophisticated evaluation. Research shows that 'the market for corporate video streaming in Western Europe is set to grow almost tenfold in the next five years, from £17.5 millions in 2001 to £140 millions in 2006' (*PR Week*, 4.10.02). Other activities include **web conferencing** and **'on-line chat'**, **'viral marketing'**, placing e-mail attachments that are sufficiently entertaining to induce receivers to forward them to friends, family and work colleagues, and, above all else, **e-mailing**, whether in text, audio or audio-video formats. Some public relations people endeavour to participate in *chat rooms* that are known to be frequented by their primary publics, as a means to *anticipating and countering criticisms*, although this may prove to be time-consuming and relatively impractical.

'The real strength of e-PR as a tool has been its ability to launch products and build awareness, rather than manage issues. Marketers are increasingly looking to the internet as a powerful tool.' However, 'E-PR is not a part of Internet marketing; it is a type of Internet marketing. That is to say that it provides a way of viewing the whole online marketing process, from promoting your site through to the way you sell your products and services. The Internet is about interactivity and information, which provide the foundation for all e-PR activity' (Haig, 2000).

While public relations people may use the web for a variety of communication purposes, clearly it is e-mail that is of primary interest to them, reflecting the overwhelming general preference. 'E-mail is being used increasingly by business managers to communicate quickly with employees and colleagues. Furthermore, you can send online newsletters via e-mail to different target audiences.' But then 'E-mail and Web-based discussion groups are also a big e-PR concern. It is important to monitor these online groups in order to prevent misinformation spreading about your business, and to keep an eye on what people are saying about you and your competition.'

So great is the flow of e-mail, and mobile phone, or cell phone, text messaging, that it has inspired a new term, **'spam'**, because it is all proving to be too much. It is estimated that about 40 per cent of all e-mails are now unsolicited, and unwanted text messages are particularly intrusive. Spam is a nuisance for both Internet users and service providers. Additionally, soon it will be possible to send a single text message to thousands of handsets, so worsening the problem.

The European (EU) Telecommunications Data Protection Directive that took effect in October 2003 requires that all commercial e-mail must include an address to which a recipient may send a request to cease such communication. All such Council Directives are 'binding as to "the results to be achieved" but … have to be enacted by national procedures within a time limit. Legal rights can be created even if a particular country fails to meet the deadline' (Smith, 1995).

The UK government and many other EU member states wanted this 'opt-out' provision instead of the original 'opt-in' proposal, similar to the US legislation, that was proposed by the EU. Then the UK government produced legislative proposals that had at their core a requirement that the senders of unsolicited e-mail and text messages must *first* obtain the permission of their intended receivers.

Meanwhile, the UK's Advertising Standards Authority decided bulk e-mailing and text messaging must be clearly marked 'unsolicited' or not be sent without *prior* permission of the intended recipients. All of this confirms that there is a real problem, but it requires a global response, and that appears unlikely at present.

11.5 The relationship between public relations and the media

The UK media comprises in excess of 4400 titles, of which about half are newspapers and consumer magazines and the balance are trade and technical publications. Throughout the EU the print media includes in aggregate an estimated 7500 titles, about 500 on average in each country. Details for France, Germany, The Netherlands and Scandinavia are good or quite good; for Greece, Italy and some others, the available data, assembled into 'reading lists', is neither so full nor reliable (Stewart-Hunt, 2003).

These estimates suggest, therefore, that *over one third* of the EU print media is located in the UK; *that* indicates the presence of *many journalists looking for a good story*, and goes some way towards explaining why the UK's Institute of Public Relations is the second largest body of its type in the world, after its US counterpart. Given this concentration, there is extensive media relations activity; some public relations people are in contact with journalists, one way or the other, throughout the working day, and the busy interaction continues over weekends.

It is, generally, an uneasy relationship, supposedly distinguished by a pronounced asymmetry, based on the widely accepted notion that public relations people need journalists but journalists do not need public relations people. In consequence the public relations side persistently refuses, usually, to say a bad word about the media, much less countenance a scintilla of criticism against a journalist, well, at least not in public anyway. And the journalistic side persistently insists, usually, in excoriating everyone who works in public relations, or may even ever have done so, at every public and private opportunity.

This, however, is for the most part a *charade*, largely played out for third party consumption. In reality the relationship is much more symmetrical. For public relations people now have the Internet, by which they may communicate *without mediation* of journalists, a significant and increasingly substantial addition to their various unmediated tools. And journalists have a *lot less time and opportunity* to originate material themselves and *much greater pressures* to consider 'ready baked' offerings that can be swiftly transformed into tempting nourishment for their customers.

There is an **interdependency** here that must not bear mention. '... journalists are complicit in the in-take of PR material. They seek the material, use it to fill expanding editorial space and benefit from any audience or reader increases,' observes Moloney (2000), who offers two related explanations for 'this contradictory mixture of hostility and complicity.'

Firstly, he considers journalists to be 'too weak as a professional group', owing to a 'marketisation' of their 'institutions', too few jobs and lesser distinction between editorial, advertising, promotion and circulation (sales). It is certainly the case that new technologies have greatly impacted on print production, resulting in ever more available space to fill, while, owing to intensified competition for advertising and readers, there are even fewer resources with which to fill the space. In consequence the media have opened their editorial pages to commercially sourced inputs on a scale that was unimaginable but 20 years ago. 'Media placement' has long since ceased to be for the public relations practitioner the arduous and painstaking endurance trial of yesteryear.

The second explanation is that the journalists are the 'news managers' who, although they never mention it, are the people who, they claim, objectively decide what goes in the space when there is too little 'hard' news to fill it. 'Now they are more likely to accept [PR material]. Journalists have increased their reliance on secondary sources (including PR), especially when these sources produce copy in a pre-prepared, journalistic form. Journalists thus rely more on official and company spokespeople as primary definers of events. This reliance gives the sources the ability to co-operate or obstruct depending upon the favourability of journalists' copy.'

Journalists have always been the final arbiters of what appears, and probably, being only human, they have often indulged their preferences and prejudices in doing so. Undoubtedly their dependence on outsider contributors, in whatever shape or form, has most definitely increased, and they have always, very sensibly, tended to prefer inputs that better understood and met their requirements.

That public relations people are the *primary* definers of events, however, is very doubtful, although they might strive to be so. Clearly, in matters politic and in reporting corporate 'hard' news such as annual results, that *may* be so, but it is difficult to see the multitude of MPR events in quite such an awesome light. And, yes, the public relations contributor does indeed seek to exert influence on what appears, much as most other people do when they are in contact with the media.

Theaker (2001c) observed 'signs that antagonism between journalists and PR people is not as widespread as commonly held. Several [journalists responding to her survey] quoted local councils, police and health authorities, housing associations and utilities as providing good service. One journalist mentioned a leisure company which were "masters at forcing us to do stories".' Although we are not told *why* or *how*. The general tone of her respondents is condescending: their tips are of the typically banal and trite variety that many journalists still use in their endeavour to patronize public relations people, often just before applying for jobs with them.

This uneasy relationship, conceived with built-in tension, nevertheless has its more subtle dimensions. For example, consider these:

- 'Journalists often have advance notice of which companies and organizations are going to do badly. Experience frequently shows that rot in an organization begins on the public relations side, with slow, inadequate and especially defensive responses. Maybe stockbrokers should employ freelances [writers] as scouts' (*Writers' News*, 6.01).
- ' "For every story I've broken, [originated] there are 20 I've stopped," he [a leading UK publicist] boasts' (*The Times*, 23.9.02).
- 'Family firms may exist in all sectors of industry ... but in the stuff of popular legend, businesses outside the traditional women's fields of hair and beauty, public relations or child minding are predominantly father / son concerns ...' (*The Guardian*, 9.6.03).
- 'It is hardly a secret among less idealistic PROs that journalists regard themselves as gatekeepers barring access to the truth, rather than facilitators on the path to enlightenment' (*PR Week*, 4.10.02).

CHECKLIST

- The media have three basic duties: to inform, educate and entertain.
- Collectively, they are the main source of information, and are said thereby to exert power, for 'knowledge is power'.
- The media provide the venues of the modern public sphere, where people 'meet' to consider current affairs and topics.
- They create the framework, or reference-point, for forming private worldviews.
- They are the main means to projecting images for gain.
- PR, by supplying the media without charge, is partly responsible for broadcasting and print output standards and values.
- The use of infomercials, product placement, advertising features, advertorials and other PR-generated devices may corrode editorial values.
- Uses and gratifications theory states that the media may be used: (1) for entertainment, (2) to find interesting items, (3) for diversion, (4) in substitution for social relationships and (5) to check on personal identity and values.
- Key elements of mass communication are (1) how and with what effect messages are received and (2) agenda setting, by which the media filter and alter messages to match their interpretation of their receivers' worldviews.
- For McQuail the media operate in two dimensions: (1) seeking either to achieve social change or reflect current conditions; (2) emphasizing either culture and

ideas or materialist forces and factors. Accordingly media relations strategy may be: (1) campaigning and focused or reserved and broader; (2) concerned more with the social content and effect or with the technical means of communication.

CASE STUDY
WHEN THE e-MAILING HAS TO STOP

The incidence of unsolicited e-mail soared in the 12 months to December 2001, according to a survey of 119 UK newspaper and magazine journalists. Almost 20 per cent reported a 100 per cent or more increase. 'Over a quarter of unsolicited e-mails received by journalists are from public relations practitioners and 75 per cent of respondents believed that there should be a formal e-mail code of conduct to govern the way in which public relations practitioners use e-mail' (Mason, 2002). Furthermore, 'only 50 per cent of respondents had received any form of training in the use of computers and e-mail.'

The survey focused on the impact of unsolicited e-mail on communications between UK print journalists and public relations practitioners. Similar studies of both print journalists and broadcasters had been conducted annually in the USA since 1994 by Middleberg and Ross. Their most recent study, in 2000, had stated that the preferred method for communicating with unknown sources was e-mail, placed by 32 per cent of respondents ahead of telephone, face-to-face, post and facsimile. Questions in the study relating to computer-aided reporting, or e-mail, were replicated in the British research, in order to compare and contrast US/UK attitudes, allowing for the US e-mail take-up levels being at least five years ahead, 'in an attempt to predict how British newspapers and magazines might react to their increasing in-box overload in the future.'

The 119 respondents who agreed to participate comprised 52 per cent of the random sample of 228 selected publications. Among respondents, 38 per cent were from trade and technical titles, 53 per cent from consumer publications, three per cent from daily newspapers and six per cent from weekly titles. All had noticed a significant increase, and 40 per cent reported an increase in excess of 50 per cent.

Principal complaints related to the receipt of large picture file attachments that take a long time to download, untargeted e-mails and incompatibility of differing operating systems. Some respondents indicated preference for faxes and post. Comments included '... information in an e-mail has less impact and is less likely to be retained in the mind ...' and '... posted press releases could have more impact and were more likely to have a longer "shelf life".'

'In comparing the findings of this study with those of the Middleberg Ross Cyberspace research, it seems that UK journalists could perhaps be approaching the point reached by their American counterparts five years earlier in 1997. Many British journalists report in-box traffic increase of up to 100 per cent and a large percentage (30 per cent) of those surveyed never open unsolicited e-mails. ... In 1997 Middleberg/Ross report that US journalists turned their backs on e-mail and reverted to sourcing many of their stories either through telephone, fax, face-to-face or postal communications.'

QUESTIONS

1 Should television news be 'slanted to a particular point of view', like newspapers?
2 What responsibility should public relations bear for 'the sterility of popular culture'?
3 Why might the media be used as 'a check on personal identity and values'?
4 Might journalism no longer seem to 'carry the weight it once did' and if so why?
5 Why might 'rot in an organization begin on the PR side'?

▨ **12 Global public relations**

The development of public relations internationally – communication factors – thinking beyond the clichés and slogans – non-governmental organizations – the European Union – the developing countries

12.1 The development of public relations internationally

The development of public relations outside the USA and the UK began to accelerate from the middle of the last century. The first talk of organizing public relations practice internationally occurred in November 1949, when a group comprising four British and two Dutch public relations men conceived of a 'para-national society' to raise practice standards and improve quality and efficiency. This led to a second meeting in March 1950, attended by PR people from the UK, The Netherlands, France, Norway and the USA, under the auspices of the Royal Netherlands International Trade Fair and the Public Relations Society of Holland (Black, 1989).

At that meeting a provisional committee was established, with the purpose of promoting international exchange of information and co-operation. This met regularly in England, occasionally observed by people from Australia, Belgium, Canada, Finland, Italy and Switzerland, and led to the establishment of the **International Public Relations Association** (IPRA) in 1955. The list of countries represented is a useful indication of where the paid practice of public relations was taking root around the world in those formative years.

IPRA adopted a **formal code of conduct** in 1961, comprising practice guidelines for members, and, in 1965, **an international code of ethics** for public relations practice, the 'Code of Athens'. The **United Nations formally recognized IPRA** 'on a consultative basis to the Economic and Social Council' in 1964 and later it was also recognized by Unesco as a non-governmental organization (NGO) in the 'mutual information category of relationship'. Over the years IPRA, whose membership comprises senior practitioners, has issued a succession of influential papers, including a 'gold paper' at each of its triennial world congresses.

In 1997 the association published a survey of eight countries in relation to the effects of *globalization* on corporate communication. The countries studied were Australia, Brazil, Japan, Singapore, South Africa, Switzerland, the UK and the USA. 'There was unanimous agreement that companies would need improved communications in the global field' (Theaker, 2001d).

Political changes

Apart from the globalization of markets, *political change* has strongly stimulated the growth of public relations. This has been most noticeable in eastern Europe and in China. In the former, following the collapse of the Communist regimes, national public relations associations were quickly formed, many in countries that are becoming EU members. At around the same time, 1991, an association was also formed in China, which is said to have 100,000 public relations students.

The spread of public relations practice around the world has been accompanied by a **slower development of related research**, which has been undertaken primarily in north America and western Europe. Corporate communication research was 'still in its infancy', according to van Riel (1995), who somewhat defensively declared 'I take the view that it is necessary to keep research progressing at full speed, yet never to lose sight of the connection with practice.' He cited a number of European academic writers whose work had been published in the previous 20 years. In the UK great emphasis is placed on the work of various American scholars, particularly Grunig and Hunt.

Global PR linkages

Several regional associations of national public relations bodies have been long established. These include the **Inter-American Confederation of Public Relations Associations** (FIARP), which stimulated development throughout Latin America, and CERP, whose members cover the whole of Europe. In 1986 the consultants formed their own discrete organization, the **International Communications Consultancy Organization**, whose membership comprises trade associations in 24 countries, with the aim of working towards 'quality, efficient PR consultancy practice across borders', including harmonization. (ICCO website, 29.5.02). It too has a professional code, the 'Rome Charter'.

And in 2000 the desire to collaborate internationally gave birth to yet another body, the **Global Alliance for Public Relations and Communications Management**. Although this was formally inaugurated in Chicago, it too was conceived in London, at a series of meetings the previous year.

The Global Alliance brings together over 20 national and international associations and has been established in response to the influence of global trends and issues; it aims through co-operation 'to strengthen the influence of the public relations industry among our constituents around the world.' In addition to the usual purposes, this new organization 'enhances networking opportunities for professionals and serves as a vehicle for examining ethical standards, universal accreditation options, and other initiatives to strengthen the profession around the world' (Alliance website, 26.5.02).

The membership of the Global Alliance provides another indication of where public relations practice is well established. Member associations are in:

- 'the Americas' (Canada, USA, Mexico, Puerto Rico),
- Europe (IPRA, CERP and 10 national associations),

- India,
- Asia (Australia, New Zealand, Philippines) and
- Africa (an association covering southern Africa and an association in Kenya).

The consultants' need of a separate international forum in order to discuss what *matters most to them* reflected what happens *nationally*. In the UK, for instance, consultants in the 1960s formed their own trade association, the Public Relations Consultants' Association (PRCA), separate from the existing institute. However, the *development of multinational and global* consultancy has been a major factor.

Ever-larger international PR consultancies

The *urge to merge* has served to **continually produce ever-larger firms**, as has occurred in accountancy and some other occupations; and being the biggest never seems to be *quite* enough, there is always the prospect, it seems, of just one more extra huge merger, the largest ever in public relations, to date. And as with other occupations, just a handful of such businesses dominate the trade; currently 10 in this case, if one network of 104 'partner firms' in 38 countries is included (*Financial Times*, 27.11.01).

12.2 Communication factors

Travel, they say, broadens the mind. But the *ease* of *apparent contact* made possible by ever-cheaper transport, together with the daily depiction of the world through televisual images and ready access to the Internet, can serve to **disguise some basic and persistent impediments to communication**. For instance, although an estimated 1900 million people the world over speak English, 'only' some 350 millions are *native* speakers. In other words, it might be tempting, certainly for the British and Americans, to assume that 'everyone speaks English' but they do not, and *barely one-sixth* of those that do have the level of command of the language implicit in such an assumption.

Speaking the same language

Indeed, the matter of **language** itself, never mind the many nuances and subtleties of communication, can represent a major obstacle that cannot be minimized or readily discounted. Apart from English, there are **no fewer than ten major languages** in use around the world. These include Mandarin Chinese, the first language of some 800 million people. That is well over *twice as many as English*, and when the 'competent speakers' are added it is thought that a billion people speak it.

With the approximate number of native speakers of each in brackets, the remaining major languages are:

- Hindi, and closely related Urdu (350 million),
- Spanish (315),
- Bengali (170),
- Arabic (165),
- Russian (165),
- Portuguese (160),
- Japanese (125),
- German (90) and
- French (75).

And these major languages are among **some 6000 still being spoken**. 'So in the key communications area of languages the public relations practitioner has much to consider when venturing abroad' (Black and Davis, 2002).

Not that a *single* language necessarily prevails in a *single* country. Even in the UK English is but one of several spoken languages, and in some countries there are *not one but two* **'official' languages**, and there are often important **regional and local dialects** as well. This is typically found in the vast countries of Africa and Asia, and even in large countries such as France, the source of the world's diplomatic language, but it can occur in small countries as well, often owing to historic migration and settlement or to climatic and geographic factors.

'Even between countries supposedly speaking the same language … it is necessary to ascertain the correct choice of words is made, both to ensure clarity of meaning and to avoid the possibility of giving offence.' Although English may be spoken by many people, 'it is essential to use the local language correctly' in public relations, regardless of the frequent use of English for advertising and packaging.

Working with cultural differences

Differing **culture** also plays its part and is readily underestimated, particularly owing to superficial appearances. **Cultures often *co-exist*, and *proximity* is no assurance of similarity**.

International public relations practice is divisible into *outward* and *inward* **activity**; that is to say, public relations practitioners may:

1   communicate with publics located abroad in their place of domicile,
2   or with publics 'at home' on behalf of foreign sources.

Often the latter is on behalf of foreign governments or non-governmental organizations (NGOs) and illustrates very well the cultural differences *without the need to travel any distance.*

Example

When a central European government sought UK media coverage for its brilliant achievements, in commerce, science, the arts and so on, the source information came from an official news agency in poorly written English that was barely understandable and took much unravelling. There was also significant need of *cultural* translation for the UK media. At the commercial section of the embassy their internationally acclaimed beers were remarkably good and everyone was diplomatic to a tee, but the cultural nuances seemed to outsiders to be at times totally inexplicable, especially given the *proximity* of the two countries, and the reluctance to better understand UK thinking was formidable. Their country was a popular holiday destination for British tourists, but to most of the UK media its presence within Europe seemed downright *implausible*.

Sensitivity to cultural differences is probably *more necessary* in public relations than in *any other* occupation. Whereas such differences routinely close to hand may be more readily understood, they are likely to provide far greater challenges when encountered abroad. And sensitivity has to be accompanied by a determination to *adapt* as necessary to meet local circumstances. The growing tendency to look across from one whole continent to another and suppose that 'the other' is homogeneous has to be resisted. **Making generalized assumptions about other cultures can be the death of communication**, and an understandable reluctance to recognize heterogeneity because it spells 'more effort' is a serious hazard; thoroughly researching and understanding differing cultures is *fundamental* to international public relations practice.

Any desire for a *uniformity* in communication soon has to come against this 'heterogeneity of the context of the environment in which the organization operates', which leads to recognition that 'it is not always desirable nor practical to stimulate "uniformity" in overall communication policy' (van Riel, 1995). This is *particularly* so given the **reputational significance of the signals that the organizations emits** and the 'rational and (apparently) irrational ways in which members of the target groups select signals from those put out by the organization.'

These considerations provide a counterbalance to the, often, extravagant claims for the Internet. The very *ease of use* creates the impression that the world has 'shrunk' to just over the horizon. 'Geographical limitations are all but eliminated when you are online' (Haig, 2000) sounds seductive, but does not quite tell the full story, for it is those very geographical factors that determine the quality of the communication, regardless of the channel used. For all that, the advent of the Internet undoubtedly is of the greatest significance in all international communication.

Example

A joke in one culture may be quite the opposite in another. Cadbury produced an advertisement showing a map of India and within it an indication of the border state of Kashmir, which is partly in India and partly in Pakistan, with the slogan 'Too good to share'. According to the BBC's man in India, it caused Cadbury 'a lot of trouble'. Clearly, what seemed amusing to the advertising people did not seem so to Indians, for whom the Kashmir dispute is certainly no joke.
(BBC *Today*, 21.8.02)

12.3　Thinking beyond the clichés and slogans

Generalizations abound in consideration of international communication. Whole races of people are readily labelled, personal experience is happily extrapolated, inferences are drawn from slim evidence and lingering doubts are soon made *fact*. And in the pursuit of *effectiveness* much wise counsel is offered. Think global, act local is the cliché of choice. Segment, segment, segment, cross-refer and cross-refer again. Public relations knows no frontiers. Communicate away the world's differences. Stretch the hand of friendship across continents. Speak the right language. Unite in common understanding. And so on. It is as if distance not so much makes the heart grow fonder as the head more woolly.

The reality of international public relations is that the ground rules are much the same, **but the conditions have changed**:

- *unfamiliar* environments have to be scanned with the *utmost* care and attention to detail
- *each* public has to be scrutinized to the *n*th degree
- the drive for *control* has to be intensified
- *consistency* has to be maintained under often challenging conditions
- measurement and evaluation has to reflect the *exact* specifics of each circumstance.

The public relations and the marketing *must be mutually complementary*, *particularly* where 'relationship marketing' begins to overlap with PR in its concentration on finding and keeping loyal customers.

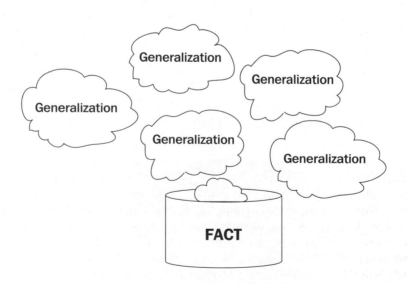

Figure 12.1　**Generalizations made 'facts'**

12.4   Non-governmental organizations

The people who appear to excel at international public relations are the NGOs, which are often referred to as advocacy groups or 'watchdogs', although there are many to whom such appellations do not readily apply. They vary greatly in size, origins and duration. Their purposes are correspondingly many and varied, from, for instance, regulating the use of the high seas to harrying corporate transgressors to distributing food and medicines.

They 'have become the new sophisticated communicators and perceived instigators of change in the global marketplace' (Wootliff and Deri, 2001). 'Some [NGOs] are pro-industry; others more cautious. Still others can find no redeeming qualities at all in multi-national corporations or global free trade.' 'Business people tend to be at least as suspicious of the NGOs as they are of the media' (Lambert, 2002). 'But this year they have been starting to talk about ideas for working alongside them in various forms of partnership.'

Example

What happened to the US sportswear manufacturer Nike both illustrates NGO communication effectiveness and explains business wariness of them. Early in 1996 CBS television broadcast a 'stunning expose' of working conditions in factories in China, Indonesia and Vietnam that were supplying the company. The wages paid were less than the local minima, conditions were appalling and there was physical abuse. The damage changed Nike's carefully cultivated youth brand image from 'urban cool' to rapacious exploiter of poorer peoples; the company sought to defend itself by rebutting the allegations (*The Times*, 23.9.02).

Then a leaked confidential report, from management consultants who had been inspecting a factory in Vietnam for Nike, did more damage. The revelations, in *The New York Times* in November 1997, led to a trenchant hail of international criticism of Nike, on both the business and sports pages, and an NGO called Working Assets Citizen Action 'generated' 33,000 letters of complaint addressed to Nike's CEO, 'urging him to pay workers a living wage and to implement a comprehensive third party monitoring system.' Other NGOs, such as Global Exchange and Vietnam Labor Watch, joined in, together with student groups, demanding that universities 'doing business with Nike' put pressure on the company to achieve higher standards. There was a telling documentary broadcast; sales fell and the share price suffered accordingly (Wootliff and Deri, 2001).

In April 1998 a prominent environmental activist and anti-corporate campaigner sued Nike under California's Unfair Competition and False Advertising Law in relation to its public relations defence. He accused Nike of making false claims about its labour record. He argued that as these claims had commercial intent and impact, they amounted to 'unfair business practice'. Soon after Nike pledged to end child labour in its suppliers' factories, to enforce US standards there and, probably most tellingly, to allow NGOs to participate in monitoring its Asian factories. 'The company also publicly stated that the conditions in its factories needed to be drastically improved.'

Nor has the damage been limited to the company. Public relations practice has been held to account for the accuracy of its statements. The California Supreme Court found that statements made by businesses were not protected by the American constitution's guarantee of free speech. 'California is the fifth-largest market in the world. ... The ruling also applies to charities, non-governmental organizations, possibly political groupings and even journalists,' according to a Harvard law professor. 'The decision [allows] any California citizen to drag a business into court and bring it to its knees unless it persuades a jury that everything it said was error-free and omitted nothing' (*The Times*, 23.9.02).

The impact of NGOs on international public relations practice probably cannot be fully calculated, because their influence extends to the most mundane day-to-day decisions, such as consumer choice of food.

Example

The UK groceries retailer Sainsbury 'believes that its customers want excellent quality and value for money, but not at the expense of people working in developing countries who may be working in unsafe conditions and for poor wages.' To that end the company participates in several initiatives designed to ensure basic human and labour rights and it has its own code of practice for 'social responsible sourcing for all its suppliers.'

The company is a founding member of the Ethical Trading Initiative (ETI), alongside retailers, labour unions and international charities. The ETI aims to improve conditions for employees of suppliers in developing countries through enforcement of a 'base code' taken from the primary conventions on labour standards of the International Labour Organization (ILO). Members' supply chains are monitored independently and members are actively applying the code directly; Sainsbury visits its suppliers to raise awareness and monitor associated issues.

The company sees several benefits that it derives for itself from this. These include greater supply chain efficiencies, enhanced risk management, higher staff retention and 'mitigation of disruption to operations caused by economic and social insecurity, shrinking markets and the depletion of available raw materials brought about by neglect of social and environmental issues' (DTI website, 9.3.03).

That the ETI benefits the company is clear, and it is most unlikely that any of its retail customers will disagree with its honourable purpose, although some may question how much they may have to pay for it. However, it is the NGOs who are entitled, and likely, to claim much of the credit for creating consumer interest in such issues and provoking the resultant corporate responses. And consumers' expectations *spread*, so that, for instance, claims relating to *all* sourcing policies are tested for their credibility.

'Sainsbury's has just sponsored a conference on organic farming. Well done. Good PR for them. But it is now two months since I have been able to find a single

> organic carrot in the sad, one-fiftieth of an aisle they call the "organic vegetables" section at my local mega-Sainsbury's. … The shop assistants are sympathetic as we stand side by side gazing sorrowfully at the empty shelves. … And so, like more and more people, I now order my veggies by home delivery' (*Marketing Business*, 11.97).

On *credibility* the NGOs score remarkably well. In a 2000 survey, by public relations consultants Edelman Worldwide, of some 1300 plus 'thought leaders' in Australia, France, Germany, the UK and the USA (Wootliff and Deri, 2001) NGOs were more trusted than government, business and the media on:

- *'the big issues* such as the environment' – by over half of the sample
- *human rights* – by almost 60 per cent of the sample
- *health* – by over half of the sample.

When it came to 'who is more "trusted to do the right thing" ':

- in the USA business scored well clear of the others, at 44 per cent
- in Australia the NGOs were strong winners at 53 per cent
- in Europe the NGOs came top again, on 48 per cent.

For the purpose of the survey, thought leaders were defined as men and women aged 35–64 who are college graduated, registered to vote and have an annual $75,000 plus 'household income'.

'Why NGOs are winning'

The researchers advance some explanations for why they consider NGOs are 'winning':

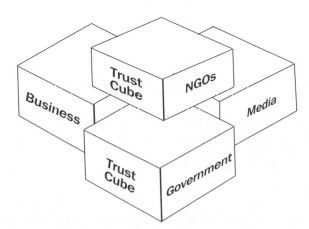

Figure 12.2   **Varying levels of trust in NGOs, government, business and the media**

- effective use of the power of images, particularly in broadcast and on the Internet
- speaking directly to consumers and appealing to their emotions
- focusing on a clear agenda with a call to action
- building coalitions, with companies, other NGOs and consumers
- being seen as selfless crusaders.

By contrast, Wootliff and Deri say that companies, government and the media have 'a myriad of agendas and audiences'; business is poor at creating coalitions and often organizations lack external support; and 'businesses might be perceived as supporting corporate greed.'

Example

An organization that needs little introduction to most people around the world is Greenpeace, which has a proven record of being very adept at the effective use of the power of images. It is particularly accomplished at waylaying ships on the high seas and occupying them, oil platforms and buildings in order to create highly televisual messages.

Typical of its activities was the boarding of a bulk carrier ship in February 2000 that was loaded with genetically modified soya, to which Greenpeace, and many consumers, object. The owners described as piracy the 'storming' of the 72,000-tonne vessel off the UK coast by five protesters using inflatable dinghies, who abseiled down the bow and onto the anchor, preventing the ship completing its passage from New Orleans to Liverpool.

They raised a flag across the bow that read 'Europe says "No GMOs"'. It was signed off with the Greenpeace UK website address, printed large enough for television viewers to find it. The action had been planned over months. 'My understanding of pirates in the South China Seas [the ship was Korean registered] is that they nick the cargo and kill the crew. We do not do any of those things,' said a spokesman. A demonstrator said 'We are happy to stay here as long as it takes.'

(*The Times*, 26.2.00)

12.5 Regional alliances and groupings

An increasingly important dimension in international public relations practice is the growth of regional alliances and groupings *between nations*, of which the **European Union** (EU) is probably creating the greatest interest, owing to its expansion to embrace most countries in the whole continent of Europe and the development of its constitutional structures in order to cope with this. The EU is now very much part of the politics of EU member states; in the case of the UK, the **European Commission** (bureaucracy), **Council of Ministers** and **European Parliament** take their place alongside 15 other components of 'the system' (Miller, 1998, cited by Theaker, 2001e). Miller is a leading UK lobbyist and well versed in the complex web that binds

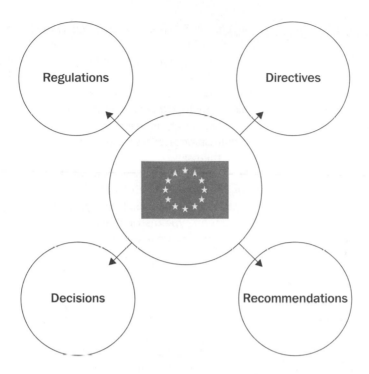

Figure 12.3 The four main forms of European Union legislation

civil service departments, special advisers, committees, task forces, bodies and regulators, and the 'cabinets' that advise European commissioners (ministers).

Directives are but one of four main forms of **EU legislation**; they also include:

- *Recommendations*, which amount to guidance for national legislation
- *Regulations*, and certain decisions, that are binding as soon as they are published in the *Official Journal*
- *Decisions*, which are directives that apply only to certain countries or companies.

'A final element in this complex political scene is the large number of Union documents produced. These are of varying status and require the most discriminating monitoring. In an average year some 7,000 pieces of draft or final legislation emerge.' The emphasis is on consultation and compromise, according to Smith (1995), another prominent UK lobbyist, '... with a marked preference for lobbies organized at a Union rather than a purely national level.' Where differences occur between the Council of Ministers and parliament, reconciliation of views is sought by the Commission, 'acting as honest broker and guardian of the treaties – the outcome of this process is known as a Common Position.'

12.6 The developing countries

In the developing countries the public relations priorities are very different. Communication itself is often constrained by the **relative lack of available media,** and that which exists may be *effectively closed to external contributions*. The **distances are likely to be made greater** by *geographic and climatic* hindrances and *inadequate transport infrastructure*. There is **widespread illiteracy** and a **multiplicity of ethnic, linguistic and dialectical differences**. **Culture** is a major factor, especially in rural areas, where various tribal and religious beliefs are likely to be strongly held.

Here public relations is **primarily about** *education*, embracing both public and market information, for, before a product or service can be introduced, it is often necessary to first explain the circumstances in terms that *make sense* within the overall context in which people find themselves.

And when products are marketed there is usually a substantial need of **ancillary explanation and demonstration**. For instance, with labelling of products 'It is not enough to print the label and instruction in the local language since the majority of people will not be able to read. Cartoon-type instructions are necessary, although rare' (Jefkins and Yadin, 1998). Similarly, weights and measures '... are incomprehensible to people who do not weigh anything nor use rulers or tape measures. This has been a problem with products such as powdered baby milk, many buyers having no means of measuring or sterilization.'

Drawing on his extensive experience of public relations training in Nigeria, Jefkins pointed to the disparities in that country's state of educational progress. On the one hand, there were some dozen universities and many technical colleges, secondary schools and private schools, and many Nigerians were being educated in western universities, but on the other, universal primary education had not been introduced until 1977. This pronounced dichotomy, apparent in many developing countries, has a direct bearing on public relations activities, since messages have to be most carefully conceived and very closely targeted to take fullest account of the **wide economic and social differences**.

He wrote scathingly of the business outsiders' misperceptions. 'Foreigners rarely understand the communication problems. They sit in London, New York or Geneva, and plan marketing schemes as if they were selling to a mass market in an industrial society.' However, Jefkins observed that many people in developing countries might have little faith in home-produced products, *preferring* foreign-made. This preference is not confined to the developing countries, as witness the popularity of German motor cars, but he thought that in the developing countries, given the circumstances, 'A PR task may well be to foster pride in home production.'

CHECKLIST

- The influence of global issues and trends and the development of multinational PR consultancy have hastened the spread of PR practice throughout the world and the creation of international PR trade associations and ever-larger PR firms.
- Sensitivity to language and cultural differences is probably more necessary in public relations practice than in any other occupation.
- The reality of international PR is that the ground rules are much the same but the conditions have changed.
- Non-governmental organizations (NGOs), alias 'advocacy groups' or 'watchdogs', excel at international PR; their influence extends even to such mundane matters as consumer choice of food.

- NGOs offer instructive examples in skilled communication, with their: (1) effective use of images, (2) direct appeal to consumers, (3) clear focus and calls to action, (4) creation of coalitions and (5) projection of selfless goodwill.
- Regional alliances and groupings between nations are increasingly important to PR practice.
- In the developing countries there are major PR impediments, including inaccessible media, geographic and climate hindrances, inadequate transport, illiteracy and multiple ethnic, linguistic and dialectical differences.
- PR practice is primarily concerned with public information and educating markets, often involving primary instruction and ancillary explanation and demonstration.

CASE STUDY
COMMUNICATING FOR SUSTAINABLE DEVELOPMENT

Shell Philippines Exploration BV decided from the outset to integrate economic, social and environmental factors into the development of the Malampaya deepwater natural gas project in the Philippines. The basic challenge was to maintain the rich biodiversity while creating a gas industry that will provide 30 per cent of the country's energy requirement, reduce dependency on imported fuel and generate $8–10 billions over two decades in government revenues.

The company consulted with both national agencies and local communities to 'promote a partnership approach based on open dialogue and co-operation.' Social and environmental impact studies were undertaken and a 'social management process' was designed, to develop health, education and employment programmes for local communities, supported by 'strategic partnerships' with 'NGOs and institutions experienced in community mobilization and capacity-building.'

This combination of local dialogue and partnership programmes was judged to be the key to gaining local acceptance of the project and making it a success. 'Early wins' were achieved in new education and health provision, employment and conservation of indigenous flora and fauna. The healthcare advance was obtained through Shell sharing its emergency medical facilities with local people; employment was stimulated through a partnership with the Pilipinas Shell Foundation aimed at stimulating local enterprise.

Recognizing that maintenance of positive relationships with stakeholders will be key to the long-term success of the project, Shell has also established a Sustainable Development Council in the Philippines, to identify issues requiring attention, and is pursuing on-going dialogue and partnership-building both locally and nationally.

Meanwhile in India, Tata Steel is similarly concerned to develop economic, social and environmental conditions, through an ambitious programme that began with 32 villages in 1979 (DTI website, 9.3.03). The company is Asia's first, and India's largest, integrated private sector steel company. It has a long history of CSR initiatives. Through the Tata Steel Rural Development Society (TSRDS), the company is addressing a wide range of issues in over 700 villages local to its diverse operations in the states of Jharkhand and Orissa.

Priority is given to assisting the poorest and most under-developed and underprivileged areas of the region. Here training is being provided to villagers on methods of multiple crop farming, water management, re-forestation, poultry and animal husbandry. Rapid progress has been achieved and many of the programmes have developed into self-sustaining schemes managed by local communities.

TSRDS also has a number of projects designed to bring about improvements that may be managed by local people trained for the purpose. These relate to education, medicine and sanitation; family planning; the supply of drinking water and irrigation; agriculture, animal husbandry and afforestation; vocational training, rural industries, entrepreneurship and handicrafts.

The Indian Chamber of Commerce and Industry has awarded the Society three times for its outstanding achievements in rural development and it has also been publicly recognized for its service to the severely disabled. Tata Steel is often cited as an example to other companies, nationally and internationally, and through the work of TSRDS it benefits from reduced dependency on it by local communities that have achieved self-sustainable health, education and other schemes.

QUESTIONS

1   What recent political changes may have stimulated the development of public relations and with what likely substantial consequences?
2   Why could sensitivity to cultural differences be 'probably more necessary in public relations than in any other occupation'?
3   What are the likely public relations implications of 'Think global, act local'?
4   When might a 'Common Position' fall victim to communication, and why?
5   What type of public relations is likely to be most appropriate in the developing world and why might that differ from practice in the developed countries?

■ ✓ 13 The occupation of public relations

Size and structure – current consultancy practice – the person specification – practitioner earnings – integrated services– image and reputation of public relations – self-regulation – education and training

13.1 Size and structure

Just how many people are employed in public relations worldwide is subject to conjecture; in the UK alone there is uncertainty. Research in the mid 1980s undertaken for the Institute of Public Relations (IPR) suggested between some 14,000–19,000 people, but could not be more specific owing to various uncertainties, including the relatively numerous part-timers, jobs that included a substantial element of public relations but were *not specified as being PR* and the use of a *confusing array of differing titles.*

Just a few years later, in the early 1990s, the IPR was reporting an estimated 48,000, which represented a dramatic increase, probably accounted for by the important qualification – 'working "in some way" [in PR]' (Moloney, 2000). And that is the central difficulty about trying to head-count this industry, as it is now described officially: the estimates depend upon accurate identification of job titles and the co-operation of people whose occupational descriptions do not spell out their public relations involvement.

Added to which, there are a welter of jobs, starting with those of chief executives, that include a *significant element* of public relations. When *they* are included it would be realistic to suppose that there are **at least half a million people** engaged, either for a living or as *part* of their occupation, in recognizable public relations activities in the UK. And to them has to be added the many people who undertake PR on a voluntary basis or their own behalf, in itself a growing trend.

Various other generalized indications of the UK trade's size and strength are circulated. For instance, that there are **some 1400 consultancy businesses**, allowing for the many self-employed and including the myriad of specialists serving one sector or another or offering particular expertise in a branch of public relations. And it is thought that **consultants outnumber in-house people by four to one**. The PRCA trade association claims that its relatively small number of member companies account for the vast majority of revenue earned, which indicates the highly fragmented structure of the trade, or is it an industry, or is it a profession? The words are used interchangeably, depending upon individual perspective and taste.

What the empirical evidence indicates with certainty is that the practice of public relations has *grown very fast* in the UK over the past quarter century, which in turn appears to maintain its position as the *largest concentration of PR people in Europe.* The IPR continues to claim second position in size among similar bodies around the world.

As to consultancy earnings, **an annual survey of 30 prominent public relations firms** (Willott Kingston Smith and Fintellect, 2002) indicated an aggregate turnover by them of over £441 million. When this is extrapolated, and taking into account previously published estimates, it seems likely that total consultancy industry turnover is currently around £2.5 billion. To which may be added the cost of in-house public relations, in commerce, government, local government, NGOs, the voluntary sector and elsewhere. In short, this is a **substantial occupational group**. And its growth is reflected elsewhere in Europe, most noticeably among the smaller eastern countries that have been famously described recently by an American politician as the 'new' Europe.

13.2   Current consultancy practice

The annual survey by Willott Kingston Smith provides illuminating data on the current condition of five related marketing communications occupations: advertising, media buying, direct marketing and sales promotion (together), design and public relations. In 2001–02 media buying proved on average the most profitable per person employed (£11,080) and had the highest operating profit margin (16.1 per cent). The designers came next, just ahead of the public relations consultants (£8790 and 11.0 per cent). The advertising agencies did worst (£7730 and 8.5 per cent). However, 'Some of these averages have been adversely affected by the results of foreign owned companies which report little profit in the UK.'

Nevertheless, all was far from golden for two-thirds of the public relations consultancies in the survey. One-third incurred a pre-tax loss, compared with only one in the previous year, and a third of the firms had shown a decrease in operating profit from the previous year, compared with 14 per cent in the previous sample. The four

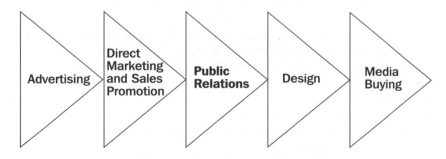

Figure 13.1   **Marketing communications profitability**

with the highest operating losses were all part of publicly quoted UK or foreign groups; probable confirmation yet again of a truism long recognized among public relations consultancy managers, that the small and independent are likely to be the best placed for reducing costs in weakening markets.

Any such survey is but a snapshot picture, and therefore extrapolation of findings has to be viewed with caution. However, during 2001–02 there were some interesting changes observed:

- *more consultancies were competing for each commission*, most certainly a long term trend observable in the UK for many years, and
- this coincided with *reduced client budgets*, that is to say, the figures that prospective customers were prepared to spend on specific proposed public relations projects and programmes.

That latter feature does not necessarily indicate, however, a reduced *number* of proposed purchases. 'Anecdotal evidence would suggest that technical, IT and financial PR have suffered the most whilst healthcare, CSR and public affairs have been more resilient.'

Public relations, as people in it never tire of saying, is a 'people business', and necessarily **employee costs account for a high proportion of total overheads:**

- *Average employee costs* in the survey were £45,500 per year, up from £41,200 in the previous year
- *Other overhead costs per head* had remained fairly static, on average £25,000.

So employee costs were back to the percentage levels that UK consultancy managements resolved in the 1970s to reduce because they were believed to account for too great a proportion of total costs. This was '... disappointing but comes as no surprise bearing in mind that competition to find high calibre staff has been tough and the costs of recruiting such staff have now filtered through to the financial results.' The aim is that employment costs should not exceed 50 per cent of gross income, an optimum ratio of 200 per cent compared with 174 per cent found in the survey.

13.3   The person specification

In addition to other marketing communications – advertising, direct marketing, sales promotion and direct sales – public relations is related, by varying degrees, to a *number* of other occupations, owing to either *the nature* of its activities or *its effects*. Marketing consultancy is the most obvious, but the list also includes

- management consultancy,
- the law,
- politics,
- diplomacy,
- journalism and
- broadcasting.

To a lesser extent, there are connections also with occupations that include photography, creative writing, theatre production and sports promotion.

Given this, it might be imagined that the public relations person, certainly the generalist, is at risk of being a 'Jack of all trades but master of none'. The early writers did little to counter any such supposition and the qualities they specified were numerous.

Example

'To sum up, one needs honesty, integrity, character, intelligence, imagination, ability to write, to speak in public, administrative capacity, a wide general knowledge and a very high ethical standard. Sympathy, understanding, leadership, sound judgement, ideas and courage' (Lloyd, 1963). 'This may sound rather like a religious cult, or some esoteric philosophy, but do not be disheartened.'

More recently the requirements have grown.

Example

'Students need an understanding of psychology so that they understand motivation and persuasion; a better background in political science for the understanding of how government functions so that it can be made more responsive to societal needs; an understanding of anthropology so that they understand change and how it takes place and the importance of cultural adaptation; and of sociology so that they are able to more accurately evaluate societal trends and human interaction.' And they also need 'common sense, curiosity, objectivity, logic and clear thinking [which are] perhaps the most important assets of a successful public relations practitioner ...'.'
(Black, 1989)

It *may* be that public relations people meet all of these requirements and many more, but the *greater* probability is that they meet *some* of them very well. So, for instance:

- a public affairs specialist may have a background in law,
- an internationalist in diplomacy,
- a publicist in journalism or sports agency,
- the consumer specialist might have come from elsewhere in marketing and
- a person working in public information may have transferred from the civil service or administration in a major public service.

There are some generally agreed *core skills* needed, regardless of the specific practice circumstances. In no particular order, they include the ability to:

- listen, and to hear, and to assimilate information
- write, cogently, to order, in a variety of styles to meet a range of requirements
- interrelate with people at all social and power levels as circumstances require
- think and plan with discipline and resource, particularly under pressure.

The third of these is often described as 'knowing how to deal with people' or 'getting on with people', but that might be equally said to be the requirement of the hotel receptionist or any one of many other customer-interface jobs. In public relations it implies *persuasive* skills, either overt or covert. Practitioners deal in impressions, and their encounters are conditioned accordingly. They aim to 'get the best' out of the situation, like most other people, but, unlike most other people, they are rather more accomplished at it.

13.4 Practitioner earnings

The average employee in UK public relations consultancy may have cost £70,500 to employ in 2002, but that was an *average*, and it related solely to *consultancy*. A survey of **fifty public relations recruitment advertisements** provides some indication of *salaries* currently offered. Of these advertisements, 30 almost entirely related to the *public and voluntary sectors* (*The Guardian*, 24.2.03) and 20 to the *private sector* (*PR Week*, 4.10.02).

The sample indicated that:

- 70 per cent offered salaries ranging from £20,000 to £39,999 per year.

Of the balance:

- 16 per cent offered £50,000 and above,
- 8 per cent £40,000–£49,999 and
- 6 per cent below £20,000.

In the *public and voluntary sectors*, the highest figure was £61,000, to be paid in local government (with the potential for 13 per cent more on top), but a similar position elsewhere in local government was set at £45,000.

In the *private sector* all the highest paid opportunities were with consultancies: these five ranged from £55,000 to £80,000. An in-house position with a global company tied on £50,000 with another 'top agency' job, in charge of fast-moving consumer goods (FMCG) MPR.

Individual earnings are notoriously difficult to average across the whole of a sector that includes a handful of global consultancy operators and a vast number of specialist small firms serving niche markets. The larger companies traditionally command the larger fees, but competition is fierce, and many smaller companies successfully premium charge because they have unequivocal competitive advantage within their markets. Medium-size firms, in this as in other similar sectors, are expected to be absorbed into their larger competitors.

One leading industry figure has predicted the appearance in the coming years of a plethora of firms so specialized that they cater for niche practices as small as biotechnology equity offerings or organic food marketing. ' "The question then will be whether these specialists get sucked in by the bigger firms, and whether the mid-size firms consolidate and also work with these smaller, niche practice firms. My guess is yes, they will." At that point … the process will self-renew as those who have sold out tire of working for somebody else and leave to set up new firms. It is a long-established money-go-round: and globalization or not, it seems unlikely to stop' (*Financial Times*, 27.11.01).

13.5   Integrated services

The formation of larger marketing services groups that bring together all marketing communication, including public relations, is designed to 'offer added value to clients via integrated work', according to a leading group chief executive. 'One of the striking features of the survey this year is the changing mix of disciplines in the Top 50. There has been a clear lessening of the dominance of advertising as a lead discipline. [Large groups] reflect the trend by declaring an intention to move their non-advertising revenue to 64 per cent of the total over the next five years' (Willott Kingston Smith and Fintellect, 2002).

However, 'One plus one has to equal more than two. For the London office of Weber Shandwick [public relations consultancy], this issue is particularly pertinent because the new outfit has nine separate units. But referring clients to sister practices isn't straightforward. Managers generally earn their bonuses by maximizing revenue for their own unit, so it's often in their interests to hang on to business, even if it would be better handled by a sister practice, or even another agency in the group' (*Financial Times*, 12.3.02). It appears that confidence about *personal rewards* and sharing clients with *known colleagues* is the key to making these large combines work.

13.6   Image and reputation of PR

There, in the cartoon, sits the British prime minister at his agency, 'Blair Self-Promotions', with his feet on the desk, surrounded by wall posters with flattering slogans to himself. Holding in one hand a sheet headed Millennium City Tony Award, showing him photographed dangling a medal bearing the large letter T, and with the telephone in his other hand, he is saying to his senior spin doctor 'Love the idea, Alastair, but isn't that the day that I receive the PR Industry 'Narcissus' Award as No. 1 pop megastar P.M. of the Millennium' (*The Times*, 20.8.99).

The joke is an easy one for readers to grasp, but it is commenting *on the public relations industry as well as on politics*, and also on the fashion for awards schemes, seemingly for just about anything, which is *indelibly associated for many people* with public relations. And in a ferocious critique of the UK's two bodies, a prominent consultant gave public vent to what many public relations practitioners may think.

'Neither the IPR nor the PRCA have done much to enhance PR's standing and for years the "industry" has amused anyone not connected with it. ... The industry ... simply lacks credibility. ...People just don't take the industry seriously enough. ... the IPR and PRCA [reflect] what the PR industry was like five or 10 years ago. PR today is much more professional, much more female, much more technical and much more international. The IPR and PRCA are none of these' (*Financial Times*, 30.10.01).

In total he made 22 points, reserving some of his venom specifically for a decision by a past president in 1993 (at her sole discretion) to give the IPR's annual president's award 'for services to public relations' to the woman writer and star of a very popular television series *ridiculing public relations*. Previous recipients had included the British Queen's daughter and a leading management writer. This outburst ended limply: 'let's stop worrying about PR's image and get on with doing a good job and adding value.'

But this *is* about PR's image, and its reputation. It is generally acknowledged that there is a deep irony that the occupational group most concerned with the fostering and maintaining of sound reputation appears to have a very poor one. Should this be of concern? Given the circumstances, it would seem sensible to suppose that its poor reputation *should* indeed be an issue for PR people.

And clearly many *are* worried by it, because they seek to avoid use of the term public relations in describing what they do. They sense that it has become synonymous with deceit and trickery, wherever that occurs, whether by their hand or otherwise. And they would be correct about this: fairly or otherwise, any attempt to distract attention or gain attention now appears to be 'all down to public relations', according to its detractors.

Senior public relations people, according to Moloney (2000), deny that they are held in low reputation. 'These conviction PR people are not faced down by low reputation; they reject the stereotypes of film and fiction ... However [with the majority of practitioners] reaction to low reputation is usually shrugged off ...'

The *greater* probability is that *all* practitioners regret the circumstances, wish very much that they were collectively held in higher regard (which would probably raise their earnings), hope that their trade bodies can do more to relieve the situation and prefer meanwhile to concentrate on the job in hand, doing it both effectively and creditably.

They must be well aware that there are several other occupations that similarly suffer public opprobrium and are doubtless comforted by the thought that none of these appear to be *that* hindered, if at all, by it. They may reason that in an increasingly questioning and critical environment there is a degree of inevitability about this, particularly for any activity that is at the *forefront of cultural change and influence*, and consequently they may adopt a relatively sanguine outlook.

13.7 Self-regulation

As to whether the criticism of the two bodies is *warranted* remains debatable. Professional bodies and trade associations generally suffer from, sometimes severe, criticism by those they seek to represent, but that does not excuse any perceived inadequacies. One sure test is the number of people who are entitled to join but *prefer not to do so.*

Those who opt to remain outside membership present problems for those who seek to represent them, in their attempts to gain greater control and thereby **enforce their ethical codes**. The member who is found wanting may be ejected, but, if the market *pays little regard to that membership*, this sanction represents no hazard. When very occasionally the IPR has expelled members these practitioners have not appeared to suffer any consequent significant material loss. And if a non-member's conduct raises a complaint there is little that may be done about it.

So self-regulation is difficult, however well intentioned. And successive waves of politicians in the UK have refused to empower the IPR, or anyone else, to certificate practitioners, on the grounds that public relations practice *does not place people at risk* in consequence of incompetence, comparable to, for instance, accountancy, law and medicine. There is, after all, a battery of legislation that applies to different aspects of practice.

By not having all practitioners or all consultancies in membership, both bodies also have a problem in asserting their credential to be *wholly* representative, and this again makes it more difficult for them to promote public relations as effectively as some of their members may wish. Politicians have been known to repeatedly question the proportion of practitioners or consultancies in membership, and the PRCA has sought to counter by laying stress on the size of the market held by its members.

These problems may be overcome through the growing web of supranational bodies and the onward growth of public relations practice around the world. Practitioners who remain outside the various bodies may come by stages to recognize that observance of the *broad intent*, if not the letter, of the codes, which heavily overlap, is *within their interests*; there are indications that this may be occurring in the UK already, since an **orderly market** for their labour and services is mutually beneficial to all practitioners.

13.8 Education and training

By some accounts public relations is a 'graduate profession', by which it is meant that only university graduates need apply. There is undoubtedly **the search for status** underlying this assertion, the supposition being that since learned professions have long since come to insist on graduate-only intake, public relations may be aligned with them, or re-positioned, by following suit.

In **higher education** public relations is now widely taught, noticeably in the USA, where 'today, one hundred colleges and universities ... provide bachelor and graduate programmes in public relations' (Black, 1989). Similarly in Europe, there is a growth in public relations education at this level. The first UK degree course in PR was offered at Stirling in 1988 and there are now some 15–20 such undergraduate and graduate courses. In addition, public relations as a distinct subject is increasingly being taught as a one-year option within marketing and other courses. A similar trend may be observed in other European countries.

In consequence, there is a growing incidence of recruitment directly from the universities and colleges, as is common in other occupations. However, many experienced practitioners, as we have noted, came into public relations via other routes and brought with them their knowledge and skills gained there, which their new employers, and, in most cases, in turn their customers, deemed both relevant and of value. Until recently it was widely assumed within UK practice that this admixture of background skills, experience, understanding and contacts was the *sinew* of public relations, what gave it relevance and depth, the surer feel for contemporary thinking, purposeful outlook and effectiveness.

The advent of public relations in higher education does not appear to have much changed *the nature of demand* **for public relations**, except perhaps to add **greater expectation**, in *some* quarters, of those levels of skill and resource expected of graduates. The trade benefits from knowing about the theory and from the various personal disciplines necessary for gaining an advanced specialist education, but in the event of any mismatch between theory and practice it insists that practice requirements are paramount. For their part, academics complain of friction between themselves and practitioners. For instance, 'Some of the material has ... been presented at conferences – with varying responses, some of which have been quite hostile. While this has not always been a pleasant experience, we firmly believe, journalistically, that if people appear not to want you to say something, then there is all the more reason to say it' (L'Etang and Pieczka, 1996).

Undoubtedly the public relations trade would be the poorer if PR was *not* taught in higher education and if its academics were deterred from undertaking research, which is necessary for the advancement of any serious discipline that offers careers as well as jobs. Practitioners may consider that they benefit adequately from their work-generated research, but it is unlikely that they would not *also* derive benefit, as a whole, from external contributions. And it is in such areas as this that claims to be a profession are fully tested.

Even the most committed advocate of the superiority of empirical learning might acknowledge of higher education courses that 'there cannot be any harm in it' as such. But many who are familiar with the nature of public relations work may question the apparent mismatch between the intellectual rigour of the courses and the frequent shortage, or even lack, of opportunity to apply the benefits of that to the work in hand in practice.

At the **further education** level, there are several diplomas available, some more demanding than others. The first appeared at the beginning of the 1970s and, over the years, study, through day and evening courses at colleges and within the workplace and by distance learning, has become increasingly expected of younger practitioners. Although in demand internationally and often regarded as being beneficial in some other occupations as well, the diploma qualifications have only gradually acquired material value in UK public relations. This appears to have been noticeably less rapid than in many similar occupations, and a surprisingly large proportion of British public relations people continue to rely solely upon qualification by experience.

There are three likely explanations for this:

1 Many people entering public relations bring with them a degree and/or qualification from another area, such as law, management, political science, sociology, psychology and anthropology. They may recoil at further study or genuinely suppose they have no need for another qualification.
2 Some newcomers have already pursued careers elsewhere, say in journalism, and view public relations as being more in the nature of a diversification than a fresh start. They perceive themselves to be already well qualified for the type of work that is expected of them. Furthermore, they may consider that combined work and domestic demands make further study impractical.
3 Often practitioners find that their intellectual and technical competences are well enough developed for handling the type of work required of them anyway and any craving they may have for more 'content' is satisfied by the levels of research and/or planning that are already part of their workload.

Many practitioners who are reluctant to engage in further study tend to emphasize that practice is 'about having plenty of common sense', which is a substantial understatement as they well know. The broad range of knowledge and skills required contradicts this simplification. Their stance is not likely to be sustainable, however. Although employers routinely complain about their difficulty in attracting 'high calibre' recruits, a common enough complaint among most employers generally, the *intensification of competition* for opportunities to work in public relations is likely to erode private doubts about, or resistance to recognizing, the wisdom of formal training and qualification. This competition is being powered by the under-graduates, among whom public relations is one of the most popular choices of career in the UK today.

For all practitioners there is also **continuous professional development** (CPD) to provide the means to obtain information and knowledge of contemporary issues and conditions of practice-based relevance. The UK public relations trade came late to this, and falteringly, judging by the IPR having to 're-launch' its 'Developing Excellence' scheme in 2001. Those members who voluntarily provide satisfactory evidence of having undertaken 100 hours of CPD over three years, a somewhat modest requirement, are accorded 'Accredited Practitioner' status, and keep going if they want to retain it.

There are three categories of such schemes in the UK:

- Some are *statutory*, and if not adhered to members lose their right to work in that occupation: this draconian approach applies, for example, to medical doctors
- Some are run by *chartered* bodies and, although CPD is not a legal requirement, members must comply in order to retain their individual chartered status (this applies with the Chartered Institute of Marketing)
- And others are *voluntary* schemes, where it is hoped that members will want the status appellation on offer in exchange for doing CPD.

It is unlikely that any prudent practitioner would wish to *not* pursue some form of CPD, and many do so anyway, without the need of schemes that offer formal inducements. The problems that arise with CPD schemes are more likely to relate to exactly *what* does or does not qualify:

- Promoters specify the number of hours they want to be spent on this or that activity, say reading or attending lectures, but these allocations can be over-prescriptive for the individual if his or her needs are not similarly balanced. For instance, the 100 hours might include 20 hours of attending lectures, conferences and seminars, but the practitioner may be accustomed to spending 100 hours *a year*, much less over three years, on this alone. Then only a small percentage of that time qualifies for CPD approval and meanwhile more time has to be found to fulfil other elements of the schedule, regardless of whether the practitioner finds them appropriate.
- The choice of 'qualifying events' and other content can be at variance with what the individual requires. For instance, lectures that win CPD points may be chosen not on their merits so much as because *they are run by the promoter*, whereas *those of a competitor are excluded*. In such circumstances the practitioner may prefer the non-qualifying alternative for its content, and may be including it anyway but without benefit of CPD accreditation.

Despite these potential deficiencies, non-statutory CPD schemes serve an excellent overall purpose of emphasizing the importance of what the UK government calls 'lifelong learning' in a relatively structured and relevant manner outside the routine of daily practice. That some people dishonestly claim to have done what they have not and others 'scramble' to complete their commitments toward the end of the allotted period without much regard for content is inevitable. Ultimately they cheat only themselves.

CHECKLIST

- At least half a million people in the UK alone are engaged for a living or as part of their occupation in recognizable public relations activities.
- Many more undertake PR on a voluntary basis or on their own behalf.
- Core PR skills are the ability to: (1) listen, hear and assimilate, (2) write cogently to order in various styles, (3) interrelate at all social and power levels and (4) think and plan with discipline and resource, particularly under pressure.
- The larger marketing services groups that include PR, formed to offer total integration of services to clients, depend upon managers having confidence about their personal reward prospects and sharing clients with known colleagues.
- The emergence of highly specialized PR practices that serve very small niche markets is likely to continue and probably accelerate.
- Trade self-regulation in the UK is difficult, however well intentioned, since a substantial number of practitioners are not in institute or association membership and far from all employers and clients insist on either one or both.
- There is a growing number of undergraduate and graduate degree courses in public relations internationally.
- UK graduate entry to PR may be via a PR degree, a management or marketing degree that includes an element of PR or a degree in a relevant field.
- Mature entry to PR may be via a variety of other occupations such as journalism.
- Formal training and qualification in PR may include one of several PR diplomas.
- Institute members are encouraged to gain formal recognition of their continuous practice development (CPD), by fulfilling on-going training specifications.

CASE STUDY
RAISING DESIGN PROVISION FOR BLIND PEOPLE

When the UK charity Action for Blind People launched the country's first ever hotel designed and built for use by blind and partially sighted people, it embarked upon a media relations campaign with the central objective to further demonstrate and encourage the adoption of best practice in adapting public space for use by people who are visually impaired.

The charity already operated three other leisure hotels around the UK, all converted for use by blind and partially sighted visitors, but the £4 million Russell Hotel overlooking the seafront public gardens at the south coast resort of Bognor Regis was the first to be purpose built. The new hotel was a joint venture with another charity, the Guide Dogs for the Blind Association, which also contributed funding for the redevelopment and expansion.

The opening of this new hotel in 2002 provided a valuable opportunity to press the case for best practice with specialist professional and technical magazines read by opinion formers, including specifiers such as architects. It also provided the means to give a valuable boost to awareness of this niche player among hotels through the travel and tourism pages of the national press and to launch the charity's hotels business regionally, through the regional media.

A core message to be communicated was that blind and partially sighted people expect hotel facilities that, in the words of the architect, 'really aren't that different from what you would expect in any hotel'. So the 40 new bedrooms have all the latest features and superior discrete bathrooms, the catering is to a high standard and available in a choice of locations and there is a heated indoor swimming pool and an instructor-attended gymnasium.

The differences are subtle and may not be that noticeable to most fully sighted people. They include, for example, enlarged corridors and bedrooms, big enough to also accommodate guide dogs, textured carpets that guide visitors to reception and plenty of handrails. These design features have been implanted so carefully that they complement the attractive interior designs. In addition, staff members are specially trained to understand the specific needs of their guests and there are also voluntary sighted guides to assist.

Consumer research had provided the architects with many pointers to requirements and left them convinced that if these can be met in a hotel they can be satisfied also in the design of any other facility or amenity for people with a range of disabilities. The strength of demand indicates that there are niche market opportunities for owners and developers who invest in quality adaptation. Occupancy levels in the chain are typically 75–90 per cent throughout the year, well above hotel industry norms, and capacity reservations for Christmas are reached a year or more in advance.

Armed with such a strong story, Action for Blind People secured valuable coverage for the opening in three national daily newspapers and heavy media reporting in London and the southeast of England, on television and radio and in the press. A few local newspapers in the midlands also reported on the new hotel.

But the most prized coverage came more discreetly, from most of the specialist press read by opinion formers. These titles deal with architecture, design, interior design, catering, leisure, the voluntary sector and the visually impaired. Often with relatively small circulations, such publications carried weight where it was wanted, prompting positive and prompt feedback requests for more information from new contacts, such as hotel owners, property developers, public authorities and their various advisers and representatives.

These specialist newspapers and magazines, often also published electronically, account for around half of the UK's entire 4400 or so publications. They provide the means, as occurred here, for public relations to demonstrate three of its prime strengths: explain complex arguments and issues; educate markets; and communicate with opinion formers, who, incidentally, may not be that readily identifiable by other means.

Like many other charities, Action for Blind People is no stranger to success in media relations, counted in terms of favourability and quantity, and it also aims for outcomes that satisfy underlying objectives based on its core purposes. The corporate mission is to inspire change and create opportunities to enable blind and partially sighted people to have equal voice and equal choice. To that end it provides housing, information and employment development services through five centres and three supported employment factories, in addition to its specialist hotels business.

The charity had no campaign budget for this project, other than staff time. The return includes substantially strengthened prospects for securing wider adoption of best practice and generation of possibilities for furthering the hotels business. And the media coverage has persisted, through national reporting under leisure, travel and tourism, where lead times extend over months; each item provides valuable ongoing support for little if any additional effort.

QUESTIONS

1 What may be the principal reasons for the rapid growth of public relations practice?
2 What may account for year-by-year changes in demand for different branches of public relations and how might levels of demand be stabilized?
3 Why might public relations consultancy remain permanently fragmented, and how?
4 Why might senior practitioners deny that PR is held in low reputation, and with what possible consequences?
5 Why might CPD be no laughing matter?

▉ ◪ 14 Futures

The Internet – the mass mediators – politics – globalization – public relations practice

14.1 The Internet

The 'global village' may very well describe the Internet, but McLuhan memorably coined the term when thinking of television, which he regarded not as a visual but an 'aural and tactile' medium that was 'thrusting the new television generation back into what he termed a "tribal" frame of mind' (Wolfe, 2000). McLuhan gained recognition as a world authority following his establishment of an extracurricular seminar on popular culture at the University of Toronto, where he taught English literature, and the publication of his first book, *The Mechanical Bride* (1951). More than that, the name of Marshall McLuhan came into popular folklore, synonymous with modern communication, but he died in 1980, aged 69, over a decade before the advent of the Internet.

Not that McLuhan got there first. Teilhard de Chardin ('usually referred to by the first part of his last name, Teilhard, pronounced TAY-yar'), who died in 1955, had the 'stunning prescience' to conceive of mankind being united through technological advance 'by a single "nervous system for humanity," a "living membrane," a single "stupendous thinking machine," a unified consciousness that would cover the earth like "a thinking skin".'

Both men, by their differing language, had foretold the Internet, which is that web or skin that connects humanity, potentially shrinking the earth to a scale of apparent familiarity and certainty that would have confounded previous generations. It is an advance that ranks with some of the greatest historic developments, including the invention of printing, which also revolutionized communication. But in the 16th century, as now with the web, only relatively few people benefited.

It took centuries for the advantages of printing to reach most people, and still there is substantial illiteracy in the world; there are some people in the advanced countries that cannot read and write. And not everyone necessarily wants to savour Caxton's legacy.

Example

According to a Book Marketing Survey (*Writers News*, June 2003), in the UK 28 per cent of the population never reads a book and only 45 per cent are really 'into' book reading. And that is despite, or because of, the heavy popularity of newspaper and magazine reading.

So how long is it likely to take for the Internet to truly cover the earth, even given our much faster modern timescales? And will everyone necessarily *want* access; much less gain it?

On the assumption that the value of the Internet is beyond question, may there be developing a new **'information poor'**, a form of *disadvantaged underclass*? A 1999 report by the UN Development Programme thought so. It pointed out that:

- 80 per cent of the language used was English, although less than 10 per cent of the world spoke it, and
- at that time a personal computer cost the equal of a month's salary in the USA but eight years' average income in Bangladesh.

The report identified a *direct correlation* **between differing levels of income, education and Internet access.** 'When people in these two worlds [those with and those without access] live and compete side by side, the advantage of being connected will overpower the marginal and impoverished, cutting off their voices and concerns from the global conversation.'

In other words, *not* **to be using the Internet is** *to be marginalized.* That is quite a threat, and measures to foster universal access without reference to personal circumstances must surely meet with general approval. The popularity of open access in public libraries and 'Internet cafes' demonstrates a strong demand. But, as with all media, what about *content*? What is it that 'information poor' people are at risk of missing, and *could they live without it*? What knowledge and conversation are they being cut out of?

Questions of content

People in a growing number of countries may indeed 'speak the language of the Internet', and have all the necessary supporting infrastructure, but the *quality* of the communication is mixed. Is it equal to the aspirations held out for it? Can a 'single seamless Web' deliver against the promise? '... the simple truth is that the Web, the Internet, does one thing. It speeds up the retrieval and dissemination of information. ... That one thing the Internet does, and only that. All the rest is Digibabble' (Wolfe, 2000).

Amidst all the commercial and 'other' content, informational and otherwise, the Internet does, nonetheless, also offer some *news*, mostly 'soft', sometimes very soft indeed, but also occasionally 'hard'. And this is an area in which the Internet is likely to become of *substantial and increasing relevance to public relations*.

The 'real' news content, however, appears in short supply so far, and independent, on-line subscription-based newspapers and magazines remain more of a prospect than a reality. Some day the newsprint publications will make their historic switch to electronic, but not before they can be sure that people who **willingly pay for news in the hand will pay for news on the screen.** The willingness of subscribers to buy their news electronically as their *first preference* is bound to develop over time, but *how much* time, and **what role might public relations play, or want to play, in trying to expedite this?**

A key feature of the Internet, from a public relations perspective, is that it also facilitates *direct*, **unmediated, communication**, and most future PR effort doubtless will focus on developing ever more innovative ways of achieving this, for instance, through 'caring and sharing' loyalty schemes. It is also a **very cost-effective channel**, not only for sending messages out but *receiving them back as well*: the Internet is a democratizing tool that tests organizational claims to wanting *genuine* two-way dialogue. In other words, **for the organization it can be a great leveller**.

One prominent public relations consultant probably spoke for many when he complained of the Internet: 'Give a bunch of paranoiacs access to cyberspace and their imagined grievances become "fact" in the twinkling of a megahertz. … The reputation managers of the future will need to understand more about activist psychology, to be fast and perceptive in their early monitoring of the internet – and know how to exploit it. They must understand that "perception is reality" and will need to learn new, more subtle psychologies to regain public confidence' (*Financial Times*, 2.10.01).

Questions of law

And this general assumption that the Internet is some place where normal conventions and rules of conduct do not apply is likely to be formally challenged more frequently.

Example

A recent decision in the Australian high court established that *those publishing material on the Internet could face legal liability anywhere in the world*. Joseph Gutnick, an Australian, brought a libel action against Dow Jones concerning allegations of money laundering and tax evasion published in its *Barron's* magazine. The magazine was published in hard copy in the USA, but in Australia, where Gutnick chose to sue, it was available only on the Internet.

Dow Jones, an American company, sought to obtain a hearing in the USA, not only for greater convenience but because US law is far more favourable to defendants in libel actions. It argued that there had been no publication in Australia because the Internet server was in New Jersey, USA, and the magazine was almost entirely directed at an American readership. It also argued that 'it would be potentially catastrophic if an Internet publisher were to be held to publish material wherever it could be received, since it could be held liable according to the laws of any country'; being aware of every country's laws was impractical (Tench, 2002).

But to no avail. 'Defamation at its heart is about damage to reputation. Since the reputation of Gutnick was damaged wherever the defamatory material was received … an action could be brought in any such place. … a special ad hoc exemption could not be invented for one technology.' And as to Australia not being a sensible place for the hearing, it was likely that the subject matter would have a predominantly Australian element. The decision is not binding elsewhere, but is 'likely to be seen as highly persuasive' throughout the Commonwealth.

There is a further element to this: the 'developing law' whereby *a defence of qualified privilege* may be available to a publisher in a libel action, 'even where the allegations complained of are wrong, if [the publisher] behaved responsibly in publishing them.' In a separate earlier case, a Spanish news agency succeeded with qualified privilege in England, partly because back home it would have had that defence available to it against any action for defamation brought in Spain. The law of the defendant's country was imported into the law of the English court.

So on the one hand the claimant can say that the matter in question *is* published, thanks to the Internet, as if it had been handed out in hard copy on the local streets, and no matter where the computer is located from whence it came. On the other hand, the publisher may say having to know and understand the law everywhere is impractical and unreasonable. Public relations practitioners will need to follow these developments closely.

14.2   The mass mediators

The new media supplement, rather than supplant, the 'traditional' media, and it seems likely therefore that the relationship between public relations and journalism *will continue to be central to PR practice* for a number of years yet. This can range from cosy to hostile, but, as we have observed, it is evolving, albeit very slowly, towards a greater measure of maturity based upon a recognizably **more balanced power relationship**. Nevertheless, there are the third parties to be remembered, so occasional outbursts of 'hack attacks' on public relations are to be expected. These tend to be so outspoken as to risk blunting their impact.

Example

A column headed 'Wacko PR stunts' that offered four 'case studies' from the fictitious FlipSide Solutions Public Relations Newsletter implied such unethical attitudes and behaviour as to be at risk of generating sympathy for public relations practitioners, rather than the reverse. Comments like 'We say: what's so wrong with diabetes?' might leave readers pondering the morals of journalists rather than PR people.
(*The Guardian*, 25.11.02)

Provocative outbursts of this nature *may well be met with less reserve* in future. Like the comment of a past president of the IPR about the practice of recruiting former journalists to senior communications roles in UK government. He told a website that some were inexperienced in PR and naïve about what they could achieve. 'Without naming names, I've met one or two people that have come from the media … with a lot of naïve ideas about the management of their post and the democratic accountability of their post' (*The Times*, 20.8.02).

Nor is it likely that the well-established journalistic inclination to loosely apply the description 'public relations exercise' and its derivatives will abate much, however inept or inappropriate its application may appear at times. It has entered the popular lexicon.

> ### Example
>
> When a US company, Advanced Cell Technology, announced that it had cloned human embryos, a former ethics adviser to the company, who had resigned following disagreement, told the media 'This is not science, it's public relations.' That resulted in the headline 'Researchers seemed to aim for PR coup' (*Financial Times*, 19.2.02). Indeed, 'PR' appears destined to appear in headlines for the indefinite future as a short, simple loose-fit, interpret-it-as-you-may term.

That journalists routinely pass judgement on public relations people, in public, *as if their audiences are as fascinated with PR as clearly they are*, may be in part at least attributable to the long-standing prejudices held within the **media schools**. The comment of an unidentified media department head at a London university is likely to be typical: 'I would be surprised if one per cent of each intake got jobs in a mainstream media outlet. A few might get into PR. ... .' This person 'spoke on condition of anonymity' (Silver, 2002).

14.3 Politics

The lead presenter of the BBC's main breakfast-time radio news and current affairs programme in the UK survived in post following an outburst in which he championed **editorial standards**, complaining that the BBC had substituted entertainment for news, gimmickry for facts, emotionalism for direct reporting. Soft, cosy journalism intruded everywhere because it was assumed that the listener preferred news pre-digested rather than delivered straight. 'If we all spent half as much time worrying about writing good, simple English free of linguistic pomposities, jargon and journalese as we do messing about with the latest wizardry, the viewer would be better served.' To which he might have added the irritating laboured over-use of currently fashionable words and the easy repetition of clichés.

This presenter is well liked and much respected. It is said that he is the one that the politicians are most wary of being interviewed by (the programme is heavily political) and his remarks struck a sympathetic chord with many. There is a widespread perception that in both television and radio news *unadulterated information* is at a premium and that much of what is presented comes through a mist or hue of emotional interpretation. Viewers and listeners who can remember when 'news was news' resent this 'lowest common denominator spoon-feeding' approach and research indicates a substantial fall in audiences for television and radio news. The people quitting are reckoned to be generally the better educated and wealthier.

This may not much concern politicians, who deal in numbers: they usually count people in their millions first before attending to their opinions. But it should concern public relations people, particularly those that are alternatively known as 'spin doctors', for the mass broadcast media are integral to their communication methodologies.

News in UK *newspapers*, by contrast, has always been suspect in the view of the more thoughtful. Early in the last century there emerged the wealthy owners with their own agendas, wanting to use their papers to influence politicians and people according to their own views. Their interest is said to be usually very keen.

Example

The Canadian owner, Beaverbrook, reportedly checked every day's proposed content in his newspapers, regardless of where he happened to be in the world at the time, and that long before the convenience of modern technology.

Now newspapers provide news 'with attitude' designed to most closely match their markets, and public relations sourcing *takes fullest account* of these differences of interpretation, editorial preferences and underlying policies.

The telling comments of the editor of *The Guardian* illustrated this very well. Talking about the scramble to find younger readers, because advertisers want them, he said of them:

'They don't read, they're not interested in politics, they don't go to the opera or theatre and they don't like heavyweight articles asking Wither Nato? They're post-modern, post-serious, post-literate ... We either adjust to meet them halfway ... or become extinct.'

That policy, pursued by the 'serious' (broadsheet) UK newspapers, attracted young readers but also alienated older people. So then three newspapers 'discovered the oldies' and began to gain sales as refugees from the other papers swapped loyalties.

What seems to be sure amidst this turmoil of change is that newspapers the world over are intent on positioning themselves in relation to their target markets, much as if they were *any other type of product*, and that has **consequences for news and current affairs**, which has to *fit their positioning policies*. Since news is largely about politics in some shape or form, this is a reality that all 'spin doctors', in particular, have to fully take into account. They have to address the subtleties of editorial worldview that result in, for example, a recent French headline 'We are all Americans now'. This trend is likely to *intensify* as markets for readers and advertisers become increasingly *competitive and fragmented*.

News is often not news at all but propaganda, and of that there is currently no shortage.

Example

Of the war in Afghanistan, 'in [a] sense the war is about belief: make-believe, in the form of propaganda, but also about which version of the truth the great mass of

> Muslims can be persuaded to believe' (*The Times*, 9.10.01). And 'It is shameful that so few organizations have challenged the [UK defence ministry] on its information policy and removed their personnel from the pool system. Hungry for footage of "our boys", the [UK] media has largely sold out on ethics and integrity' (*The Times*, 10.5.02).

And the greatest casualty of propaganda is **trust**; how readily can viewers, listeners and readers **believe the veracity of the news**?

This too has implications for public relations practice, *as a whole*.

> 'Only 18 per cent of the [UK] population thinks that politicians are trustworthy and 15 per cent believe journalists are trustworthy. ... Both sides [politicians and journalists] believe the other to be deeply untrustworthy and ready to lie,' according to a prominent politician.
> (*The Times*, 31.7.02)

This debasement of the news and current affairs coinage can *contaminate other areas of media*, as well as **reducing the credibility, and therefore value, of the media as communication intermediaries** between a public relations source and its public. It is likely to hasten the greater PR use of all *direct channels* of communication, such as the Internet, and a *corresponding reduction* in use of the mass media for relaying 'serious' content.

14.4 Globalization

Historically, public relations has been most closely associated not with marketing but with **notions of democracy**, so much so that there is 'the public relations obsession with democracy' (L'Etang, 1996) and 'a nervous preoccupation with the perils of democracy that has chaperoned the growth of corporate public relations for nearly a century' (Ewen, 1996).

But there is a strong link discernible, for public relations in recent times has come to play a full part in the development of 'McWorld', which 'celebrates market ideology with its commitment to the privatization of all things public and the commercialization of all things private. Consequently it insists on total freedom from government interference in the global economic sector (laissez-faire)' (Barber, 2001). And McWorld has not been obtaining a universally good press. Every time political leaders gather in numbers, 100,000 or more protestors turn up to demonstrate and seek as much media coverage as they can contrive.

These 'children of McWorld' hold grievances concerning '... not world order but world disorder. ... They understand ... that globalization's existing architecture breeds anarchy, nihilism and violence.' Globalization's 'freedom from interference – the rule of private power over public goods – is another name for anarchy. And terror is merely one of the contagious diseases that anarchy spawns.'

The economic consequences of this, it is argued, means that while many in the developed countries benefit from free markets in capital, labour and goods, as a result ordinary people in the developing countries are 'largely unprotected'. Recent 'summits' of the World Trade Organization (WTO) have provoked demonstrations about this by protestors from developing countries. Other effects include 'a wage race to the bottom' as jobs are relocated around the world in search of lower employment costs.

'Collective consciousness'

In this globalized world, communication is instantaneous and geographical location very nearly irrelevant. So, it is argued, the **'market paradigm'** has within it the means to spawn economic abundance and misery *with equal facility*, through 'what sociologists call a "collective consciousness" ' that is shared by all the principal players, the senior managers of the multinational and global companies, their investors, brokers, analysts, bankers and so forth (*Financial Times*, 10.11.01). When a few members of that community feel bullish or depressed *it can rapidly become infectious*.

The main financial markets of the world, in New York, London and Tokyo, watch each other very closely, continually making adjustments accordingly. Companies and *other types of organizations are at it too*, observing each other and individually trying to decide what future actions are likely to be in their best interests. However, 'the aggregate results of many individually rational decisions are often far from rational for all the agents considered as a group.' For instance, universal cost-cutting reduces aggregate demand for the output of the cost-cutters, thereby increasing the risk of recession.

Globalization *of communication*, needed for this new market-driven world, brings public relations back to its roots *even as it takes a more central and critical role in commerce*. For 'the process of globalization has transferred so much decision-making power to individuals and companies that the collective irrationality of their separate decisions may prove much harder to counter through government action than in the past'. Where does that leave the public relations 'obsession with democracy'? Can McWorld and democracy co-exist, and could PR be the *glue of reconciliation*?

14.5 Public relations

Whether the public relations trade would want to raise its game in this way must surely depend upon, perhaps more than any other single factor, its **standards of conduct and outlook**. Public relations people are to be admired for their many fine qualities, but they are driven:

- by endlessly successive time deadlines,
- changing circumstances,
- competitive pressures and
- often-hostile environments.

They are paid to articulate the views of others, represent their interests and promote their products, services, causes, personalities and so on. In doing so they seek to meet the needs of many differing publics, not least those of the mass media. Not for them is there much scope for reflection beyond counselling where necessary on matters of the day. And therein lies the kernel of the problem. Their occupation is based on careful research, planning, measurement and evaluation, *but techniques and tactics dominate it.*

It is argued that public relations is a powerful force for democracy, because it provides **a forum for pluralism**, but *in reality* it is usually only those who can *afford the admission charges* that get to play. As yet public relations advice is not available at public expense, free at the point of access for anyone who needs it.

Whither excellence?

Nor is the application of the excellence theory of public relations much in evidence, for total two-way symmetry *is not tolerable* to most purchasers of public relations services. For many of them the mere *thought* of giving ground to a public is anathema: any practitioner who seriously advised it they might well consider unfit. And that despite the many examples where its application has been most rewarding to its initiators.

Furthermore, it might be supposed that this 'tension [in the concept of symmetry] has implications for the potential disintegration of organizations as we know them and their possible transformation as they reintegrate in some different form' (L'Etang, 1996), although consequent organizational disintegration must surely be a relatively remote risk.

And nor is the theory universally accepted. L'Etang, for instance, complains that it lacks substance, suggesting that the term is merely a euphemism for 'good'. In addition, ' "symmetry" appears to offer liberation and free expression simultaneously, but it is also a potentially totalitarian ideology.' Practitioners with the relevant experience might well regard this as excessive, particularly in the context of conciliation and dispute resolution.

Despite such reservations, however, it is conceded that public relations practice may be applied in the service of diplomacy and international relations, not only for 'publicity' but 'because [public relations] is linked to fundamental positions about the way individuals organize themselves into collectivities (whether publics or nations), form identities and relate to other collectivities.'

That may be so, but is the public relations fraternity as a whole in command of its destiny, much less capable of helping others to sort out theirs? It is, often unfairly, pilloried for allegedly unethical behaviour and low morals by vested interests that know full well these are widespread among many other trades, where they go unremarked. Much of what PR people do is determined, and sometimes dictated, by their employers and customers, yet the so-called 'dirty tricks' are held to be entirely of their own making. In short, the poor reputation of public relations is not *entirely* self-earned; to a degree it is 'planted' by a variety of interests, which PR people appear to have little ability or will to counter or overcome.

The struggle for status

For all this, there seems *no collective desire* to disprove the detractors, even though it may be fairly stated that much PR practice would probably not attract opprobrium in another context. And quite a fair proportion of public relations might be regarded dispassionately as being *positively beneficial to society*. So why the reluctance to beat their own collective drum?

Public relations practitioners usually opt for the back office, which may be variously interpreted as proof of their manipulative, 'something-of-the-night' machinations or as self-effacing discretion in order to fully benefit the interests they serve, albeit in these pushy times. Those that put themselves forward almost always do so in order to compete one with another, not to advance the interests of the trade as a whole, and they have a remarkable casualty rate.

On one matter, however, public relations people *do* appear to speak with a single voice. They all **seek admission to 'dominant coalition' circles**, to be accepted as a senior management function, to be 'taken seriously', and they offer some compelling arguments in support of their contention. In a few, and growing, instances, they are being taken at their word, and in a proportion of *those* cases their arrival in the power play has brought demonstrable benefits that may be observed externally. 'High end' public relations most certainly deserves to be taken this seriously by organizations, as by government, but *most times* it is assigned solely 'low end' tasks, cast in roles that invariably underestimate its value.

Might the time have come for the trade to *strike for the higher ground* that is implied by talk of democracy and international relations, and thereby **do a bit of re-positioning** for itself? Could it turn to greater effect its evident taste for international conferences and solemn self-regulatory declarations based on the high-minded principles of international diplomacy? Might it see in the present state of the world an opportunity to *contribute its expertise and skills on a bigger board*?

CHECKLIST

- Internet news content is likely to become of substantial and increasing relevance to PR, especially once major publications become only available electronically.
- The Internet facilitates direct, unmediated communication; ever more innovative PR practices are likely to be developed in order to optimize this benefit.
- The Internet is a democratizing tool that tests organizational claims to wanting genuine two-way dialogue, being a very cost-effective channel to use. PR will educate its masters about this new reality and seek ways to benefit from it.
- Increasingly those who publish on the Internet will face the risk of legal liability anywhere in the world, since defamatory material is now held to be published, and therefore actionable, wherever it is receivable. This will rein in the informality of the net and affect the content and presentation of PR messages.
- Journalistic attacks on PR are increasingly likely to meet with PR counter-attacks as the power relationship between the two comes into greater equilibrium.
- Loss of audience for broadcast news is likely to further erode PR access by this means to better-educated and/or wealthy people, who are said to be quitting.

- The tendency of newspapers to adopt positioning policies designed to most satisfy their readers is likely to intensify, thereby increasing the need for news and current affairs to be made to fit the subtleties of their editorial worldviews.
- Propaganda, presented as news and current affairs, can contaminate other areas of the media and reduce the credibility and value of the media to PR. Its growing incidence is likely to hasten PR's greater use of all direct channels and lessen dependence upon the media for relaying 'serious' content.
- As PR continues to help develop McWorld, it may use its global communication skills to play a pivotal role in seeking reconciliation between the 'market paradigm' and democracy, in which it has a deeply embedded historic interest.
- Depending upon its standards of conduct and outlook, PR will continue to steadily advance its occupational status, through association and admission to 'dominant coalitions', and it is likely to become increasingly active in the service of diplomacy and international relations.

QUESTIONS

1 Why might the Internet be a great leveller and a great unleveller?
2 Why might ageism in editorial policy be an asset or an obstacle to communication?
3 What may be the results of changing news and current affairs reporting standards?
4 What are the communication implications of the 'collective consciousness'?
5 When might public relations be a powerful force for democracy, and how?

◪ References

Barber, B.R. (2001) 'Ballots versus bullets', in *Financial Times* (20.10.01)

Black, S. (1989) *Introduction to Public Relations*, Modino Press

Black, S. and Davis, A. (2002) *Public Relations*, 3rd edn, Old Bailey Press

Bland, M. (1995) 'Strategic Crisis Management', in Hart, N.A. (ed.), *Strategic Public Relations*, Macmillan (now Palgrave Macmillan)

Bowman, P. and Ellis, N. (1977) *Manual of Public Relations*, 2nd edn, Heinemann

Campbell, A., Devine, M. and Young, D. (1990) *A Sense of Mission*, Economist Books

Cartwright, R. (2001) *Mastering the Business Environment*, Palgrave Macmillan

Cutlip, S.M., Center, A.H. and Broom, G.M. (1985) *Effective Public Relations*, 6th edn, Prentice Hall

Davenport, T.H. and Beck, J.C. (2001) *The Attention Economy*, Harvard Business School Press

de Bono, E. (1978) *Opportunities*, Associated Business Programmes

DeSanto, B. and Petherbridge, J. (2002) 'BBC in America', in Moss, D. and DeSanto, B. (eds), *Public Relations Cases – International Perspectives*, Routledge

Doyle, P. (2000) *Value-Based Marketing*, Wiley

Dozier, L.D. (2002) 'Oklahoma City and Kerr–McGee – managing internal communication during an external crisis', in Moss, D. and DeSanto, B. (eds), *Public Relations Cases – International Perspectives*, Routledge

Drucker, P.F. (1980) *Managing in Turbulent Times*, Heinemann

Ehling, W.P. (1992) 'Estimating the value of Public Relations', in Grunig, J.E. (ed.), *Excellence in Public Relations*, Lawrence Erlbaum

Ehling, W.P., White, J. and Grunig, J.E. (1992) 'Public Relations and Marketing Practices', in Grunig, J.E. (ed.), *Excellence in Public Relations*, Lawrence Erlbaum

Ewen, S. (1996) *PR! A Social History of Spin*, Basic Books

Fawkes, J. (2001) 'What is Public Relations?', in Theaker, A. (ed.), *The Public Relations Handbook*, Routledge

Fifield, P. (1992) *Marketing Strategy*, Butterworth–Heinemann

Grunig, J.E. and Grunig, L.A. (1992) 'Models of Public Relations and Communication', in Grunig, J.E. (ed.), *Excellence in Public Relations*, Lawrence Erlbaum

Grunig, J.E. and Hunt, T. (1984) *Managing Public Relations*, Holt, Rinehart and Winston

Grunig, J.E. and Repper, F.C. (1992) 'Strategic Management, Publics, and Issues', in Grunig, J.E. (ed.), *Excellence in Public Relations*, Lawrence Erlbaum

Grunig, J.E. and White, J. (1992) 'The Effect of Worldviews on Public Relations Theory and Practice', in Grunig, J.E. (ed.), *Excellence in Public Relations*, Lawrence Erlbaum

Grunig, L.A. (1992) 'Power in the Public Relations Department', in Grunig, J.E. (ed.), *Excellence in Public Relations*, Lawrence Erlbaum

Grunig, L.A., Grunig, J.E. and Ehling, W.P. (1992) 'What is an Effective Organization?', in Grunig, J.E. (ed.), *Excellence in Public Relations*, Lawrence Erlbaum

Haig, M. (2000) *e-pr The Essential Guide to Public Relations on the Internet*, Kogan Page

Handy, C. (1989) *The Age of Unreason*, Century Hutchinson

Harrison, S. (2000) *Public Relations: An Introduction*, 2nd edn, Thomson Learning

Hart, N.A. (1995) 'Marketing Communications', in Hart, N.A. (ed.), *Strategic Public Relations*, Palgrave Macmillan

Henderson, T. and Williams, J. (2002) 'Shell: Managing a Corporate Reputation Globally', in Moss, D. and DeSanto, B. (eds), *Public Relations Cases – International Perspectives*, Routledge

Ind, N. (1995) 'The Practice of Corporate Identity', in Hart, N.A. (ed.), *Strategic Public Relations*, Palgrave Macmillan

Jefkins, F. and Yadin, D. (1998) *Public Relations*, 5th edn, FT/Prentice Hall

Johnson, G. and Scholes, K. (1999) *Exploring Corporate Strategy*, Prentice Hall

Kidder, R. and Bloom, S. (2001) 'Ethical Fitness in Today's Business Environment', in Moon, C. and Bonny, C. (eds), *Business Ethics*, Economist Books

Kitchen, P.J. (1997) 'The Interaction between Public Relations and Marketing', in Kitchen, P.J. (ed.), *Public Relations: Principles and Practice*, International Thomson

Kitchen, P.J. and Papasolomou, I. (1997) 'The Emergence of Marketing PR', in Kitchen, P.J. (ed.), *Public Relations: Principles and Practice*, International Thomson

Kotler, P. (1991) *Marketing Management*, 7th edn, Prentice Hall

Lambert, R. (2002) *The Lambert Challenge*, Business in the Community

Lancaster, G. and Massingham, L. (1988) *Essentials of Marketing*, McGraw-Hill

L'Etang, J. (1996) 'Public Relations as Diplomacy', in L'Etang, J. and Pieczka, M. (eds), *Critical Perspectives in Public Relations*, International Thomson

L'Etang, J. and Pieczka, M. (1996) 'Introduction', in L'Etang, J. and Pieczka, M. (eds), *Critical Perspectives in Public Relations*, International Thomson

Lloyd, H. (1963) *Public Relations*, The English Universities Press

Mason, L. (2002), unpublished public relations masters dissertation

McCorkell, G. (1997) *Direct and Database Marketing*, Kogan Page

McDonald, M.H.B. (1989) *Marketing Plans*, 2nd edn, Heinemann

McNair, B. (1996) 'Performance in Politics and the Politics of Performance', in L'Etang, J. and Pieczka, M. (eds), *Critical Perspectives in Public Relations*, International Thomson

Moloney, K. (2000) *Rethinking Public Relations – The Spin and the Substance*, Routledge

Moss Kanter, R. (1984) *The Change Masters*, Allen & Unwin

Newman, W. (1995) 'Community Relations', in Hart, N.A. (ed.), *Strategic Public Relations*, Palgrave Macmillan

Oliver, S. (2001) *Public Relations Strategy*, Kogan Page

Peters, T. (1987) *Thriving on Chaos*, Alfred A. Knopf

Pieczka, M. (1996) 'Paradigms, Systems Theory and Public Relations', in L'Etang, J.

and Pieczka, M. (eds), *Critical Perspectives in Public Relations*, International Thomson

Porter, M.E. (1980) *Competitive Strategy*, Free Press

Portway, S. (1995) 'Corporate Social Responsibility: the Case for Active Stakeholder Relationship Management', in Hart, N.A. (ed.), *Strategic Public Relations*, Palgrave Macmillan

Quirke, B. (1995) 'Internal Communication', in Hart, N.A. (ed.), *Strategic Public Relations*, Palgrave Macmillan

Regester, M. and Larkin, J. (1997) 'Issue and Crisis Management: Fail-safe Procedures', in Kitchen, P.J. (ed.), *Public Relations: Principles and Practice*, International Thomson

Shaw, C. (2002) 'TV News with Attitude', in *The Times* (29.11.02)

Silver, J. (2002) 'Newcastle? It's a city in Scotland', in *The Times* (5.7.02)

Somerville, I. (2001) 'Public Relations, Politics and the Media', in Theaker, A. (ed.), *The Public Relations Handbook*, Routledge

Smith, D. (1995) 'Parliamentary and European Union Relations', in Hart, N.A., (ed.), *Strategic Public Relations*, Palgrave Macmillan

Smith, P.R. (1999) *Great Answers to Tough Marketing Questions*, Kogan Page

Stewart-Hunt, C. (2003) in conversation with author (5.3.03)

Stone, N. (1995) *The Management and Practice of Public Relations*, Palgrave Macmillan

Tench, D. (2002) 'Long arm of the Internet – Web publishers face worldwide legal liability', in *The Guardian* (16.12.02)

Theaker, A. (2001a) 'Corporate Community Involvement', in Theaker, A. (ed.), *The Public Relations Handbook*, Routledge

Theaker, A. (2001b) 'Research and Evaluation – PR grows up?', in Theaker, A. (ed.), *The Public Relations Handbook*, Routledge

Theaker, A. (2001c) 'Media Relations', in Theaker, A. (ed.), *The Public Relations Handbook*, Routledge

Theaker, A. (2001d) 'Future Challenges for PR', in Theaker, A. (ed.), *The Public Relations Handbook*, Routledge

Theaker, A. (2001e) 'Public Affairs and Issues Management', in Theaker, A. (ed.), *The Public Relations Handbook*, Routledge

van Riel, C.B.M. (1995) *Principles of Corporate Communication*, Prentice Hall

Varey, R. (1997a) 'External Public Relations Activities', in Kitchen, P.J. (ed.), *Public Relations: Principles and Practice*, International Thomson

Varey, R. (1997b) 'Public Relations: The External Publics Context', in Kitchen, P.J. (ed.), *Public Relations: Principles and Practice*, International Thomson

White, J. and Dozier, D.M. (1992) 'Public Relations and Management Decision Making', in Grunig, J.E. (ed.), *Excellence in Public Relations*, Lawrence Erlbaum

Wolfe, T. (2000) 'Digibabble, Fairy Dust, and the Human Anthill', in Wolfe, T., *Hooking Up*, Random House

Wootliff, J. and Deri, C. (2001) 'NGOs: The New Super Brands', in *Corporate Reputation Review* (Summer 2001)

◾ ⌄ Index